The Mind Stealers

The Mind Stealers

PSYCHOSURGERY AND
MIND CONTROL

Samuel Chavkin

Houghton Mifflin Company Boston   1978

Library of Congress Cataloging in Publication Data

Chavkin, Samuel.
The mind stealers.
Includes bibliographical references and index.
1. Violence. 2. Social psychiatry. 3. Social
control. 4. Psychosurgery. I. Title.
RC569.5.V55C47   617'.481   77-19284
ISBN 0-395-26381-6

Printed in the United States of America

V 10 9 8 7 6 5 4 3 2 1

The extract on pages 48 and 49 is from "The
Children" by Ned O'Gorman. © 1975 by The New
York Times Company. Reprinted by permission.

TO SYLVIA AND WENDY

Acknowledgments

I want to express my appreciation to the following for their cooperation in the preparation of some of the material for this book:

Ernest A. Bates, M.D., University of California Medical School, San Francisco; Diane Bauer, formerly *Washington Star* news staff; Lyle W. Bivens, Ph.D., Chief, Neuropsychology Section, National Institute of Mental Health, Bethesda, Maryland; Peter R. Breggin, M.D., Washington, D.C.; M. Hunter Brown, M.D., Santa Monica; Professor Stephan L. Chorover, Department of Psychology and Brain Science, Massachusetts Institute of Technology; Lee Coleman, M.D., Berkeley; José M. R. Delgado, M.D., Chairman, Department of Physiology, Madrid Autonomous Medical School, Spain; Professor Frank R. Ervin, M.D., Neuropsychiatric Institute, University of California, Los Angeles; Paul Fedio, Ph.D., National Institute of Neurological and Communicative Disorders and Stroke, Bethesda, Maryland; Robert J. Grimm, M.D., Assistant Director of Neurology, Good Samaritan Hospital and Medical Center, Portland, Oregon; Professor Robert G. Heath, M.D., Chairman, Department of Psychiatry and Neurology, Tulane University School of Medicine, New Orleans; Eric Holtzman, Professor of Biological Sciences, Columbia University; Irv Joyner, Coordinator, *Criminal Justice Issues*, Commission for Racial Justice, United Church of Christ; Gabe Kaimowitz, Senior Attorney, Michigan Legal Services, Detroit; Herbert Lansdell, Ph.D., Fundamental Neurosciences Program NINCDS, Bethesda, Maryland; Richard Levins, Professor of Population Sciences,

Harvard University; Richard S. Lewontin, Professor, Biology and Zoology, Harvard University; Petter A. Lindstrom, M.D., San Diego; Vernon H. Mark, M.D., Associate Professor of Surgery, Harvard Medical School; Matthew L. Myers, Staff Attorney, National Prison Project, American Civil Liberties Union, Washington, D.C.; Edward M. Opton, Jr., Senior Research Psychologist, The Wright Institute, Berkeley; Justine Wise Polier, former Justice on New York Family Court, presently Director, Childrens' Defense Fund, New York; Arpiar G. Saunders, Jr., Staff Attorney, National Prison Project, American Civil Liberties Union, Washington, D.C.; Professor Ralph K. Schwitzgebel, California Lutheran College; Professor Michael H. Shapiro, University of Southern California Law School; B. F. Skinner, Ph.D., Professor Emeritus, Harvard University; Representative Louis Stokes (D–Ohio); Professor L. Alex Swan, Chairman, Department of Sociology, Fisk University, Nashville, Tennessee; the late Professor Hans-Lukas Teuber, Massachusetts Institute of Technology; Sharland Trotter, Editor of *APA Monitor* (organ of the American Psychological Association); Professor Elliot S. Valenstein, Department of Neurosciences, University of Michigan; J. M. Van Buren, M.D., National Institute of Neurological and Communicative Disorders and Stroke, Bethesda, Maryland; Isidore Ziferstein, M.D., Associate Professor, Neuropsychiatric Institute, University of California, Los Angeles.

I realize, and so should the reader, that some of those mentioned above will not agree, or will disagree, with my views and conclusions. I am nevertheless indebted to them for their time and counsel.

I am also grateful to Mary Heathcote for early readings of some of the sections of the manuscript and to Judy McCusker for her editorial sensitivity and her impeccable typing of the text.

I am particularly appreciative of the patience and encouragement of my editor, Ruth K. Hapgood, considering the many months that went into the gathering and preparation of the material.

Contents

The Mind Stealers

1. Who Owns Your Personality?

A SO-CALLED SCIENTIFIC rationale is being spawned to explain some of the critical dilemmas of the day — such as the rising tide of violence — by blaming them on individuals who don't make the grade genetically, or whose uncontrollable behavioral problems are associated with faulty neurological wiring. These people are said to be afflicted with a case of bad genes, or suffering from some brain disorder, or carrying around an extra chromosome, or victims of all three conditions.

Ever-mounting crime — the muggings, burglaries, and killings — according to this theory, is only partly the result of ghetto frustrations, unemployment, and overall economic despair. More significant, these theorists hold, is the presence of a large number of Americans, as many as 15 million,[1] who are afflicted with certain brain dysfunctions; their damaged brain cells may suddenly go awry, triggering impulsive outbursts of rage and uncontrollable seizures of assaultive behavior.

The solution to this problem, proponents of this view declare, is to have these individuals submit to a behavior reconditioning program in prisons or other "corrective" institutions. Failing this, such persons would undergo a brain operation, psychosurgery, that would permanently rid them of their aggressiveness and other obsessive, hostile characteristics. Yet there is no actual proof that sick or malfunctioning brain cells are the causes of their violent dispositions. Psychosurgery is expressly designed to alter the behavior and overall emotional character of an individual.

As bizarre as it may sound, this theory, for nearly a dozen

years, has been making headway. It has received considerable encouragement and experimentation at the Veterans' Administration and possibly other government agencies.[2]

For law enforcement people, the failure of whose methods is reflected by the steady rise in street crime, the biological approach with the surgical twist is especially appealing. Psychosurgery might even become part of the police armamentarium, along with mace, the club, and the service revolver. It would enjoy respectability, since the rationale would originate in the medical community. No one has proved that millions of our citizens are about to run amok because of brain dysfunction, however, nor is there proof that psychosurgery can "cure" violence. We know that cutting away certain sections of the brain or destroying brain cells will subdue patients, make them docile, and in some instances leave them in a permanent, zombielike state. For once brain tissue is destroyed, it will never again regenerate. The late Dr. Walter Freeman, a pioneer in the early psychosurgery called lobotomy, commented on this phenomenon by saying that "lobotomized patients seldom came into conflict with the law precisely because they lack the imagination to think up new deviltries and the energy to perpetrate them."[3]

"Murder of the mind" is how critics refer to the end-result of psychosurgery. "The role of psychosurgery has little if any applicability for violent behavior,"[4] says Dr. A. K. Ommaya, acting chief of the Surgical Neurology Branch of the National Institute of Neurological and Communicative Disorders and Stroke (NINCDS).

A similar view comes from Dr. Elliot S. Valenstein, who states that "there is no convincing evidence that . . . episodically occurring violence caused by brain pathology represents anything more than a very insignificant percentage of the violence in our society." He contends that "there is no reason to believe that brain pathology is contributing to the accelerating rate of assaultive behavior."[5] Dr. Valenstein is professor of psychology at the University of Michigan and author of the book *Brain Control*.

Lest the reader find solace in the belief that it can't happen to her or to him, that the application of the brain-damage violence theory is confined only to criminals with bad brain cells, there may be an unpleasant surprise in store. Already this theory is being extended to include other types of "deviant" individuals who would be candidates for psychosurgery — mental patients, hyperactive children, homosexuals, alcoholics, drug addicts, and political nonconformists.[6]

There is much concern about the growing acceptance of behaviorist and psychosurgical remedies for what basically are socioeconomic problems requiring political solutions. There is an ominous reminder of the period just before and during the Nazi regime in Germany, when some of that country's leading psychiatrists described the emotionally ill as an "economic drain," persons of "no value." Their solution? Doing away with the mentally ill.

Eventually these psychiatric "healers" in Germany played key roles in the physical extermination of some 275,000 mental patients. Dr. Fredric Wertham, in his extraordinarily well-documented work on violence, *A Sign for Cain*,[7] cites psychiatrist Alfred Hoche, who published a book some twelve years before Hitler took power, in which he set the basis for the concept that mental patients were socially nonproductive and therefore expendable.

Hoche was professor of psychiatry and director of the psychiatric clinic at Freiburg until 1934. He was a highly respected scientist and had trained some of the outstanding psychiatrists in Germany. As Dr. Wertham points out, however, because of his reactionary views, his rigid judgmental values as to who was fit or not fit to live, Hoche paved the way for looking at the mentally sick and the physically handicapped as a drag on the nation's economy. As early as 1920 he urged that the killing of "worthless people" be legally permitted.

Eventually this thinking led to the *Untermenschen* theory: that is, that these were people who didn't quite make it to the human level. These theories were interwoven into the criterion for the elimination of non-Aryans, such as Jews, Slavs, and Gypsies.

There were dozens of psychiatrists directly involved in the execution of these hapless people, including many thousands of children. Such well-known physicians as Dr. Werner Heyde, professor of psychiatry at the University of Würzburg, was a key figure in overseeing the use of carbon monoxide as a method for killing mental patients. Yet another internationally known scientist, Dr. Werner Villinger, an authority on epilepsy and acute psychosis, began popularizing the view that rehabilitation of juvenile delinquents was hopeless and that sterilization was the answer.[8]

What is equally startling is the revelation that Hitler didn't force these psychiatrists to assume their executioner roles; they in their various ways contributed to the Hitlerian myth of the Aryan superrace and the need to rid it of physical or mental defectives. Many less prestigious doctors, at first hesitant to break their Hippocratic oath, ultimately were swept up into this macabre operation as they watched their medical "betters" lead the way.

While the pro-Nazi psychiatrists were drafting "therapies," the geneticists were laying down the "scientific" foundation for the eradication of second-class humans. No less a notable than Konrad Lorenz, who in 1974 was awarded the Nobel Prize for his pioneering studies of animal behavior (ethology), had earlier proclaimed the theory of the need to cleanse the Third Reich of its pool of inferior genes. His observations of the animal kingdom, he explained, led him to understand that when domestication of animals takes place, much of the competitiveness in mating is gone and so degenerative mutations take place. A similar phenomenon, he said, surfaces in certain phases of civilization so that "socially inferior human material is enabled . . . to penetrate and finally annihilate the healthy nation." In the year 1940, at the height of Hitler's regime, Lorenz wrote:

> The racial idea as the basis of our state has already accomplished much in this respect . . . We must — and should — rely upon the healthy feelings of our Best and charge them with the selection which will determine the prosperity or the decay of our people.[9]

Currently it would be both presumptuous and reckless to suggest that psychiatrists and neurosurgeons are drafting plans to do away with those Americans who are mentally ill or are deemed incorrigible, uneducable, or noncontributory to the overall economy of this land. But it would be equally inexcusable to forget or to gloss over the Nazi experience. And it would be even less justifiable to overlook similar trends in this country. Certainly there are enough puffs of smoke on the horizon to suggest that a fire may be smoldering underneath. The tendency in dealing with crime and delinquency is to bypass the social roots of violence (the nation's economic upheavals, unemployment, etc.) and to focus instead on the "pathology," genetic or otherwise, of the culprit who fails to "shape up."

It is scarcely believable that so soon after the Nazi era consideration of race as a cause of ethnic depravity has once again surfaced to the degree that it has. The notion of hereditary flaws in ethnic groups is offered as an explanation for the increase in the number of blacks and Hispanics in the prison population. There is not even an attempt at disguising the blatant racism implicit in this approach. It is no longer confined to the mutterings by frustrated, bigoted members of various hate groups. It has become an open issue for debate by academicians.

R. A. McConnell, research professor of biophysics at the University of Pittsburgh, commenting on the biological explanation of this nation's current social and economic disarray, declared:

> I estimate that somewhere between 10 and 30 percent of the U.S.A. population has inadequate genetic endowment to make a net zero or greater economic contribution in a modern industrial society. Or to say it more precisely, this many people are in excess over the possible need for their level of ability. Unless the average genetic competence can be raised, a large (and presently growing) fraction of our people must remain permanently in the spiritually degrading position of charitable dependence upon the rest of us. This, I believe, is one root cause for our present social malaise. A fortiori [even more certain], a still higher fraction is so restricted by genetic endowment as to be unable to understand many of the intellectually complex issues that are submitted to public vote.

In short, our civilization based on science and technology, which are the creation of a miniscule elite, has grown too complex for the ordinary man.[10]

This, of course, could set up the assumption that a section of the population, by reason of hereditary deficiency, is unable to keep up with modern civilization and therefore is deprived of the privileges enjoyed by the elite. It would follow that some of its members inevitably turn to criminality to achieve what they could not attain through talent or skill.

Professor McConnell draws his inspiration from such modern-day apostles of genetic determinism as Jensen and probably Shockley and Wilson of Harvard, the architect of the new genetic school — sociobiology. Arthur R. Jensen, professor of educational psychology, University of California at Berkeley, has become the center of debate for the last half a dozen years, following the launching of his thesis that black children, except to a very limited level of development, are simply uneducable. The sooner this country wakes up to this fact, he argues, the sooner it will rid itself of costly illusions. "Compensatory education has been tried and it apparently failed," he declared in a 123-page article in the *Harvard Educational Review*, in 1969.[11] So, he asks, why continue draining the nation's treasury on special programs for the disadvantaged minorities? Jensen's entire case rests on his claim that blacks do poorly compared to whites on standard IQ tests, even after they have been exposed to especially designed remedial efforts. And the reason for this poor performance, he insists, is genetic, and it is passed on from one generation to the next.

Jensen has found strong support from physicist William Shockley of Stanford, who has stated that "there is a difference in the wiring patterns" in white and black minds.[12]

Just how seriously the Jensen views have been considered at the highest levels of the American government was reflected by President Nixon's report in 1970. His review of Head Start and other governmentally sponsored educational programs indicated a very dim view of these undertakings. While he did not mention Jensen by name, there was little doubt as to Jensen's influence. Senator Daniel Patrick Moynihan, then a White House advisor, is reported to have said, "the words of Jensen were gusting through the capitol." Moynihan has admitted to having been questioned about Jensen by Nixon and others at a presidential cabinet meeting. According to a *Life* magazine account, Moynihan stated that even though there was only "inferential knowledge [about the role of the gene] . . . and that nobody knows what a 'smart gene' looks like, that Dr. Jensen is a thoroughly respectable man, that he is in no sense a racist . . ."[13]

In the 1975–1976 Boston race riots relating to school busing, handbills were circulated with headlines that read, "Heredity Determines Intelligence," and "What's Responsible for Negroes' Low I.Q.?" In one of these leaflets Jensen was cited as the source for those diatribes, quoting him and others that "genes — the strand of protein coded to determine all that we are, inherited by us at conception — play an overwhelmingly predominant role in determining one's basic level of intelligence."*

Rejecting the Jensen-Shockley thesis, a Harvard genetic scholar and population expert says that it has no scientific credibility. Professor Richard Lewontin states that "the basic error is to suppose that coded in our genes — and there is no evidence of anything like it — are determinative behaviors of individuals."[14] The fact that some traits differ genetically between individuals, he adds, does not point to the causes of differences between groups, such as races or social classes.

The racist-genetic approach quickly falls apart when exposed to the test of experience. As early as World War I, for instance,

---

* Early in 1977 Dr. Jensen seems to have done somewhat of an about-face on the question of blacks and IQ. In a recent study involving 653 youngsters in an unnamed town in Georgia, the Berkeley psychologist noted a downward trend in the IQ of black students as they grew older. He conceded that this may be the result of environmental factors — a standard of living much lower than that of the white population and the disadvantages of being a rural southern black. Writing in *Developmental Psychology* (May 1977), Jensen said: "I cannot say exactly what those factors are . . . They may have to do with nutrition . . . health and a disadvantaged home environment." Despite this observation he still believes that there is a basic IQ difference between blacks and whites.

black soldiers from certain northern areas who were privileged to have the same kind of education as northern whites scored significantly higher in the IQ tests than whites from impoverished sections of the south.[15]

It would appear that the prime objective of some of the proponents of the Jensen-Shockley school of philosophy is to absolve the existing social and political institutions from responsibility in ameliorating the continuing crises of the cities. The main thrust is to place all the onus for antisocial behavior — attributable to ghetto life, deprivation, and unemployment — on "genetically flawed individuals" with a supposedly damaged heredity.

It is interesting that at the other end of the spectrum, the environmental determinists — such as those led by B. F. Skinner, who stress overall environment as the principal influence on the development of the individual — also bypass the responsibilities of governmental and societal institutions with regard to the rise of crime or other social upheavals. It is the early influence and the initial circumstances in which a person has been reared, the Skinnerians argue, that will make the individual either a solid, respectable citizen or a mugger or a swindler.

Inherent in both schools of thought, whether based on genetics or environment, is a rigidity that freezes the individual into whatever station of life he has found himself. In effect, it offers a "scientific" validity to justify the existing scheme of things in terms of social stratification and therefore of inequality — whether it touches on one's wage-earning capacity, educational opportunities, or social status.

The revival of genetic determinism represents a leap backward to primitive Darwinism: a period in which Herbert Spencer proclaimed that Darwin's findings did indeed corroborate that the world operated on the basis of "the survival of the fittest."[16] Those at the helm of power — whether in government, in industry, or in commerce — have long subscribed to this thesis. John D. Rockefeller, who was much inspired by Spencer, once declared that "the growth of a larger business is merely survival of the fittest . . . the working out of the law of nature and the law of God."[17]

Given this premise, it is inevitable to infer that those less fit would simply have to accept their lot in life and resign themselves to the jobs they may hold, the places where they live, and whatever they can provide for their children, however limited. As the British Nobel Prize winner, Dr. P. B. Medawar puts it, "thus it is a canon of high tory philosophy that a man's breeding — his genetic makeup — determines absolutely his abilities, his destiny, and his desserts." This belief, he adds, "lies at the root of racism, fascism, and all other attempts to 'make nature an accomplice in the crime of political inequality,'" quoting the French philosopher Condorcet.[18]

It is in keeping with this overall philosophy that government authorities at all levels — national, state, and city — point the accusatory finger at the delinquent per se. But they continue to drag their feet in dealing with the basic causes — the ever-deteriorating social and economic conditions that dog the inhabitants of the ghetto enclaves. Instead, the emphasis made in terms of money and planning is to improve the efficiency of the law enforcement agencies in subduing the culprit and recycling him or her into a conforming individual, one who will accept the very conditions (drug traffic, unemployment, slum housing) that precipitated his or her criminal acts to begin with.

In 1970 more than 3 percent of this nation's nonwhite male population between the ages of eighteen and thirty-four, six times the percentage for whites, found themselves behind bars.[19] Despite these soaring figures and in spite of the veritable building boom in the construction of new penitentiaries to house the increasing prison population, there seems to be no indication that those charged with making this country's policies are ready to come up with new concepts in dealing with the situation.

The Law Enforcement Assistance Administration (LEAA) and other government agencies are pouring hundreds of millions of dollars into programs designed to reshape the delinquent by a host of behavior-modification techniques. In many instances, the

LEAA, by its own admission, does not follow up on how this money is spent and on what. It may not even be aware that some of the programs it funds include the use of torture procedures so horrifying as to remind us that sadism is not the monopoly of any one country. Among the rehabilitative instruments: powerful drugs, electric-shock devices, and most devastating — psychosurgery. And those exposed to these procedures for the most part are juvenile delinquents, prisoners, and mental patients. LEAA's failure to monitor such activities stems from the fact that it has never developed review guidelines for the protection of human subjects involved in the programs it supports.

Youthful detainees, some only twelve years of age, are kept in isolation for months at a time; some are known to have been gassed and abused in many juvenile centers across the country. Prisoners are often chained to a steel bed-frame, which has come to be known as the rack; thrown into solitary confinement in dingy, damp cellars; and injected with such drugs as Anectine, forcing the person to gasp for breath — a sensation described as closest to drowning.

But what is most alarming is that these attempts to "cure" the violent are in reality aimed at controlling the mind, to make the individual submit to whoever wields authority. Behaviorist James McConnell, professor of psychology at the University of Michigan, has welcomed these developments. In an article titled "Criminals Can Be Brainwashed — Now," he stated:

> . . . the day has come when . . . it should be possible . . . to achieve a very rapid and highly effective type of positive brainwashing that would allow us to make dramatic changes in a person's behavior and personality . . .
>
> We should reshape our society so that we all would be trained from birth to want to do what society wants us to do. We have the techniques now to do it . . . No one owns his own personality . . . You had no say about what kind of personality you acquired, and there is no reason to believe you should have the right to refuse to acquire a new personality if your old one is antisocial . . . Today's behavioral psychologists are the architects and engineers of the Brave New World.[20]

On the other hand, former Senator Sam J. Ervin, Jr., who headed a Senate subcommittee studying the government's role in behavior modification, expressed great alarm at the "widespread and growing interest in the development of methods designed to predict, identify, control, and modify individual human behavior."[21]

In his introduction to the subcommittee's report, late in 1974, the senator declared that "behavioral technology . . . in the United States today touches upon the most basic sources of individuality, and the very core of personal freedom. To my mind," he added, "the most serious threat . . . is the power this technology gives one man to impose his views and values on another . . . If our society is to remain free, one man must not be empowered to change another man's personality and dictate the values, thoughts and feelings of another."[22]

With reference to psychosurgery, Dr. Robert J. Grimm, a research neurophysiologist at the Good Samaritan Hospital and Medical Center, Portland, Oregon, sees it as an issue comparable in dimension to the debate that arose among nuclear physicists after Hiroshima over the question of the bomb. "Do scientists have the right to pursue projects potentially destructive of human life, and in this era, destructive of the individual?" is the question he put to the Fifth Annual Cerebral Function Symposium in California in March 1974. He felt that such moral issues "were repeatedly raised during the Vietnam War over weapon development, germ warfare and massive forest defoliation." These dilemmas, he told his listeners, "surface now over the issue of psychosurgery and technical efforts to deal with aggression and dyssocial behavior."

Dr. Grimm then warned that "neuroscientists will be under increasing pressure to examine their individual and collective positions vis-à-vis the widening issue of brain control application in a democratic society. We cannot escape this responsibility."[23]

The warnings sounded by Dr. Grimm and Senator Ervin could not have been more appropriate: only three years later the nation was stunned to learn that a large-scale behavior control experimentation program had been going on in the United States for upward of twenty-five years. What most of us traditionally felt — that "it can't happen here," was indeed happening. At a Senate hearing on August 3, 1977, Admiral Stansfield Turner, director of the Central Intelligence Agency, disclosed that the CIA had been conducting brainwashing experiments on countless numbers of Americans, without their knowledge or consent. Some were prisoners, others were mentally ill patients, still others were cancer patients. But there was also an unknown number of nonpatients who unwittingly became experimental subjects; for instance, patrons at bars in New York, San Francisco, and other cities were drugged with LSD and other psychotropic agents by the CIA. Nurses and other members of hospital staffs underwent sensory deprivation experiments, and some of them experienced the onset of schizophrenia.

These CIA activities were clearly illegal and were carried out with the participation of at least 185 scientists and some eighty institutions: prisons, pharmaceutical companies, hospitals, and forty-four medical colleges and universities.

One of the scientists contacted by the CIA was Dr. Robert Heath, a pioneer in psychosurgery and depth-electrode stimulation in the pleasure and pain centers of the brain. Dr. Heath, who is chairman of Tulane University's Department of Psychiatry and Neurology, told the *New York Times* that he declined a CIA offer of financial aid to investigate the potential for the manipulation of the pain region of the brain. He said he found it "abhorrent." The *Times* reported, however:

> Dr. Heath has acknowledged agreeing to do one research project for the agency in 1957 after an agent asked him to test a purported brainwashing drug on monkeys and then, if practicable, on prisoners at the Louisiana State Penitentiary . . ."[24]

Dr. Heath said he did the work on the animals but not on humans. But what about other investigators who may have been involved in psychosurgery experiments? The full story may never be known because many of the documents, according to Admiral Turner, are missing or have been destroyed.

The main objective of this mammoth CIA effort, which cost the taxpayers at least $25 million, was to program an individual to do one's bidding even if it would lead to his own destruction. As quoted by the *New York Times*, a CIA memorandum of January 25, 1952, asked "whether it was possible to 'get control of an individual to the point where he will do our [CIA's] bidding against his will and even against such fundamental laws of nature as self-preservation.'"[25]

Commenting on this disclosure, the *Times* said editorially:

> We are not sufficiently schooled in ethics to know how this differs from murder . . . The means as well as the end were outrageous.

It added that

> no one seems to know how many citizens were used as guinea pigs and how many were directly harmed.[26]

Needless to say, this type of behavioral technique could be used for more purposes than just breaking down an international spy. Any person could become a target should his or her behavior or thinking fall out of favor with those in authority.

Considering the scope of the CIA revelations, the recent recommendation by a congressional commission to have the federal government become more active in funding and extending psychosurgery research has raised questions in some quarters. The commission, known as the National Commission for the Protection of Human Subjects of Biomedical and Behavioral Research, has given its blessings to psychosurgery in the belief that it could be significant in treating a variety of psychiatric ailments that resist psychoanalysis or drugs. The commission feels certain that the safeguards contained in its recommendations would block the use of psychosurgery in experiments to control behavior (see Chapter 7).

It is important to remember, however, that nothing is foolproof, particularly if a powerful government agency takes it upon itself to break the rules. The CIA began its brainwashing projects in 1953, the very year that the United States government signed the Nuremberg Code that prohibits human experimentation on captive populations, such as prisoners, or anybody else for that matter, unless the person is fully informed on the nature of the experiment and freely gives his or her consent.

2. Guilty Brain Cells

HIS MOOD WAS one of brooding preoccupation. Then his face began to twitch with pain. Moments later, seized with panic, he cried out, "I'm losing control . . . I'm losing control." A few seconds more and Thomas R., a patient undergoing electrical stimulation of the brain, would have gone into violent rage and perhaps into a physical attack on those near him. The electrical charge appeared to have sparked a specific cluster of neurons to bring on this uncontrollable anger.

Thomas's brain was wired with strands of electrodes, sunk deep in both temporal lobes and entering the amygdala nucleus of the limbic system,* the so-called emotional brain. Every time a low-voltage current was allowed to pass through the electrodes — thin wires, each planted in a different part of the brain — Thomas would respond with a variety of reflexive movements and emotions. He complained of weakness; of pain in the ears and teeth; of fuzzy thinking; and of "everything going wild" — depending on which electrode was being activated at a given moment.

But a fraction of an inch away from the point at which Thomas was flung into depression, another activated electrode

---

*The limbic system, among the least understood areas of the brain, is associated with emotion, creativity, pain, pleasure, smell, control of certain bodily functions, sex, and rage. (Its amygdala region is said to be especially related to aggression.) One neuroscientist described the limbic system as being involved with the four Fs: feeding, fighting, fleeing, and sex.

produced a contrary effect; a sensation of well-being and relaxation.

The purpose of all this electronic probing was to get a fix on the specific area of the brain suspected of harboring diseased neurons that the doctors thought triggered Thomas's occasional episodes of impulsive, violent behavior.

The examination was being conducted by Dr. Vernon H. Mark, a tall, no-nonsense surgeon who peers at you through dark-rimmed glasses, and Dr. Frank R. Ervin, a big man with impish green eyes and a high-domed forehead set in a face overrun by a Tolstoyan beard. Dr. Mark is director of the Neurosurgical Service at the Boston City Hospital and associate professor at Harvard Medical School. Dr. Ervin, formerly associate professor of psychiatry at Harvard, is now on the faculty of the Neuropsychiatric Institute at the University of California at Los Angeles.

Since both are among the principal exponents of the much disputed theory that impulsive violence is tied directly to malfunctioning brain cells, Thomas was referred to them for treatment. According to these physicians, Thomas, "a brilliant, 34-year-old engineer, with several important patents to his credit,"[1] had suffered serious brain damage because of a prolonged drop in his blood pressure following surgery on a peptic ulcer while he was in the army fourteen years before. This resulted in brain anemia and serious cerebral damage.

When discharged from the service Thomas educated himself as an engineer. Despite his muscular physique, the doctors said, "it was difficult to believe he was capable of an act of violence . . . for his manner was quiet and reserved, and he was both courteous and sympathetic." But his behavior at times "was unpredictable and frankly psychotic."[2]

Thomas's chief problem, the two Harvard professors reported, was his violent rage; "this was sometimes directed at his coworkers and friends, but it was mostly expressed toward his wife and children." He suspected his wife of carrying on with a neighbor. His wife's denials "were enough to set him off into a frenzy of violence. He would sometimes pick up his wife and throw her against the wall . . . These periods of rage usually lasted for five or six minutes, after which he would be overcome with remorse and grief and sob as uncontrollably as he had raged."

His psychiatrist finally had him hospitalized, and brain-wave examination "disclosed epileptic electrical activity in both temporal regions . . ."[3]

And now Dr. Mark and Dr. Ervin were hovering over Thomas, noting his responses to the different electrical stimuli. With the current turned off, the electrodes became the conduits of information on brain-wave activity at the various points in which the electrodes were lodged. The flow of electroencephalograms (EEGs) was interpreted as additional confirmation of the presence of brain pathology. EEG tracings showed cascading and spiking patterns at the point where stimulation triggered anger or rage. These seemed to be telltale signs of where the trouble lay.

This brain investigation continued for ten weeks, and throughout this period Thomas ate, slept, and walked about with the electrodes implanted in the pink gray, jellylike substance that makes up the human brain.*

Dr. Mark and Dr. Ervin say they were able to control Thomas's violent behavior every day by stimulating a particular section of the brain — the lateral amygdala, which countered the rage reaction. But to continue stimulating the brain indefinitely to inhibit his temper tantrums was considered impractical. Finally, certain that they had zeroed in on the "guilty" brain cells, they decided that the long-term answer lay in psychosurgery.

---

*Among the many interesting oddities about the brain is that although it functions as the headquarters for transmitting and controlling pain throughout the body, it does not reflect sensation itself except when stimulated at specific points.

Thomas agreed to this course of action "while he was relaxed from lateral stimulation of the amygdala" — described as a rather pleasant sensation. When the effect had worn off, however, "Thomas turned wild and unmanageable . . . The idea of anyone's making a destructive lesion in his brain enraged him," the Harvard professors report.[4]

But after many weeks of persuasion Thomas consented. And so Dr. Mark and Dr. Ervin passed a current through the electrodes, more powerful and at a different frequency than that used for stimulation, and the patient found himself minus a cluster of "defective" brain cells and presumably freed of his hostile ways.

There are two endings to the story. The first: In their book, *Violence and the Brain*, the two doctors cite the case of Thomas R. as a successful example of how surgical intervention liberated the patient from impulsive outbursts of rage and aggressive behavior. Four years following surgery they reported that "Thomas has not had a single episode of rage."[5]

The second ending: Thomas R. is now suing Dr. Mark and Dr. Ervin for $2 million. Filed on his behalf by his mother, the suit alleges that his episodes of rage are worse than before the operation and that he has become unemployable.

Harvard-trained psychiatrist Peter R. Breggin, a leading opponent of psychosurgery, who conducted his own follow-up investigation, charges that "Thomas is chronically deluded and hallucinates frequently: lives in constant terror that surgeons will again control his mind." He says that Thomas will often pile books on his head so as to ward off the possibility of another operation.[6]

According to Dr. Breggin, who interviewed the patient and the family, Thomas's mother describes her son as someone "who is almost a vegetable." Following surgery, Dr. Breggin reports, Thomas moved to California, where he developed a series of psychological abnormalities he never experienced before. His wife divorced him and remarried. He is frequently picked up by the local police when found disoriented and delusional. The VA hospital in which he winds up from time to time describes him as a "schizophrenic, paranoid type."[7]

The upcoming trial may reveal where most of the truth lies.

On the West Coast, a young schizophrenic, 22 years of age, moody, with a background of unpredictable, aggressive behavior, came under the care of Dr. Petter A. Lindstrom, formerly of San Francisco and now in San Diego. The young man's school history was spotty. He never was able "to reach high school grades." Periodically he did chores on a farm, but as time went on he became ever more aggressive and even violent. He was institutionalized three times, usually receiving psychotherapy as well as drugs and electroshock. But all to no avail.

With Dr. Lindstrom, who specializes in the use of ultrasound on the prefrontal area of the brain, the young man began to show such improvement following this procedure that he was able to return to work on a farm. Four months after treatment, however, Dr. Lindstrom reports, "the old symptoms gradually recurred" and additional ultrasound irradiation also failed.[8] The young man was returned to a psychiatric institution, increasingly losing contact with reality. Despite such occasional failures, Dr. Lindstrom says, his method generally leads to substantial alleviation of a variety of mental ailments. Dr. Lindstrom's strong advocacy of ultrasound therapy is based on his belief that these high-frequency vibrations, under the control of the surgeon, bring relief without causing the complications that frequently accompany the use of the scalpel in brain surgery. "There is no destruction of neural tissue," he told me, in the course of a phone conversation.[9] As for the side effects, the California surgeon doesn't feel they are too serious. If the irradiation dosage is too high and if the treatment is repeated several times, paresis (paralysis) may develop. But most of the time this condition may be temporary, he says.

Dr. Lindstrom calls his technique the Prefrontal Sonic Treatment (PST). He directs an ultrasound beam, about 20 millimeters in diameter, through two or three small holes drilled in the skull onto the prefrontal area, involving the white matter of the brain tissue. This is not a true lobotomy procedure, he contends, "since neither the surface of the brain nor the brain sheets are cut or punctured." He compares his approach with a "regional electro-shock," affecting "part of the prefrontal white matter instead of the cortex."[10] The operation is carried out in two stages, two days apart. The dosage schedule (exposure time and intensity of sonic beams) is related to the age and condition of the patient. Hospitalization time is nine days.

Citing a group of 383 patients made up of psychotics and psychoneurotics who underwent ultrasound therapy, Dr. Lindstrom said he was heartened by what he felt were a substantial number of favorable results. Many of these, Dr. Lindstrom pointed out, "had reached the point when other treatments had failed . . ." But a number of patients, he said, "did not admit the improvement which their postirradiation behavior according to all observers implied," and this he attributed to their basic "negativism."[11]

In a paper that he presented at the Second International Conference on Psychosurgery in Copenhagen, 1972, Dr. Lindstrom further elaborated on this matter by stating that

> the symptoms which were the reason for the PST, i.e., anxiety and depression, may have improved but then the basic schizophrenic condition may have continued, slowly leading to other symptoms, as irrational behavior or paranoia, altering an early good result to a late poor one. This may have been the basis for the fact that three of the psychotics and two others, classified as neurotic, committed suicide months or years after the treatment.[12]

Interestingly enough, Dr. Lindstrom himself points out that the effect of "PST on patients has been an improvement or eradication of certain disabling symptoms," but "not necessarily a cure of the basic disease."[13] Critics raise the question as to whether some of the symptoms that Dr. Lindstrom was attempting to correct were actually related to disease altogether, even though, he said, the patients were chronically ill. Dr. Lindstrom reported to the Copenhagen conference that

> There is a possibility that some of these patients could have improved
> . . . *if they could have been placed in an entirely different social and economic*
> *milieu. Other impractical solutions like a new spouse or a different mother-in-*
> *law might have precipitated a turn for the better.*[14]

Although most enthusiastic about his PST development, Dr. Lindstrom does suggest a few caveats with respect to patients who may not respond favorably to such treatment. This list includes persons with "sociopathic personality disorders" and those with severe negativism, alcoholism, paranoia, severe social maladjustment, or immaturity. Finally, he adds, if there is little or no familial or environmental support during convalescence or rehabilitation, "the prognosis is more doubtful."[15] Barring such conditions, Dr. Lindstrom feels there is every reason for success. Since 1954 Dr. Lindstrom has performed 550 psychosurgical operations via ultrasound.

Whether by electricity or by ultrasound, Thomas R. and Dr. Lindstrom's patients had this in common — they underwent psychosurgery — a procedure designed to alter their behavior. It was not done to remove actual physical problems such as a tumor or a blood clot, nor was it aimed at modifying a neurological disorder such as Parkinsonism. It was done on the assumption that there were certain defective brain cells or faulty neurological circuits that were the root of these patients' aberrant behavior. And the remedy consisted of either removing or destroying those cells.

The National Institute of Mental Health (NIMH), the federal government agency charged with the guidance of diagnostic and therapeutic research in the field of mental health, categorically declares that psychosurgery is performed in the absence of direct evidence of existing structural disease or damage of the brain.[16] Critics refer to the modern procedure as "laundered" lobotomy. Lobotomy, with its appalling side effects, has come into such disrepute since the forties and early fifties that most of the medical profession would just as soon forget it, sweep it under the carpet. According to Dr. Bertram S. Brown, NIMH director, the lobotomy "cure" was "often worse than the disease." He feels that "no responsible scientist today would condone a classical lobotomy operation."[17]

Psychosurgery is usually referred to as the sophisticated spin-off of lobotomy, which involved the lopping off of the prefrontal or frontal lobes of the brain. This is the area where emotional and intellectual processes may interact in high-level thinking and decision making.

Lobotomy was first applied on human patients in 1935, when a Portuguese neuropsychiatrist, Dr. Egas Moniz, became so impressed with a report on how neurotic chimpanzees became passive and compliant after experimental surgery in the frontal lobes that he decided to use it on several of his highly agitated psychotic patients. The initial results seemed dramatic and almost overnight Moniz received worldwide acclaim as the man who had triumphed over schizophrenia.

Sadly enough his "triumph" turned out to be a mixed blessing. He was awarded the Nobel Prize "for his discovery of the therapeutic value of prefrontal lobotomy in certain psychoses."[18] But one of his "successful" lobotomized patients went berserk, got hold of a gun, and fired deliberately at the doctor. The bullet pierced Moniz's spine and he wound up a hemiplegic (having one side of his body paralyzed).

Although clinical data were still sparse and the basic rationale for the operation considered to be on shaky grounds, it didn't take long before lobotomy was introduced to the United States. Pioneers in the American application of lobotomy were Dr. Walter Freeman and Dr. James W. Watts. At first critical of Moniz's haste to move from animal experiments to human patients, they themselves in a relatively short time became the leading exponents of the procedure. True to American technology, Dr. Freeman improved upon Moniz's technique by simplifying it so that the operation could be performed in the doctor's office.

Using what became known as the "ice-pick" method, Dr. Freeman would force an ice-pick-like instrument through the skull immediately above the eye into the prefrontal lobes of the brain. It would then be manipulated in such a way as to cut or separate the bottom sections of the frontal lobes; however, the surgeon was operating blindly and destroying not only the presumed targeted area but also a good deal of the surrounding tissue.

By the early forties lobotomy was applied wholesale. This was the time when thousands of emotionally broken, battle-fatigued soldiers returning from World War II were crowding the psychiatric wards of the Veterans' Administration hospitals. Traditional psychoanalytic techniques did not alleviate their problems, and tranquilizing drugs had not yet made their debut. Vast numbers of nurses and paramedical aides were needed to help restrain the frequently violent veterans. The cost of maintaining such custodial personnel was staggering.

So the use of lobotomy was not altogether motivated by sympathy and desire to relieve the war-torn patient of his torment. Perhaps equally significant was the need to pare the expense of maintaining a large attending staff. As Dr. Freeman once admitted, this type of surgery "proved to be the ideal operation for use in crowded mental hospitals with a shortage of everything except patients."[19]

Veterans' Administration hospitals rushed to set up crash programs to train surgeons in lobotomy techniques and with this encouragement many an overzealous surgeon unsheathed his scalpel and proceeded on his own.[20] It was open season on the luckless "agitated" mental patient, whether a veteran or someone languishing in the back ward of a state mental asylum.

The upshot: Thousands of mental patients soon found themselves with bits of their frontal lobes gone. It is reported that some surgeons did as many as fifty lobotomies a day.[21]

The immediate results usually pointed to a kind of sedation and passivity in the patient. According to Dr. Freeman, many of the formerly turbulent patients, subject to frequent episodes of rage, became quiescent, tamed, and amenable to command. They were then discharged as "cured," to the extent that they no longer crowded the overburdened facilities of the veterans' and state mental institutions.

The real degree of "cure" was never fully evaluated because there were few follow-up studies. Experts describe the lobotomy period as one of the shabbiest in mental health care in this country's experience. Few records were kept and scarcely any controls maintained.[22]

As enthusiastic as Dr. Freeman was about lobotomy (he himself is said to have performed or personally supervised 4000 such operations), he nevertheless conceded that results in many cases were disastrous. Frontal lobotomies, he reported, often led to epileptic seizures, with their onset totally unpredictable; in some instances they began shortly after surgery and in others five or ten years later. The epilepsy incidence was put at 30 percent. There was also a 1 to 3 percent mortality from cerebral hemorrhage that could not be controlled.[23]

In addition, there were bizarre personality changes, ranging from "invisible inertia" to "perpetual overactivity." The frontal lobe syndrome, he quipped, might be epitomized as "all the Boy Scout virtues in reverse": for instance, a total indifference to one's personal appearance and, therefore, a lack of restraint in food intake. Many of those "cured" became irritable, profane, rude, and developed other disagreeable traits they had not shown before.[24]

Many patients were no longer able to introspect, project conceptually into the future, make plans, or work on anything more than the lowest menial level. "On the whole," Dr. Freeman once said, "psychosurgery [lobotomy] reduces creativity, sometimes to the vanishing point."[25]

Urging the need for family assistance to the patient following surgery, Dr. Freeman also pointed to the great difficulties connected with such care. "The patient who has undergone extensive psychosurgery is at first immature in his reactions, going about carelessly dressed, responding hastily and sometimes tactlessly, and indulging his appetites for food, drink, sex, repose, and spending money with little regard for the convenience or welfare of others.

"At the same time, the patient has lost his sensitiveness to criticism. He may flare up in anger but does not sulk for long. The function of the family is to help the patient grow up from this surgically induced childhood."[26]

Adverse reports on lobotomy began drifting in from different parts of the country just as the tranquilizers made their dramatic impact in freeing thousands of patients from their straitjackets. As suddenly as lobotomy shot into the therapeutic firmament as the answer to whatever ails one emotionally, so did it plummet down in disrepute. By the early 1950s it was definitely on the way out as a cure, but not before leaving a "lobotomy wasteland" littered with some 50,000 human "retreads," many of whom had slid into a vegetablelike state.

Present-day psychosurgeons admit that the early lobotomy techniques were primitive. But now, they insist, the picture has changed. A lot more has been discovered about brain function and its various neuron pathways, and many new technological developments, they claim, have made it feasible and safe to tame impetuous aggressiveness through surgical intervention. The science of neurophysiology, they say, has advanced to such a degree that different behavioral patterns can be correlated with specific locations in the brain. With the availability of sophisticated instrumentation, such as depth electrodes, diseased cells that get in the way of normal brain functioning can be pinpointed with exactitude and then removed or destroyed with little damage to the surrounding tissue. Modern stereotactic surgical methods involving geometric coordinates and X-ray inspection make possible the positioning of the tiny electrodes precisely in the right spot.

Scientists critical of psychosurgery argue that as yet there exists no proof of a direct tie between specific brain cell abnormality and corresponding behavioral disorder. But even if there were such a link, these scientists point out, reaching the diseased or abnormal cells with electrodes would be nothing less than a miracle.

The brain is believed to be made up of billions of cells and thousands of electrical circuits, all closely intertwined. For these electrodes to reach the right cell would be equivalent to elbowing one's way through the proverbial multitude of angels standing on the head of a pin and attempting to make contact with only one of the angels for a private, uninterrupted conversation.

But in addition to finding the exact "diseased" point in the brain, there is the enormous danger of mutilating much of the surrounding cellular "wiring" in which it is swathed. It's like trying to pluck out one thread in a closely spun spider web without tearing into the rest of the fabric. When that happens in the brain, destruction of the "defective" cells that are suspected of causing aggressiveness or other disordered behavior usually spells annihilation for the cells in the adjacent areas. Thus, healthy cells that influence personality, individual sensitivities, or intelligence potential may also go down the drain.

Ordinarily, the debate on psychosurgery might have remained confined to neuroscientists, surgeons, and psychiatrists. But the issue has spilled over beyond the medical community. Increasingly it has generated shock waves of concern that psychosurgery, as well as electrical brain stimulation, may hold more promise as brain-control methods than as cures for emotional disturbance.

Psychosurgery began surfacing as a political issue in the late sixties, when civil disorders began shaking the country. With the dust hardly settled following the Detroit riots of 1967, Dr. Mark and Dr. Ervin, together with Dr. William H. Sweet, professor of surgery at Harvard, advanced the theory that "brain dysfunction" in some rioters might have been as strong a reason for the disorders as the social and economic causes.[27] Others, however, felt that this was a way of stigmatizing social activists with the label of sickness — persons who were impelled to lead demonstrations because of brain pathology.

3. Behavioral Surgery

EXPERIMENTS WITH electrical brain stimulation in animals began early in the nineteenth century. By mid-century, scientists in Italy, England, Russia, France, and Germany were already sticking electrically charged pins and needles into the brains of dogs, frogs, and cats in an attempt to learn more about the nature of the nervous system.

But it was not until the 1920s that two European scientists came up with separate discoveries that gave neurophysiological research a dramatic push forward and paved the way to modern psychosurgery and brain conditioning techniques in general.

The Austrian psychiatrist Hans Berger discovered in 1924 that the brain gave off electrical signals, which he was able to record via tracings on paper, similar to the method used in recording heart action (ECGs) by the electrocardiographic apparatus. He named these signals electroencephalograms — EEGs for short — the first recorded clues to the neural activity of the brain.[1]

That same year the Swiss physiologist Walter R. Hess began investigating behavioral responses in animals with electrical stimulation of various intracranial regions through wires implanted in their brains.[2] Working mostly with cats, Hess was able to pinpoint upward of 4000 neural sites in the hypothalamus that related directly to specific reactions of the animals. Stimulation at one point threw the animal into violent rage. At another point, the cat began to sweat. In yet another area the cat would eat voraciously.

In a strange kind of way, the two researchers had begun communicating directly with the brain. On the one hand, Berger was eavesdropping on what was going on inside the brain by spelling out its electrical activity through the EEGs. Hess, by prodding various cell clusters of the brain with electrical charges, was ordering them to activate different body functions and possibly emotions of the animal undergoing the experiment.

Berger's first experimental subject was his own teen-age son. By attaching silver strips to his son's scalp and wiring them to a galvanometer, Berger was able to develop the first EEGs. The initial tracings were hazy and frequently difficult to make out. Brain activity was reflected by a steady waxing and waning rhythm on the tracings, which Berger called alpha waves.

He was as excited as he was baffled by this phenomenon. This rhythmic brain-wave oscillation would be quite well defined while the person lay quietly with his eyes closed. But if his eyes were open, or if his attention was diverted, this rhythmic pattern would dissolve or disappear. When the person undergoing EEG examination was confronted with a challenge, such as a mathematical problem, the EEGs would begin to vary in size, and Berger, as well as other scientists, began to ponder the possibility that the EEG might provide the clue to certain intracranial disturbances.

For a time Berger's findings spurred a number of scientists, and certainly the pseudoscientists, to seize on the notion that the EEGs would be the keys to reading a person's innermost character secrets. As a matter of fact, for many years the role of EEGs was relegated for the most part to vaudeville performances and freak acts. The scientific significance of EEG remained moot at best and questionable. It wasn't until two British physiologists, E. D. Adrian and B. H. C. Matthews, of Cambridge University, replicated Berger's findings that scientific interest in EEGs was renewed.[3]

Eventually the entertainment interest in this brain phenomenon began to flag. On the other hand, refinements in equipment and EEG technique led to improved diagnosis of such conditions as epilepsy.

But even though improvements in the Berger technique continued, encephalograms taken via scalp attachments are still not as clearly defined as those recorded by means of electrodes sunk deep in the brain. Unless there is an urgent need to locate a major brain disorder, however, many neurologists feel that the risks associated with implanting depth electrodes would scarcely be justified.

Hess's findings have made an even greater impact on neurophysiological research. Once again, the prospect of controlling man's physical and emotional behavior at will, a fond notion of many a dreamer inclined to redirect the course of human history by brain manipulation, seemed at hand. But it was a mixed bag of discoveries.

Stimulation at one point would make the cat "angry, spitting, hostile and ready to attack."[4] Applying the electrode just a few millimeters away would elicit purring.

On further experimentation Hess found that just as he was able to have these electrical stimulations turn on a cat's wrath almost instantly, so too was he able to douse the animal's fury by cutting off the current. This phenomenon became known as "sham" rage, since it did not stem from the complex emotions that customarily lead to anger. Scientists could scarcely accept this display of anger or other electrically induced moods as being connected with other than psychomotor activity.[5]

Hess was also able to trigger voracious appetites in animals that had already eaten and ordinarily would have been considered satiated. When Hess stimulated the hypothalamus, the animal began devouring food all over again. "As a matter of fact," Hess reported, "the animal may even take into its mouth or gnaw on objects that are unsuitable food, such as forceps, keys or sticks . . ."[6] The question arises, therefore, whether this "appetite" was induced by true hunger or by a motor activity forced upon the animal by brain stimulation.

The debate on this issue has not ceased. To this day there are investigators who feel strongly that these emotional reflexes are the real thing and not at all a "sham."

One of the most dramatic experiments related to this question was the famous demonstration performed in a Madrid bullring some years ago by the eminent neurophysiologist Dr. José M. R. Delgado, formerly of Yale and now back in his native Spain. Dr. Delgado outfitted a bull, one especially bred for bullfights, with a radio-controlled electrode within its brain and a battery-powered receiver fastened to its horns. Standing dressed in a sweater and slacks, Dr. Delgado's only identification with the matador image was a red cape, which he waved at the oncoming "brave bull" — hundreds of pounds of unbridled fury charging directly at the scientist. At the moment when the bull was only several yards away, Dr. Delgado felt for his transmitter, his only counterweapon, and pressed a button. This signaled the receiver at the horns, which in turn activated the electrode that stimulated the caudate nucleus, a brain structure involved in controlling muscular and movement responses. The bull came to a roaring full stop.[7]

Dr. Delgado believes that stimulation of this section of the brain will inhibit aggressiveness. "Brave bulls [especially trained for the bullring] are dangerous animals that will attack any intruder into the arena. The animal, in full charge, can be abruptly stopped by radio stimulation of the brain. After several stimulations, there is a lasting inhibition of aggressive behavior."[8]

His critics, however, feel that the bull came to a stop not because, like the legendary Ferdinand, he became transformed into a beatific and kindhearted animal, but because the caudate nucleus, which controls such motor activity as walking and running, was inhibited by the electrical charge that was passed through the electrode. These scientists contend that the animal's coming to a halt was more of a motor than a mood phenomenon.[9]

Whatever the interpretations of the induced rage phenomenon, there is little question that advances in electronics and surgical technique have ushered in a new era in brain research. The availability of thinner and better refined electrodes that could be implanted with less mutilating effect on the surrounding neural tissue was hailed as a boon to investigative research. Improved procedures for placing the electrodes with greater accuracy in the desired regions of the brain, with the help of anatomical atlases and three-dimensional X-ray monitoring devices, was another new benefit. And what with telemetric amplifiers adapted from space exploration and computer data analysis, the stage appeared set for sensational revelations about the elusive brain.

As a result, there is now a race to determine who will be the first to find the key that will unlock the door to the mysterious brain — provided, of course, that there is such a door.

From coast to coast, American neurophysiological laboratories are busy experimenting on animals and, in some cases, on people. Whether in New York, Boston, New Orleans, Chicago, or San Francisco, thousands of laboratory animals — cats, mice, rats, and primates — are wired with electrical gadgetry in an attempt to learn what it is that triggers their various behavioral patterns. Rhesus monkeys, looking like little, old wizened-faced men, are strapped into chairs (resembling a baby's high chair), their arms shackled to their sides, with dozens of electrodes anchored at the skull and embedded in the brain. They sit there, in the fullest sense a captive population, from time to time baring their teeth and snapping at the attendant who is adjusting an electrical setting or testing a reaction by thrusting his fingers in front of the primates' eyes.

At regular intervals the current is switched on and passes through these electrodes into the various inner parts of the monkey's brain. The animal may dart in one direction, try to lift itself up, or make some other gesture at an impossible escape, while laboratory technicians are busily scribbling down observations of its behavior.

Buoyed by the new technology, a number of neuroscientists

quickly overcame the inhibitions caused by the disappointing experience with lobotomy. Most psychosurgeons have now abandoned the basic principle of lobotomy, involving the cutting of the neural fibers in the prefrontal lobes, an area considered to be the decision-making and perceptual frontier of the brain, and have shifted their attention to the limbic system, which is situated much deeper inside the brain.

The limbic system consists of the cingulum, the hippocampus, the hypothalamus, and the amygdala. Experimentation has shown that extensive destruction of any of these components of the limbic system radically alters the behavior of both animals and people.

Interference with the cingulum, which is a sort of information-disseminating station for various parts of the brain, especially for the frontal lobes, leads to a dramatic change in character. Monkeys whose cingula have been destroyed tend to lose what has been described as a "social conscience." They become oblivious to their companions, bumping into them, and grabbing their food without regard to possible resistance, as though their fellow primates were inanimate objects. The American neurosurgeon Arthur A. Ward, Jr., describes their seeming unawareness of how their movements may affect others as equivalent to a "loss of ability to accurately forecast social repercussions of their own actions."[10]

The hippocampus and the hypothalamus, together with the amygdala, make up an interrelated complex that regulates a variety of life drives. In the human being, the hippocampus is strongly involved with memory. When it is damaged on both sides of the brain, the individual's ability to remember — particularly to remember recent experiences — is severely impaired.

Memory function is not regulated by the hippocampus alone. Damage to other parts of intracranial systems can affect memory related to cultural rules governing behavior. Dr. Mark and Dr. Ervin tell the story of a 62-year-old bank executive who underwent surgery in the frontal lobe to alleviate severe pain caused by cancer. The operation was a success and the man recovered enough to return to his normal work and social routines. As a matter of fact, he felt so well that he persuaded his wife to join him to go to the opera. The man "dressed himself immaculately in formal evening attire and walked with his wife from their house to the theater. His conversation was witty and urbane. About halfway there, he said 'Excuse me,' and in full view of on-coming traffic and pedestrians, he urinated in the street!" His brain, according to Mark and Ervin, "had lost the use of a basic cultural taboo, and hence some of its capacity to predict the consequences of behavior."[11]

The hypothalamus is like a general headquarters in directing such physical functions as sweating, eating, drinking, waking, and sexuality, among others. As in the amygdala, there are points in the hypothalamus that, when stimulated, will throw a usually friendly animal into frenzied rage. When the current is turned off, the animal soon returns to its calm self.

But it is the amygdala, an almond-shaped mass of gray matter, that has taken the limelight over the past decade. It is the amygdala that is most strongly identified with rage, violence, and aggression. Some neuroscientists tend to agree that when this region of the brain is stimulated, many individuals (but not all) will have a variety of unfriendly or downright hostile reactions.

Doing away with the amygdala reportedly brings about a "taming" effect. Frequently, this taming transforms the individual into a sluggish, unresponsive, flat and, in many instances, compliant and accepting personality. But again all this is unpredictable, since many of those who have had their amygdala destroyed suddenly erupt into assaultive outbursts months and even years after the operation.

These discoveries about the limbic system, however shadowy and insubstantial, have nevertheless rekindled anew the hope that curing or controlling brain pathology linked with emotional crisis or aberrant behavior is within immediate grasp through various forms of psychosurgery.

Although some neuroscientists have heady visions of success, others, such as Dr. Donald Rushmer, associate director of the Neurophysiology Laboratory at Good Samaritan Hospital, Portland, Oregon, continue to warn against the use of psychosurgery. "We have just begun to reach a rudimentary understanding of how the brain functions and a primitive awareness of how the brain might control behavior in animals such as cats, rats and monkeys," Dr. Rushmer holds. In testimony before the Oregon legislature in 1973 on the need to declare psychosurgery an experimental procedure, Dr. Rushmer stated:

> It is no understatement to say that we have barely scratched the surface with our present knowledge of how even the simple nervous system of the frog really works, let alone how the billions of nerve cells in the human brain interrelate to give the range of emotions, intellect and abilities we so often take for granted . . .[12]

A similarly cautious note comes from Dr. Seymour S. Kety, a Harvard professor of psychiatry and former director of the Laboratory of Clinical Science at NIMH. "We don't really know enough about the brain or about its functions to be really sure of what we are doing when we do psychosurgery," he told me at a scientific meeting in 1974, in New York. He added, "We don't know enough of how the brain works. We don't know enough of the mechanism of action of the brain pathways to offer a rationale for psychosurgery."[13]

Interestingly enough, even the psychosurgery enthusiasts differ among themselves. There is disagreement as to the kinds of surgery to be employed. There is little concurrence on what emotional disturbances are best suited for this operation. And there is even greater disagreement about what part of the brain structure should be destroyed to effect the desired cure.

This was dramatically illustrated some years ago at an international psychosurgery meeting in Copenhagen. It was somewhat reminiscent of the poem "The Blind Men and the Elephant." Each of the six blind men touched only one part of the elephant's body, but each quickly came to a firm conclusion about the overall appearance of the beast. Opponents of psychosurgery believe the situation is exactly the same with psychosurgeons. Although they are groping like the blind men to get a fix on the *cause* of aberrant human behavior, they will not hesitate to state decisively what specific course to take in treating the *condition*.

What emerged at the meeting, according to Dr. Grimm, the Oregon neurophysiologist, is that "psychosurgeons are not in agreement as to the technique, the specificity of the lesion site, the size of the lesion, the nature of the psychiatric illness amenable to procedures, the extent or format of follow-up studies, or long-term consequences for any proposed operations."[14]

One of the participants at the meeting, a prominent British lobotomist, Dr. Eric Turner of the Queen Elizabeth Hospital, Birmingham, England, pleaded with his confreres for some order in arriving at diagnostic conclusions. He declared:

> A plea is made for accuracy of anatomical description of any operative procedures, and accuracy of psychiatric description of clinical states, even if this means abandoning sophisticated psychiatric terminology and limiting psychiatric description to a simplified but generally agreed nomenclature.
>
> It is clear that in many cases different people have different conceptions of what is meant, for example, by aggression, paranoid schizophrenia or obsessional neurosis; so that this last diagnosis may be confused with involutional depression in a previous obsessional personality, a condition entirely different from a true obsessional neurosis and *with an entirely different prognosis* after frontal lobotomy.[15]

In view of this disarray among the psychosurgeons themselves, critics ask, what chance has the patient, or those committing him to such procedures, of arriving at a considered decision?

Of course those who take a dim view of psychiatry could make similar criticism. There is probably an even greater variance of opinion among the different psychiatric schools of thought about the causes of emotional illness and the preferred therapeutic approach to it. Orthodox Freudians feud with Jungians, who in turn take issue with Reichians, who for their part may disagree with the followers of Stekel, etc.

Although the beneficial effects of these respective therapies may be very much in question, no psychiatric technique in itself is damaging to the brain structure of the individual — but psychosurgery is. Once brain tissue is surgically removed or burned out with electricity, it is gone forever. Neural cells cannot regenerate. The patient's personality is different for the rest of his or her life.

While Dr. Mark and Dr. Ervin attack the "defective" amygdala in the belief that it is most culpable for violent behavior, Dr. Orlando J. Andy, of the University of Mississippi Medical Center, is concerned with the thalamus. (Dr. Andy is known especially for his many operations on hyperkinetic-aggressive children, some only six years of age.)

The British Dr. Turner prefers a combined operation, involving the temporal lobe, the prefrontal lobe, and the cingulum.[16] Dr. M. Hunter Brown, of California, is an even greater champion of combined operations. He invades the brain on both sides of the amygdala, the cingulum, and the substantia innominata — six simultaneous targets. "I'm the only multiple target surgeon in the world and I do more target surgery than anyone in the world," he told me during an interview in his office in the spring of 1974.[17]

According to a survey by the American Psychiatric Association for the year 1972, there were upward of seventy neurosurgeons in the United States who performed psychosurgery.[18] Many of them are involved in various surgical attempts at modifying or "curing" so-called antisocial behavior, whether it be violence, alcoholism, homosexuality, drug addiction, or different neuroses or psychoses.

The two physicians who have become most closely identified with the concept that violence and aggression can be treated surgically are Dr. Mark and Dr. Ervin. Their book, *Violence and the Brain*, put forward the theory and treatment rationale for aggressiveness that has since become one of the most controversial within the medical community.

The two doctors agree with the generally accepted thesis that the limbic system, except in animals who live by hunting, "is present for self-defense as a response to perceived threat . . ." A healthy state, in terms of self-preservation. "Thus the limbic brain cannot be thought of solely as an aggression system."[19]

"In a well-ordered brain," they add, " the mechanisms of violence are there, but they need never be out of control."[20] When things go awry, however, one of two things has happened: either the limbic system has become pathologically hyperactive due to a lesion or stimulation; or, early environmental and cultural influences have programmed the brain in such a way that it "will perceive threats more intensely or more frequently" than usually considered normal. In either event it will "call the limbic organization into action for violent attack."

According to Mark and Ervin, if the undesirable environmental programming takes place at an early age, then there are no remedial ways left open except surgery.

> If environmental conditions are wrong at the important time, then the resulting anatomical maldevelopment *is irreversible,* even though the environmental conditions may later be corrected . . .
>
> The kind of violent behavior related to brain malfunction may have its origins in the environment, but once the brain structure has been permanently affected, the violent behavior can no longer be modified by manipulating psychological or social influences. Hoping to rehabilitate such a violent individual through psychotherapy or education, or to improve his character by sending him to jail or giving him love and understanding — all these methods are irrelevant and will not work. It is the brain malfunction itself that must be dealt with, and only if this is recognized is there any chance of changing behavior.[21]

Within this frame of reference, neither the usual psychotherapeutic approaches nor the extension of new opportunities to those whose delinquency might have stemmed directly from frustrations tied to economic privation have any bearing. In this view, the irreducible fact is that the mechanics of brain function have been impaired and that only by altering the brain structure is there any hope for relief or cure.

The approach outlined by Dr. Mark and Dr. Ervin has two other features with wide appeal. First, it could be considered humane, since assaultive individuals, freed from their aggressiveness through psychosurgery, would no longer be kept in mental institutions or in jails. Second, there is a substantial economic fringe benefit. The confinement of a prisoner is said to cost as much per year as the tuition and upkeep of a Harvard undergraduate. As Dr. M. Hunter Brown, the exuberant California psychosurgeon, assured me, "This thing [psychosurgery] will pay off in great measure to the citizenry. You know, it costs up to $250,000 to keep a young man imprisoned for life. So just financially, let alone the humane reasons, psychosurgery pays off."[22]

Considering the number of potentially violence-prone individuals in this country, as estimated by Dr. Mark and Dr. Ervin, the economic aspects of crime could take on formidable proportions. The two doctors claim that those suffering from brain dysfunction may run into the millions. Not all, of course, they point out, will necessarily wind up as burglars or murderers, but an impressive percentage of this group have such low thresholds of tolerance that they are likely to explode in some form of violent outburst.

Large-scale experimentation with psychosurgery and other behavior-reshaping techniques therefore becomes urgent. Critics of this view charge that in all likelihood the subjects of such experimentation will be those who are least able to resist the power of those wielding authority: the jail inmates, the mentally ill, children, and adolescents.

4. Reshaping the Child

UNDER THE GLARE of operating room lights, a seven-year-old boy, heavily anesthetized but awake enough to respond to questions, is strapped down on an operating table. Standing directly behind is the surgeon, his eyes riveted on a scalpel that he carefully slides down a penciled line, making an incision of several inches across the boy's shaven head.

While a nurse is sponging away the blood, another hands the surgeon a drill, a conventional type or one that is power-driven, which he applies to different points of the exposed skull. A few brief bursts of the drill, accompanied by the sound of a shrill metallic whine and the smell of burning bone, and the skull openings, or burr holes, are completed.

The surgeon then begins pushing electrodes, thin wires, into the target areas of the brain. Depending on the particular approach, some surgeons will implant twenty or thirty electrodes, others may use several dozen. The electrodes are activated to stimulate different sections of the brain so as to elicit EEG tracings. The cascading, spiraling EEG patterns from a given site of the limbic system are considered to be the indicators of the area in which the trouble lies. And so with a stronger charge of electricity than is used to spark the brain responses, the "pathological" tissues are burned out. The operation takes about three hours.

Variations of this type of surgery on children are quite fre-

quent in Japan and India.* In this country, the surgeon usually
associated with psychosurgery for children is Dr. Orlando J.
Andy, Department of Neurosurgery, University of Mississippi
Medical Center. The objective is the same, wherever the operation is performed: to quiet what Dr. Andy might describe as the
"hyperresponsive syndrome." This he defines as an erratic, aggressive, emotionally unstable pattern of behavior.[1]

Quite obviously, the young boy undergoing psychosurgery is
no longer going to be obstreperous or drive his teachers up the
wall, as he used to when he flailed about in bursts of blind fury to
express something he himself could not define in words. Critics
contend that with his brain function now altered by electrical destruction of parts of the thalamus or of the amygdala, the boy is
likely to begin living an emotionally flat, subdued existence.
Much of his intellectual or perception potential may be gone
forever. In sum, he was forced to forfeit his original personality
and take on a new one that would be of convenience to those
about him, rather than being of primary benefit to him.

Convenience, apparently, plays a role in Dr. Andy's thinking.
Psychosurgery, he told a Senate subcommittee hearing a few
years ago, "should be used for custodial purposes when a patient
requires constant attention, supervision, and an inordinate
amount of institutional care." Judging by much of the previous
experience with psychosurgery and lobotomy, the probability is
that as the boy grows up he is going to be submissive and ready
to take orders rather than assert himself. And his range of imagination, his abstractive powers, and his thinking potential in
general — his endowment at birth — will begin shrinking. Dr.
Andy's own report on a nine-year-old patient — brought out at
the Senate subcommittee hearing — revealed that after the op-

---

* Because of the prevailing mores in some parts of the East, a family may feel
stigmatized if one of its children is institutionalized because of emotional problems. To save face relatives will consent to having a child undergo psychosurgery
in the hope that he would become manageable at home, once his unruly or
hyperactive behavior is diffused.

eration the boy was "intellectually . . . deteriorating."[2] But there
were also successes, Dr. Andy told the committee.

Scarcely allowing for the possibility that children's emotional
outbursts may also be related to a host of environmental and
family difficulties, Dr. Andy sees hyperactivity as a disorder resulting directly from "structurally abnormal brain tissue." This is
a fact, he said, "which some psychiatrists and psychologists do
not know or tend to forget." The remedy, he insists, is surgery.[3]

Moreover, he contended, the sooner psychosurgery is done on
the "hyperresponsive" child, the better. Psychosurgery, he declared, "should be used in the adolescent and pediatric age
group in order to allow the developing brain to mature with as
normal a reaction to its environment as possible."[4] This view
runs counter to the prevailing thinking of many neuroscientists
who believe that children usually recover from a variety of
psychiatric disorders during the process of maturation.*

In another era, perhaps even twenty years ago, such operations might have caused an outcry of indignation, with dozens of
humane and child-shelter groups clamoring for a halt to this
type of surgery, since it is still based on a questionable scientific
rationale. But in the 1970s, with a soaring crime rate and a
breakdown of national morale, there are those who choose to
look the other way. Any restraining means, even if draconian in
character, are accepted in the grim hope that somehow they will
stem the tide of juvenile disquiet and lawlessness.

The degree to which Americans are willing to mortgage their
conscience in exchange for the promise of security against crime
raises quite a number of questions about what we are doing to

*The National Commission for the Protection of Human Subjects of Biomedi-
cal and Behavioral Research, in the preliminary draft of its psychosurgery recommendations (August 24, 1976) stated: "There are too few studies on the effects
of psychosurgery on children to present a clear picture of the advisability of such
procedures at this time, especially inasmuch as very little is known regarding the
long-term effects of such surgery on the immature brain . . . Thus, extreme caution should be exercised in considering the application of psychosurgery to
young patients."

our children. There is much public hand-wringing about child abuse, but very few attempts to deal with the problem at its source — the hopeless abyss of the slum that spawns hundreds of thousands of youngsters destined to become victims and killers at the same time.

More than half a million children are locked up in adult jails each year in the United States, and another half million are held in detention facilities. Many of these juveniles find themselves behind bars even though they have not committed any crimes.

In upper New York State, for instance, 43 percent of the children held in prison were "persons in need of supervision." They had not been charged with a misdemeanor or a felony. A great number were "naive" offenders.[5]

Their crimes? They had been arrested for wandering about on the street until late into the night, or had been caught smoking cigarettes at school, or had sneaked away from class, or been generally truant. These are known as "status" offenses. The interesting part is that if these youngsters had committed these same indiscretions when they were three or four years older, there would be no legal reason for putting them in jail. Adults have the right to keep late hours and to smoke. These children committed a type of "infraction" that, in the protection of a middle-class home, would probably have earned them a scolding or at worst a spanking.

But in the absence of child-shelter facilities in many parts of the United States, and because "some judges . . . explicitly chose jails for juveniles to 'teach them a lesson,'" these children were lumped together with adult criminals for indefinite periods of time. Eventually most of these youngsters were released, but their jail experiences will be a lifelong damaging experience. In those cases where an attempt was made to keep them apart from the adult inmates, separation took the form of solitary confinement, "which apparently led to suicide in several instances."[6]

A University of Michigan research group, the National Assessment of Juvenile Correction, which made public a nationwide study, reports that the situation in other parts of the country is even worse than in New York State. Over a two-year period in Indiana, there were at least forty-five deaths reported among youthful detainees, largely because no special care or supervision was provided. "No one was responsible for the juveniles' daily welfare or for preventing their mistreatment."[7]

What's it like for a child to be in jail? Some examples:

> Well, I was locked up in a cell all by myself. I was up on the upper floor because the boys were down below. And I was the only girl in there, so I was up there by myself. And I was just locked up day and night. And the only time I saw anybody was when they brought my food up to me. I mean, I thought I was going to go crazy for a while, just being locked up all the time . . . there were (books and magazines) there, but I mean, I just didn't feel like reading.[8]

A far harsher picture of maltreatment of status offenders was revealed when a district judge in Texas ordered the closing of several so-called training schools administered by the state of Texas in 1974 [*Morales* vs. *Turman*, 383 F. Supp. 53 (1974)]. In addition to these cases, there were also juvenile delinquents who were transferred from other schools "for such essentially non-violent, uncooperative behavior as swearing at correctional officers, refusing to work, or running away." All told there were some 2000 young people incarcerated, nearly half of whom were girls held in separate quarters. About 56 percent were Mexican-Americans and blacks, and the remainder were "Anglos." Frequently boys caught speaking Spanish would be punched or kicked by way of punishment.

The brutality and dehumanization of these children, the court declared, "were so severe as to be unacceptable to contemporary society." The boys were exposed to cruelty and repression from the very day of admission into these institutions. They were "tested" by "various forms of physical abuse applied by staff or other boys with the encouragement of staff." By way of example: a boy was initially beaten by other boys in his cottage. Later that day "the boys who administered the beating were, in turn, 'racked'" by the correction officer. This meant that the boys were "forced to line up against the wall with their hands in their pockets while the correctional officer punched each one in the stomach."

In the evidence supporting the judge's opinion, many instances were cited in which the mildest of infractions were met with violent reaction from the supervisory staff. When a boy attempted to run away from a work detail he was chased, caught, and then thrown into a cell where tear gas was administered. He was then taken to the hospital but remained unattended and was forced to return to the work detail the following day. There were numerous such tear gassing incidents.

Running away from work detail becomes more understandable when it is learned how "nonfunctional" some of these tasks were. One such work detail involved "useless, strenuous, degrading exercises performed five hours a day . . . boys were lined up foot to foot, heads down, and were required to strike the ground with heavy picks, swung overhead as the line moved forward. Nothing was ever planted in the picked ground . . . The regimen consisted of working for an hour and a half at a time with fifteen-minute breaks. During the breaks, the boys were required to sit in a line with their hands between their legs, looking down; they were not allowed to look in either direction or to talk . . ." Any violation of rules relating to the "'picking' detail was the subject of summary, brutal punishment." Boys were beaten because they dropped their picks or became ill.

On the national scene, the Michigan investigators found that the average age of boys and girls suddenly put away behind prison walls in various parts of the country ranged between twelve and fifteen years. In 1974, when the study was being conducted, of those incarcerated nearly 900 were of primary school age and 254 were under the age of six. The length of their stay in prison might depend on the whim of the individual jailer. Some children were known to have been detained for months.

According to the Michigan study, the detainees "disproportionately" represent the "lower socio-economic and minority" sectors of the population. Girls "have a greater probability of being detained, and held for a longer period than males, even though the overwhelming majority are charged with status offenses" and not with felonies.[9]

In 1973, a presidential commission charged with the task of formulating policies on criminal justice indicated strong disapproval of the imprisonment of youthful delinquents in county jails. As far back as 1961, the National Council on Crime and Delinquency warned that such incarceration would have a most devastating effect on the development of these children, with a ricocheting effect on society.

"To place them behind bars at a time when the world seems to turn against them and belief in themselves is shattered or distorted," the council stated, "merely confirms the criminal role in which they see themselves. Jailing delinquent youngsters plays directly into their hands by giving them delinquency status among their peers. "If they resent being treated like confirmed adult criminals, they may — and often do — strike back violently against society after release."[10]

Instead of working to ameliorate this social destruction, the vast machinery of government and community law enforcement seems to be poised to do battle with the end-product — the spiritually mutilated, blighted adolescent whose fate was sealed while still in the cradle.

Such agencies as the Law Enforcement Assistance Administration and the Department of Health, Education, and Welfare and its various subgroups are spending millions of dollars every year to create new programs designed to hold the growing army of juvenile malcontents at bay.

It is scarcely surprising, therefore, especially in the "law and order" atmosphere cultivated by the Nixon administration, that a move was under way to organize "preventive" detention camps for children and juvenile delinquents who might be prone to violent behavior. As reported in the *Washington Post*, the program was conceived and drawn up by Nixon's former physician, Dr. Arnold A. Hutschnecker. The proposal, reviewed by Daniel Moynihan and then submitted by John Ehrlichman to Robert H.

Finch, then the secretary of HEW, called for the testing of children at the age of six for future criminal tendencies. Those found unruly, or otherwise emotionally suspect, would then be confined to camps where they would learn more socially accepted behavior patterns.[11]

Dr. Hutschnecker later denied this version of his proposal in an article in the *New York Times*.[12] He said that all he suggested was that children "eight to ten years old (and later up to 15) who show delinquent tendencies should have 'guidance counsellors, possibly graduate students . . .' who are trained and work under the supervision of psychologists and psychiatrists who must have empathy (most important) but also firmness."

He did admit, however, that his proposal for early detection of future delinquents called for "mass testing of all six-to eight-year-old children (and possibly the total child population up to the age of 15)," and he cited a test developed by two Harvard Law School professors claiming that "nine out of ten (delinquents) could have been correctly identified at the age of six."

It doesn't take much imagination to predict which group of children would get the short end of the stick under such testing procedures. Since the aim was to single out those who were sulky and angry, those slow in learning (frequently associated with unresolved frustrations), and those whose intransigence had become the only form of communication, the odds are that the greatest percentage would be among the disenfranchised minorities — the Chicanos, the blacks, and the Puerto Ricans.*

Once the story of the Hutschnecker proposal leaked to the press, the Nixon administration sought to play it down. Presumably the plan could be revived at a more propitious time.

The work of Dr. Andy and others who perform psychosurgery is seen by some observers as the extension or, as neurophysiologist Dr. Stephan Chorover of M.I.T. puts it, the "cutting

---

*A recent study of 431 delinquents in New York found that 80 percent were from severely economically deprived black or Puerto Rican families; 59 percent were from families on some form of welfare; and only 21 percent were from families where both parents were present.[13]

edge" of a nationwide program aimed at reconditioning not only a hyperactive child, or those who run afoul of the law, but also those who fail to conform with society's existing mores and modes.[14]

"Behavior modification" is the name of the game and the tools it uses are many:

- Drugs, such as Ritalin, Dexedrine, Anectine
- Peer pressure in massive "encounter sessions," together with social ostracism (having the child led away to an isolated area, frequently tied to a bed or to a wall, as punishment for insubordination)
- Electric shocks
- Psychosurgery

Dr. Bertram S. Brown, director of the National Institute of Mental Health, has estimated that in the past five years the number of psychotherapists using behavior modification methods has risen from one hundred to several thousand.

The specter of behaviorist specialists — a substantial number of whom are "outright quacks" according to Dr. Brown[15] — fastening themselves on thousands of hapless children and adolescents is a frightening one. In whose image are these youngsters to be remade? Is behavior modification a form of therapy or is it a technique leading to mass mind control and compliance?

Today there is great confusion about the child disorder known as hyperkinesis. The usual symptoms are hyperactivity, an inability to concentrate or to follow the simplest directives from teacher or parent, and general disruptiveness. There has always been a relatively small number of neurologically damaged children who have speech difficulties or poor physical and mental coordination, and who often flail about, seemingly without rhyme or reason.

But what about the vast army of children whose emotional and intellectual deficits are directly attributable to searing poverty? A California team of neuroscientists has published a study covering a two-year period, 1968–1970, indicating that more than one million American children have suffered damage to their brains due to poverty. Another million children yet to be born are expected to run the same risk because nearly a million pregnant women, living at or below poverty levels, are ingesting food below their minimum daily requirements for either energy or protein.

These infants show "serious chemical deficiencies," and have very small head circumferences, "so small that the likelihood for their constituting a normal population is less than one in a million." These findings were reported at a meeting for the Society for Neurosciences, in November 1975, by Dr. Robert B. Livingston. "The difficulties that these children will experience in school and later on in their career development," he stressed, "are linked directly to the undernutrition affecting the brain growth in utero and during early life . . ." Dr. Livingston held out a future in which, he declared, "We may be putting one-third to one-half million youngsters into the school system who are deprived in this regard and who will need remedial education and will have less achievement and competitive potential in their jobs." Dr. Livingston spoke for a group of researchers at the Department of Neurosciences, University of California, San Diego.

But even when there is no neurological damage present, the devastating effect of poverty on childrens' sensitivities can be catastrophic. A glimpse of how poverty, so frequently accompanied by the absence of parental affection or stimuli, may maim or still the basic growth impulses of these youngsters is provided by a series of vignettes by Ned O'Gorman, a New York poet, who has been running a sort of day care center in Harlem for the past decade. Typical are the following, from an article in the *New York Times*:

> Henry's speech and gait were faulty. (Often, the first faculty that has been stricken in the children we meet in our school is their ability to speak. It is usually diagnosed as a speech defect, but most often I have found it to be simply the result of hearing bad English, listening to nothing but television and being spoken to hardly at all.)
>
> Henry is crippled by numb resignation. He had never experienced affection, meted out wisely, consistently. He did not know what to do with feelings. He sought life and comfort, and saw nothing but a

ruined television set that flashed white, jagged lines across its surface
. . . and his grandfather rotting away in his armchair.

Henry was six years old.

Stella is 3 and nearly mute. There is nothing clinically wrong with
her. She merely does not know yet how to talk. Her mother stands in
the doorway of her apartment like a chained totem. Stella smiles a
mute smile when I see her in the morning, jumps up a little and runs
toward me. She looks at nothing, recognizes nothing. She has no notion of what to do with toys, blocks, crayons, scissors.

She loves to play with Link, a boy of 3, who, like Stella, has developed over the months, since he has been coming to my liberation
camp, from a screaming, weeping mess into a beautiful little boy,
stricken but fighting to know his world. Stella, mute; Link, always
with nerves and chaos. Link's mother, like Stella's, is a woman of in-
tense unhappiness. Her life, her children, her flat, all are in a state of
rigor mortis. Nothing changes from day to day; her eyes grow duller
and duller; she never laughs, and the children take on her morbidity.

Daniel, now 19, came to my school when it first opened. He was 9
then. A year ago, I saw him in a doorway on 128th Street. I had re-
membered him as one of the loveliest kids on the block. He had a special kind of hilarity about him, a clean, direct presence.

But when I said hello he looked at me, eyes and body in an embat-
tled, razor-sharp fury. I walked down the street and turned once toward him, and he heaved a Coke bottle at me. I ducked. He missed
me by an inch. I've not seen him since.[16]

There is so much crossover between the impulsively "mis-
behaving" youngster and one who may be reacting in a form of
vendetta against society that no diagnosis can be made without
qualification. Writing in the *New England Journal of Medicine* recently, Dr. L. Straufe and Dr. M. Stewart, who probed the question of treating problem children, concluded that "to date no
neurologic sign or test or combination of tests has been established . . . to differentiate hyperactive children or those with
minimum brain dysfunction from normal control subjects. Fur-
thermore the existence of a unitary syndrome of minimum brain
dysfunction has not been established."[17]

In spite of these reservations, the terms "hyperkinesis" and "minimum brain damage" are becoming household words. The overtaxed teacher in many an overcrowded classroom, trying to cope with forty children about to commit mayhem, is only too ready to seek relief, even if it means branding the unruly child a hyperkinetic. Many a time it is the teacher or the principal who becomes the diagnostician and persuades the parents to put the child on a Ritalin or Dexedrine regimen. The parent, all too often on the lowest rung of the socioeconomic ladder, helpless in dealing with the problem, and for whom the schoolteacher represents authority, will submit and allow the child to enter an indefinite period of drugging.

Judge Justine Wise Polier, for thirty-five years on the bench in the New York Family Court, and now a director of the Childrens' Defense Fund, deplores what she considers the "short cut" methods. "I don't think we can use short cuts that end up in the destruction of the individual any more than we can solve the problem of a juvenile delinquent by throwing him into jail and locking him up," she said to me in the course of an interview.

"It gets down to this: Are we willing to have a great many children destroyed so as to make life easier for the teacher or more helpful to another group of children? I think it is a high price to pay in any society that places a value on the individual child."[18]

Currently there are between 250,000 and 750,000 children on a diet of Ritalin or Dexedrine, but no definite statistics are available. (Ritalin, a seemingly paradoxical compound, quiets the restless youngsters but may act as a mood lifter for depressed adults.) The basic rationale is that disruptive children and those slow in learning would perform better if their hyperactivity were calmed and their attention span extended. A study by Dr. Herbert E. Rie, professor and chairman, psychology department, Case Western Reserve University, School of Medicine, challenges this theory. "The kids look like they are doing better — they are out of people's hair — but they are not performing one bit better," he says. Moreover many become zombielike, "humorless and almost emotionless. Children have to be excited and involved to learn."[19]

In many instances there is little or no medical monitoring. Since many a child learns that taking the pill will earn him a pat on the shoulder, he will willingly volunteer for it and frequently consumes a much greater dosage than prescribed. Many of these children are maintained on Ritalin and similar drugs for years.

Is all this developing a new generation of drug-dependent youngsters? What the end results will be is generally unknown. One of the few long-term studies found that hyperactive children fed Ritalin or Dexedrine didn't gain as much weight or grow as much in height as the controls; that is, the hyperactive children who were not given the drugs. When withdrawn from these pills, their weight increased but still didn't catch up with that of the other children. Dr. Daniel A. Safer and Dr. E. Barr, who reported on their work in the *New England Journal of Medicine*, felt that this weight phenomenon indicated a retardant effect on hormone activity which, in turn, might also affect the child's sexual development.[20]*

Dr. Leon Eisenberg of Harvard is critical of physicians who prescribe drugs indiscriminately for hyperactive children and warns that this practice has "the potential for producing a flagrant psychosis which closely mimics schizophrenia."[22]

While hundreds of thousands of such children may be drugged into a temporary passivity and a kind of compliance, what about the thousands of youthful muggers and assailants armed with knives, lead pipes, and guns? The daily toll of victims at the hands of these marauders, whether in New York, Kansas City,

---

*The newest environmental factor suspected of exacerbating the condition of the compulsively overactive child are the chemical food additives. They are said to trigger an allergic response which, in turn, leads to many of the symptoms associated with hyperkinesis. These additives are injected to make food more attractive to the eye and the palate, especially in diets designed for children. Some 2000 artificial substances to enhance flavor are found in everything from cereals to soda pop, from vitamins to doughnuts, and TV dinners. Dr. Ben F. Feingold, an allergist from the Kaiser-Permanente Medical Center in San Francisco, has been making these observations for about five years. Working with several hundred children, he found dramatic evidence that hyperkinetic symptoms disappeared just as soon as the children's diets were freed from the allergenic additives. The Food and Drug Administration, after several years of indecision, is about to begin testing these additives to check Dr. Feingold's findings.[21]

Chicago, or Los Angeles tells the sickening statistical story that juvenile delinquency is increasing at an alarming rate. As a matter of fact, serious juvenile crime for the past twenty years has risen by 1600 percent, according to the National Council on Crime and Delinquency.[23]

Does it mean that an epidemic of structural brain deformities has stricken America's young to produce this phenomenon? Is there a sudden rise in the number of boys born with an extra Y chromosome, the newly suspected cause of criminality?

Many observers feel that apart from the obvious economic reasons, a good deal of the violence is inextricably interwoven with an array of environmental factors that hardly existed a generation ago. Television, for instance, has played an especially important role. Inevitably it has helped heighten the discontent of the "have not" section of the population simply by opening a window onto a world of opportunities and luxurious living that the disenfranchised minorities can never hope to achieve. The pictures of clean, rat-free, beautifully appointed dwellings with their smartly dressed, well-fed occupants constantly dangled before the eyes of ghetto inhabitants rub salt into an open wound. The constant reminder of the availability of comfort and good living to those on a treadmill trying to make ends meet sparks smoldering resentment into outbursts of violent indignation.

As Dr. Judd Marmon, the California psychiatrist who has written extensively on violence in this country, put it:

> The sources of most violence can be found in man's life situation. Indeed, the fact that in all societies rates of violent behavior can be demonstrated to be clearly correlated with certain types of social patterning (e.g., poverty, urbanization, social class, etc.) is an effective argument against the assumption that human violence arises spontaneously on the basis of biological needs or simple idiosyncratic propensities.[24]

Coupled with this development was the growing awareness, fueled by the civil rights movement of the sixties, that the underdog was finally entitled to greater share in what the country's economy had to offer. It is what sociologists have been referring to as the "revolution of rising expectations."

But the promises of the sixties were never fulfilled as disappointment upon disappointment began to pile up. Eventually these frustrations were translated into civil disorders, street riots, and spin-offs in the form of robberies and assaults.

At the same time, many psychologists believe that children's constant exposure to the "boob tube," with its steady fare of violent melodrama, has contributed to the twisting and distorting of emotional attitudes to life and death. In effect, it has served to desensitize many a viewer to pain, to torture, and to killing. The long years of the Vietnam war have so inured the country to horror that many an American family began to schedule its dinner hour to coincide with the evening television news programs, which invariably would trot out some of the worst obscenities of battle to public view — such as the reportage of human mutilation in the course of "body count" procedures. Psychiatrist Fredric Wertham, one of the world's great authorities on the subject of violence, says that "children learn how men are killed before they learn how to read."[25]

Desensitization manifests itself on different levels, he points out.

> Children have an inborn capacity for sympathy. But that sympathy has to be cultivated. This is one of the most delicate points in the educational process. And it is this point that the mass media trample on. Even before the natural feelings of compassion have a chance to develop, the fascination of overpowering and hurting others is displayed in endless profusion. Before the soil is prepared for sympathy, the seeds of sadism are planted. The clinical result is that feeling for the suffering of others is interfered with.

These youngsters, Dr. Wertham says, "show a coarsening of responses and an unfeeling attitude." But, he adds, their indifference to acts of brutality on the screen and in life "is not a simple, elementary quality" consisting merely in an absence of emotion.

I have studied children who were profoundly blasé about death and human suffering, yet showed spontaneously the most generous and altruistic impulses. While some adults winced, seven-year-old children watched the murder of Lee Harvey Oswald by Jack Ruby with unruffled equanimity. They had seen quick, remorseless killings so often! Hurting other people is the natural thing. They had learned in the School for Violence that the victim . . . is not a person but a target . . . They have been conditioned to identify not with the victim but with the one who lands the blow.[26]

Television's murder operas, in a warped, distorted fashion, have kindled hope in the beaten-down, frustrated adolescent that there may be a way out of the miasma of despair. He has come to identify himself with the characters who "make it" via the gun, regardless of whether they are "good guys" or "bad guys." The next step is to become the perpetrator himself.

After Robert Kennedy was assassinated, the *Christian Science Monitor* made a survey of 85 hours of television viewing, which included prime evening hours and Saturday morning cartoons. In seven evenings of viewing the investigators

recorded 81 killings and 210 incidents or threats of violence; an additional 162 incidents reported on Saturday morning. The most violent evening hours were between 7:30 and 9:00 — at a time when an estimated 26.7 million young people between the ages of two and seventeen are watching television. In these hours violent incidents occurred at an average of once every 16.3 minutes.[27]

Drug addiction and ready availability of guns are additional factors that have contributed to a rate of delinquency scarcely known a generation ago. The narcotics pushing industry, running into billions of dollars a year, which obviously involves some mammoth interests, whether of the Mafia type or those of more respectable participants hiding behind a variety of fronts, has been aiming at the young to make of them long-term "clients." The need to support a drug habit is now the everyday story of purse snatching, store pilfering, house breaking, and murder.

Society's answer to all this is to lay the blame on the individual transgressor, putting him away behind bars and spending untold millions of dollars in the hope of reshaping him in the image it finds most manageable. In the meantime societal irresponsibility and delinquency move along on a "business as usual" basis. No one hears of a federal crash program to break the drug traffic. And there is not a scintilla of evidence that anything is being seriously considered to inhibit the ever more gruesome crime sagas on television.

While the hyperkinetic children are being pacified with drugs, other behavior-modification techniques thrust upon the juvenile offender present an even grimmer picture.

Basically much of the behavior-modification theory stems from the philosophy of B. F. Skinner, of Harvard, who for the past forty years has been the inspirer of the idea that with so-called positive and negative reinforcement techniques, people, just like animals, can be reconditioned to behave in accord with preconceived design. In direct translation this amounts to a simplistic "carrot-and-stick" approach: reward for performance that the reconditioners consider desirable, and punishment (emotional and/or physical) for action deemed undesirable.*

Negative reinforcement in its milder forms deprives an individual of privileges when he or she fails to toe the line. In its coercive forms, according to a recent study by a Senate subcommittee, negative reinforcement "through what is referred to as 'aversive' therapy or 'aversive conditioning' uses drugs, beatings and electric shocks as painful punishment for violation of rules or accepted norms."[28]

Application of some of these negative-reinforcement techniques are known to be taking place in many so-called rehabilitation institutions for children and adolescents, frequently supported by federal funding. For instance, the program of SEED, Inc., a Florida-based, nonlicensed drug abuse "treatment" center, focuses on the rehabilitation of adolescents, whose aver-

---

*Skinner himself, until recently (see Chapter 9), has advocated positive reinforcement and avoidance of coercive control.

age age is 16.[29] In operation for nearly five years, it has been receiving substantial subsidies from various agencies of the Department of Health, Education, and Welfare as well as from the Law Enforcement Assistance Administration. For the year 1974, alone, it was slated to get nearly $370,000, with additional funds coming from private sources.

These boys and girls, some only 13 and 14 years of age, are placed on a 12-hour program of rap sessions that begin at 10 A.M. and, except for mealtime breaks, go on until 10 P.M. Each of these encounter sessions calls for the participation of 500 to 600 young people, with a staff member directing the discussion through a microphone.

The objective is to create peer-group pressure through intensive "encounter sessions," and thus wear down the psychological defenses of the individual and create in her or him a dependence on the group. In the course of these meetings, these young people are bullied and humiliated until they are ready to bare their souls. Each of them is expected to admit his most intimate follies and then make open confessions over the public address system.

Those committed by their parents must stay for at least two weeks. Those placed there by the courts are obliged to stay for a minimum of thirty days. In either case, most children find themselves undergoing these purge sessions for months.

Fourteen-year-old Carolyn told the *St. Petersburg Times* (September 16, 1973)[30] how the SEED staff would bear down on the children and persuade them to believe that everything in their past was "ugly." "They told us we thought of ourselves as failures" before coming to SEED. "They say you screwed up your family really bad . . . They say your problems are brought on by yourself."

Another SEED graduate, eighteen-year-old Pat, claims never to have been on drugs. Nevertheless, he was placed in the program for two months. Throughout this period Pat was never alone, "not even for a minute." He said staff people accompanied him to the bathroom and slept in the same room with him at night. He was not allowed to communicate with anybody outside SEED. He talked to his parents only over a microphone at the open meetings before all those in attendance.*

Is this type of behavior modification lasting, once the person leaves the peer group? This was among a number of questions raised by the Comprehensive Health Planning Council of South Florida when reviewing the SEED program activities. The council found that SEED was operated by a staff that had "limited professional training and experience" in the field of drug abuse or youth counselling.[32]

"Children have reported to me that when they wanted to leave SEED they were threatened with commitment to a State School," according to Dr. Jeffrey J. Elenewski, a clinical psychologist formerly associated with the Dade County Department of Youth Services. "They were made to sit without speaking while listening to others berate them for hours. I have interviewed children who made suicide attempts following their running away from SEED."[33]

Helene Kloth, a guidance counselor at North Miami Beach Senior High School, reported that many of the returned "Seedlings" are "straight," that is, "quiet, well-dressed, short hair and not under the influence of drugs, compared to their previous appearance of being stoned most of the time. However," she added, "they seem to be living in a robot-like atmosphere, they won't speak to anyone outside of their own group. Seedlings seem to have an informing system on each other and others that is similar to Nazi Germany. They run in to use the telephone daily, to report against each other to the SEED, and it seems that an accused Seedling has no chance to defend himself because if enough persons accuse him of something he is presumed guilty.

---

*As reported by the *St. Petersburg Times*, parents in the community were haunted by the fear that their children might turn into hardened drug addicts. In a number of instances they were quite willing to commit their children to SEED even though they had misgivings as to whether their son or daughter might indeed be a "druggie." They were told by SEED that a "druggie" could be recognized by his tastes and habits — "If he has posters on his bedroom walls, or keeps his room dark, if he has a hi-fi or burns incense, he is a druggie."[31]

"I used to think SEED was the saving program . . . Now I know that a number of the children are back on drugs . . ."[34]

SEED has received no federal subsidies since February 1974, but it continues to function with the help of community chambers of commerce and confused parents, despite the view of many professionals that children can be maimed for life because of its "therapy."

In addition to various behavior-modifying procedures, there has emerged a technology that makes available a variety of instruments to help the behavioral practitioner in his reconditioning chores. These are especially popular with those advocating the use of aversive-type therapy.

Many reform schools and corrective institutions in different parts of the country are still employing the electrically charged cattle prod to shock the recalcitrance out of one's system. The voltage is high enough to destroy the skin on contact. Recent entrants into the field boast of greater refinements in the kind of electric-shock devices they produce; for instance, the Farrall Instrument Company of Grand Island, Nebraska, claims to have overcome the crudity of the cattle prod by having its electric shockers include a voltage control.

The Farrall Company, which exhibits its wares at the meetings of the American Psychological Association and other professional conventions, distributes literature rejecting the views of many professionals that aversive methods are more punitive than corrective. It contends that zapping is the panacea for "antisocial behavior, for psychosomatic disorders, self-destructive behavior and sexual deviance."[35]

Advances in space technology, such as telemetry, have helped in the development of electric-shock equipment. The Farrall Company is now able to manufacture a long-distance wireless shocker with an "increased shock output." It has a range of around 75 feet indoors and 300 feet outdoors. The Farrall catalogue explains that the long, outdoor range "makes the unit useful on the playground and in similar situations. The control unit is a small, hand-held device. The receiver shocker is a small unit housed in a leather case and is usually attached to the patient by a belt around the waist."

Every time the child is about to break an institutional rule or do something that is frowned upon by the staff, the person at the controls presses a button, thus sending a signal that delivers the electrical shock either to the waist, the arm or the leg.

According to the Farrall booklet, the wireless shocker gives clinicians and researchers "aversive control over situations without the encumbrance of wires. The patient can now move with unrestrained freedom and yet be under control." Another advantage: "The physical separation of the patient from the therapist, at the time when the shock comes on, makes the patient think less of the therapist as a punisher, and associate the shock with the undesired act he is doing." (Shock is adjustable from 9 to 800 volts. The shock is a narrow 1 to 2 milliseconds in width. Current is 5 milliamperes.)

A so-called Personal Shocker, the Farrall Company says, is "ideal for the doctor to carry with him. The compact size and appearance of this shocker makes it less frightening to the patient. Despite this appearance, the apparatus has a very aversive shock."[36]

"Correctional" methodology is taking on an ever greater repressive character, whether it be electric zapping, long prison sentences, or psychosurgery. There is little patience with those who plead for the understanding of the basic causes that are at the root of juvenile delinquency. The adult section of the population is much too involved with its own frustrations, much of it associated with economic despair. And as a result this nation's traditionally compassionate approach to helping a youngster overcome some of her or his dilemmas is fast becoming a sentimental memory.

5. Prisoner Guinea Pigs

IN THE FORBIDDING compound that houses the California Medical Facility at Vacaville, a maximum security state penitentiary for the criminally insane, prison administrators decided one day in 1968 to try out an experiment.[1] They had a vexing problem on their hands. There were three inmates, a black, a Chicano, and a white convict who were spirited, young (in their twenties), uncooperative, and resisted the restrictions usually found in a maximum security setting. Two of this trio were under sentence for relatively light crimes. Finding it difficult to contain them, the authorities decided on experimenting with psychosurgery.

From what little information could be coaxed out of the prison staff, it appears that the operations were not successful. The condition of the Chicano prisoner, who was twenty-five years of age at the time of surgery, has steadily deteriorated. His resentment has taken on a violent character and for many years he has been languishing in solitary confinement. The one prisoner who, authorities said, was most improved and therefore released on parole, wound up in the Montana State Prison on a burglary conviction. There is little information about the third prisoner.

Three years later, despite the failure of this experiment, Vacaville and the University of California at the San Francisco Medical Center were about to undertake more psychosurgical experimentation. As outlined in a confidential communication by R. K. Procunier, director of corrections of the State of

California, the proposal would be designed to provide "neuro-surgical . . . treatment . . . for the violent inmate." He said that "surgical and diagnostic procedures would be performed to lo-cate centers in the brain which may have been previously dam-aged and which could serve as the focus for episodes of violent behavior." He then added, "If these areas were located and ver-ified that they were indeed the source of aggressive behavior, neurosurgery would be performed, directed at the previously found cerebral foci."[2]

According to the official affidavit, one such candidate for psy-chosurgery was "25, older and more mature than the bulk of the . . . inmates. He was aggressively outspoken, always seeking re-cruits for his views that the institution and its staff were oppres-sing all the inmates and particularly the black inmates. He was proficient at karate, and his files showed that he had been ob-served teaching other inmates karate techniques at another in-stitution . . . [he] had been one of a half-dozen men who led a work-stoppage and attempted general strike which had lasted for several days . . . he was continuously in contact with friends and attorneys on the outside who encouraged his activities and provided him with books attacking society. He set a fire in May as a demonstration of his political views."[3]

When news of the impending operations got to the world out-side, a number of community leaders, psychiatrists, black and Chicano activists set up a widely organized protest, and the Va-caville authorities bowed to the pressure. And so the psychosur-gery experiment was halted.

In the quest to instill prison discipline with maximum effec-tiveness, various penal institutions throughout the United States have been hard at work experimenting with a variety of additional "aversive therapies": vomit-inducing drugs, the "hole" (solitary confinement), and electric-shock therapy.

These procedures are not referred to as punitive in character. The usual term is "corrective" or even "therapeutic." The pris-oner may be chained to an iron bed for days on end, compelled to wallow in his own wastes — it's all for the prisoner's own good; a sort of transitional rehabilitative experience that will help speed his return to the normal fold.

Thus when surgeons at Vacaville pushed electrodes deep into the brains of the three prisoners to zero in on the suspected cluster of damaged cells, and then shot through a voltage strong enough to kill these cells, they were doing it to help the prisoners, not to crush them or punish them.

Despite the fact that conditions in most prisons are so difficult to endure — no matter how much even a repentant inmate tries — despite the endless series of prison riots that seem to underscore the validity of the prisoners' complaints, the emphasis is on forcing the prisoner to accept these conditions rather than on having the conditions ameliorated.

Interestingly enough, even John Mitchell, when in the post of U.S. attorney general in the Nixon administration, charged that "the state of America's prisons comes close to a national shame. No civilized society should allow it to continue."[4] According to the United Nations, the United States is second to Turkey in having the worst prisons in the Western world.[5] Scarcely a month passes without a major prison incident, what with the appalling overcrowding and the idleness to which prisoners are subjected and which inevitably lead to explosions of the Attica type.

According to the National Prison Project of the American Civil Liberties Union (ACLU), even in the federal penitentiaries, supposedly the best run of more than 4000 jails and prisons that sprawl across this country, only 26 percent of the inmates are engaged in some kind of work. In testimony before a government commission studying prison experimentation, the ACLU stated that prisoners live in "noisy, unsanitary, overcrowded, poorly lit cellblocks with no privacy, subject to hostile guards and in constant fear of assault."*[6]

---

*The ACLU charges that inmates in most American prisons are forced to purchase, with their own money, the most basic necessities of life, such as personal hygiene items. Paid work becomes essential, therefore, if only to make it possible

From time to time, suits on behalf of prisoners prompt the courts to order prison wardens to correct the abuses. One recent development, and a unique one, was the order to Governor George C. Wallace and Alabama correction officials to revamp their state prison facilities in a matter of months or have them closed down forthwith. The order came from Federal Judge Frank M. Johnson, Jr., who charged that the Alabama prisoners "suffered from cruel and unusual punishment" prohibited by the Eighth Amendment of the Constitution. What is also unique is that the blame for the prisoners' restiveness was placed directly on prisons and the authorities, rather than on outside influences, a frequently ascribed cause of prison protests.[8]

Alabama is not the only state found violating the constitutional rights of prisoners. Since 1970 federal courts have placed similar charges against Arkansas, Maryland, Mississippi, and Massachusetts. Jessica Mitford in her book *Kind and Usual Punishment* has solidly documented the accusations that cruelty foisted upon the caged prison population is not "unusual punishment" but more likely to be the usual condition throughout most of this country's penitentiaries.[9]

But instead of allocating what resources there are to create programs to ease the conditions that lead to "rampant violence and jungle atmosphere,"[10] as Judge Johnson put it, state and federal governments spend most of their available funds on programs designed to make the prisoner accept the conditions imposed upon him. Upward of 90 percent of all prison budgets are spent on control and security.

No effort is spared to develop behavior-modifying programs that submit the prisoner to the indignities and abnormalities to

---

to get a toothbrush and shaving cream. ACLU's data showed that "six states pay no prison wages at all, 17 states pay less than 50 cents a day and 21 states pay between 50 cents and one dollar a day. Only 6 states pay more than $1.00 a day. In those states that do pay wages, work opportunities are few. For example, in Illinois a prisoner can earn only from 32 cents to 55 cents a day; there are enough jobs for only one-third of the prison population. In Alabama, prisoners receive no pay for working and are allotted by the State the equivalent of only 25 cents a week."[7]

which Judge Johnson and former Attorney General Mitchell referred.

Over the past dozen years there has been a steady changeover from the reliance on traditional theories on the rehabilitation of prisoners to the belief that behavior modification is where the answer lies in dealing with prison problems. Basically it is a switch from the idea of preparing the inmate to find a legitimate way of earning a living once he is outside the prison walls, to that of altering his total personality; to making him submissive, unquestioning, and unchallenging.

This trend is tied to a number of developments, some directly associated with the civil rights movement of the sixties. The inmates are younger and much more assertive; many are politically conscious, angry and rebellious, and frequently organize their fellow prisoners into resistance groups against oppressive conditions.

A simultaneous development is a more active role for psychiatrists and psychologists dedicated to behavior modification as the solution for prison problems. Theoretically these behavior programs are designed for the welfare of the prisoner, but it is the prison system that pays the behaviorist's fees. And thus the question: Is the behaviorist there to create a program that would lead the inmate to becoming a better citizen or is he or she there to make the inmate a better prisoner?

The shift away from rehabilitative measures is attributed to the realization that these efforts simply do not work. There is abundant evidence to indicate that however sensible a rehabilitative program may be, it cannot but fail because it is operating within a prison setting. Genuine rehabilitation hasn't been tried on any reasonable scale. Normal human interactions are kept to a minimum, with few humane incentives.

The accepted purpose of a rehabilitative program is to provide the prisoner with skills to make it on his own once he is released and to channel his energy in positive ways. But how can a prisoner develop initiative and drive when a prison environment calls for his or her constant regimentation and control? If he is to be a successful prisoner, of necessity he must be docile and obedient. And once outside, all his newly acquired submissiveness will once again put him at a disadvantage in the competitive and individualistic American society.

Thus, as ACLU's Matthew L. Myers put it, those in authority who argue that "traditional rehabilitation programs are a failure and that very strong behavior-modification programs are essential have either intentionally or negligently ignored the reasons for the failure . . . Perhaps what we are learning is that by placing individuals into a punitive setting, where control and fear of assault are the primary considerations day in and day out, that these may be the causes of the failures of the rehabilitative programs . . . What we ought to do is to begin thinking about changing the prison setting itself and then go on from there."[11]

For the foreseeable future, consideration of changing the prison setting is not even on the horizon. Although the word "rehabilitation" continues to be used, more and more it begins to sound like "behavior modification," which, in turn, emerges as a cluster of punishing techniques for the control of the prisoners — to make them compliant and manageable.

Together with the physical measures traditionally used by prison wardens, the behaviorist specialists now offer technological weaponry to intrude into the individual's innermost thinking processes, an area generally considered sacrosanct even for the prisoner, an area the Constitution is understood to protect fully. Thus, in effect, the psychologist and the psychiatrist have become part of the prison constabulary. They have steadily taken on the role of architects of programs aimed at giving the jailers maximum effectiveness in keeping their wards at bay. Their chief contribution to maintaining discipline is the introduction of more subtle means of keeping the inmate off balance, in a perpetual state of fear, with the hope that once some of this dread and terror is instilled, it will become a permanent part of his psyche and inhibit him from defying those representing authority, even when he leaves the prison walls.

Since the majority of the prison population is black, Hispanic, or Chicano, it is legitimate to ask whether this terror approach is taking on a racist quality. (According to the ACLU, between 80 percent and 90 percent of those held in solitary confinement are members of minority groups.)[12] As more angry young men and women, questioning and politically rebellious, come in conflict with the law, we must also ask whether the wish to change society is reason enough for our young people to be subjected to these brain-retread operations?

There are those who are profoundly worried that prisons are being converted into proving grounds for psychosurgery and a host of other procedures designed to break the human spirit. Are these prisons to become laboratories for the testing of technologies of behavior alteration aimed at nonconformists in general, at the so-called deviants — alcoholics, homosexuals, and disturbed persons — as well as those out of step politically? As James Baldwin once put it in a letter to Angela Davis: "If they come for you in the morning, they'll be back for me at night."[13]

Among those who seriously weigh the implications of this trend is former Senator Sam J. Ervin, Jr., who chaired a three-year study of this question by the Senate Subcommittee on Constitutional Rights. "As disturbing as behavior modification may be on a theoretical level," he warned in his report, "the unchecked growth of the practical technology of behavior control is cause for even greater concern." He said that "as technology has expanded our capacity for meeting society's needs, it has also increased, to a startling degree, our ability to enter and affect the lives of individual citizens."

Senator Ervin reported that his committee "watched with growing concern as behavioral research unearths vast new capabilities far more rapidly than we are able to reconcile the many important questions of individual liberties raised by these capabilities." He deplored the fact that with the speedy proliferation of these techniques "few real efforts have been made to consider the basic issue of individual freedom involved, and to minimize fundamental concepts between individual rights and behavior technology."[14]

But others, such as Dr. Bertram S. Brown, director of the National Institute of Mental Health (NIMH), a unit of the Department of Health, Education, and Welfare, welcomes the government's participation in behavior research. Designed to counter the sort of anxiety and controversy voiced by Senator Ervin and others, the NIMH published a brochure on policy in 1975 in which Dr. Brown states:

> The Federal Government continues to support and encourage research and demonstrations that test new behavior modification techniques, that seek to refine existing ones and apply them to new clinical populations and new settings, and that promote the dissemination of techniques that have been positively evaluated . . . Research is also needed in ways to deliver behavior modification techniques to larger numbers of persons in less restrictive settings than the institutions where much of the research, until now, has been done.[15]

Acknowledging that behavior modification "currently is the center of stormy controversy and debate," Dr. Brown attempts to calm those concerned that behavior techniques "may be used by those in power to control and manipulate others." In reply to charges that "the use of behavior modification methods is inconsistent with humanistic values," Dr. Brown blandly states that, "all kinds of therapies involve attempts to change the patient in some way."

Throughout the pamphlet the NIMH director uses an "on the one hand" and "on the other hand" exposition of the merits of behavior modification. But after weighing the pros and the cons, he votes decidedly yes. There are occasional abuses in the use of behavior-altering procedures, he concedes. And he reproves those prison authorities who may be employing them as oppressive devices. But he cautions against opponents who advocate the elimination of behavior-modification programs in prisons on the grounds that such therapy is coercive. "It would seem far better," he says "to build in safeguards than to discard all attempts at rehabilitation of prison inmates," thus glossing over the basic issue of whether mind alteration is a legitimate rehabilitation technique.

Dr. Brown has kind words for aversive-control methods. Low-level electric shock, he declares, "has been highly effective in ameliorating severe behavioral problems. When properly used, the shocks are very brief. Shock used this way causes no lingering pain or tissue damage and can be administered with precise control." Dr. Brown also speaks of advantages in the use of certain aversive drugs.

Notwithstanding Dr. Brown's public relations effort to serve up behavior modification as something new and modern, the fact is that much of it is based on such primitive expedients as solitary confinement, which has been in vogue through the ages. Despite its proven record of failure as a reforming device, present-day behavior modifiers lean heavily upon solitary confinement and try to mask it by labeling it a "segregation area," or some other euphemistic term.

As far back as 1821 the New York legislature tested the effectiveness of total isolation as a means of altering the behavior of prisoners. Eighty prisoners were put into solitary confinement. Within a year five men died, at least one went insane, and so many became depressed that the governor pardoned twenty-six and allowed the others to be released from the project. Did this technique help rehabilitate the prisoners? The warden reported that there was "not one instance of reformation."[16]

Yet 151 years later, in March 1972, the Federal Bureau of Prisons launched a program known as START,[17] the acronym for Special Treatment and Rehabilitative Training, whose centerpiece was the "hole." The program called for the incarceration of the individual in solitary confinement in a small, tiled cell, 10 feet wide and 8 feet 4 inches in height. The prisoner was allowed to leave the cell twice a week for showers, once a week for a brief exercise period. This stretch of forced withdrawal from human contact — not seeing or associating with other inmates — was designed to last a long time, a year or more.

This was only part of a comprehensive program aimed at pummeling the prisoner psychologically into just so much mush, destroying his spirit and shattering his personality. All contact with relatives and friends on the outside was broken. There was no outgoing or incoming mail. No visitors. Personal harassment was also part of the program. START participants were subject to cell and body searches at any time the prison guards felt it appropriate. The inmate's isolation was as near complete as possible. Even religious services were denied to him.

One would scarcely guess from reading the Bureau of Prisons operations memorandum that this treatment was the basic component of the START method. One could almost detect a sigh of solicitous concern for the wayward felon when it declared that the program was "designed to provide care, custody, and correction of the long-term adult offender in a setting separated from his home institution."[18]

The program was predicated on the classic approaches to behavior modification in which positive and negative reinforcement techniques would reshape the behavioral patterns of the prisoner. By stripping the individual at the outset of the few privileges usually accorded the general penitentiary population, the prisoner would have to work up the ladder of "cooperation," or obeisance before authority and guards, before any of these privileges would be restored.

When the prisoner was ready to start behaving, that is, when presumably he began addressing the guards as "sir," when he started tying his shoes according to regulations as some inmates quipped, when his face would light up in a beatific smile of acceptance of any order given him, then the authorities would say, "O.K., you can begin getting back your privileges. You can now shower three times a week," and so on.

Even though the program was ostensibly aimed at reconditioning the noncooperative, belligerent individual, the START authorities appear to have been concentrating on breaking the new breed of prisoner, the political malcontents who were agitating for prison reforms. START withheld from its inmates the popular black periodicals *Jet* and *Ebony*; books and periodicals concerning black and Chicano problems; and Marxist literature.[19]

The START program originated in the federal penitentiary at Marion, Illinois,[20] where inmates were involved in a protest action. Seemingly unable to cope with this situation, the Marion authorities, some of these prisoners charged, decided to get rid of them by tagging them psychopaths and shipping them to the federal medical facility at Springfield, Missouri. The psychiatric evaluation of the prisoners was done by Dr. Martin Groder, the Marion psychiatrist at that time, according to ACLU attorney Arpiar G. Saunders, Jr. On their arrival at Springfield, however, the medical staff there, Saunders says, would not concur that these men were indeed psychotic. Nevertheless, the decision was made to have them remain in Springfield in a specially designated psychiatric area.

Because they protested this action, the prisoners were subjected to continued abuse by the guards. As Saunders recalls it, "the prisoners said they were physically beaten, submitted to forceable administration of psychotropic drugs, and were denied food, exercise and recreation."[21] (Saunders, together with ACLU attorney Barbara Milstein, pressed the anti-START court action that eventually led to the demise of START in 1974.)

These "psychopathic" recalcitrants began smuggling out letters telling of their ordeal (a number of the inmates were highly articulate and began composing habeus corpus writs to the courts). It was at this juncture that the Springfield authorities got together with the Federal Bureau of Prisons and decided on a program that eventually became known as START. It began in September 1972. A totally segregated area was established, with its own staff and its own program, and the prisoners who originally came from Marion began their tour of behavioral treatment without their consent or understanding of what it was all about.

As the program unfolded, its abusive and coercive character began to surface. Court cases began challenging the constitutionality of START for depriving prisoners of their basic constitutional rights. In one case, pressed by the American Civil

Liberties Union (*Sanchez* v. *Ciccone*) a prisoner's affidavit described how an alleged minor infraction of discipline (his unwillingness to follow an order from a guard) led to his being seized by members of the prison staff, who threw him into a cell. When four other prisoners protested, they too were flung into a cell, where they were beaten and tear-gassed.[22]

The affidavit went on: "We were then placed on our stomachs with feet shackled to the bed frame and hands handcuffed behind our backs. We remained shackled for several days. During this period I refused to eat because I would have been forced to eat 'dog style' . . . I was forced, because of the refusal of the guards to release me, even for short periods, to void my bodily wastes upon myself, the bed and floor."

Testimony such as this, as well as those of other cases placed before the courts, made it quite obvious that the START program was nothing like the attempt so gently described by prison authorities: "to help these individuals gain better control over their behavior so that they can be returned to regular institutions where they can participate in programs designed to help them make a successful community adjustment."[23]

Despite these revelations, which led to the closing of START, Norman A. Carlson, director of the Bureau of Prisons, declared that the Bureau of Prisons "profited by this experience." He told *Time* magazine seven months later (March 11, 1974) that "we're going to start [behavior modification] programs in all of our penitentiaries' segregation units, only they won't have any titles that cause such emotions."[24]

Soon afterward, similar programs were indeed under way in federal prisons in Virginia, in Michigan, and other areas. And state prisons across the land are conducting almost identical maiming "rehabilitative" programs. The justification is always Skinnerian: none of these harassments is to be viewed as torture of those who do not respond enthusiastically to whatever they are subjected to. The method is usually referred to as negative reinforcement, or aversive conditioning.

The Patuxent Institution, a state prison in Maryland, for the treatment of "defective delinquents," employs a "restraining sheet" for its noncooperative inmates. As described by a reporter in the *Washington Daily News*, this "is a device in which a naked inmate is strapped down on a board. His wrists and ankles are cuffed to the board and his head is rigidly held in place by a strap around the neck and a helmet on his head. One inmate testified he was left in the darkened cell, unable to remove his body wastes. He said he was visited only when a meal was brought. Then, one wrist was unlocked so he could feel around in the dark for his food and attempt to pour liquid down his throat without being able to lift his head."[25]

An additional terror tactic used at Patuxent is that of holding the prisoner for an indefinite sentence, his liberation being dependent on the psychiatrist's prognosis as to the inmate's dangerousness in the future. According to the ACLU, which has been in litigation on a number of Patuxent cases, many individuals have been picked up for such infractions as joyriding, given a two-year sentence, and held at Patuxent for as long as eighteen years.* A recent study showed that 75 percent of the people committed to that institution with a sentence of up to five years, served beyond that time.

The Patuxent theory of incarcerating an individual in "therapy" for as long as the staff feels it appropriate, to cure the inmate of personality traits that would lead him to commit new crimes, runs counter to the findings in a variety of studies by some of the most eminent psychiatrists and criminologists in the United States. For example, the American Psychiatric Association Task Force on Criminal Justice, which included, among others, such experts as Dr. Norvel Morris, dean of the University

---

*At the present time, 39 out of 50 states, plus the District of Columbia and the federal government, use indeterminate sentencing in one form or another. In Patuxent this could mean anything from one day to life; in other instances the judge will sentence an offender by saying "you are to serve from 2 to 10 years," with the ultimate decision as to the length of time to be spent in prison being made by the parole board. Myers states: "The ACLU feels therefore that currently 80 percent of the prison population is serving indeterminate sentences."[26]

of Chicago Law School and formerly dean of the university's Graduate School of Criminal Justice, concluded that it could not predict an individual's potential dangerousness with any regularity.[27] The only other prison in the world run along the lines of Patuxent is located in South Africa.[28]

Deploring the manner in which the Patuxent prisoners remain solely at the mercy of the prison psychiatrists, ACLU's Matthew Myers thought it unusual that oftentimes a psychiatric interview with an incoming prisoner might take less than a half hour. On innumerable occasions, he says, he has found "the information on the prisoner's social history inaccurate, and sometimes almost unbelievable. At one time I saw an individual's school record reporting that he wouldn't share his milk and cookies in the first grade, and this apparently was held against him . . . In another prisoner's social record I found this comment: 'This individual was not a breast-fed baby.'"[29]

Further complicating the Patuxent picture is that many of the psychiatrists are foreign-born and scarcely able to understand the ghetto jargon of the inmates, since the majority come from the Baltimore slums. And yet they are the experts who are called upon to render a judgment as to the prisoner's psychological state and his chances of going straight once he is out of prison.

In the nearly sixteen years of its existence Patuxent had cost the taxpayers some $40 million. In this period about 100 men were declared "cured" — a rather expensive course of therapy, averaging upwards of $400,000 per person.[30]

In California two penitentiaries, Vacaville, which made the headlines because of its psychosurgery experiments, mentioned earlier, and Atascadero, a treatment facility for the criminally insane, are among the many prisons that are in the lead with torture procedures aimed at "driving the devil" out of the refractory prisoner.

Atascadero State Hospital, a maximum security prison, houses 1500 mentally disturbed sex offenders and criminally insane. It has pioneered with such aversive "therapeutic" chemicals as

Anectine (succinylcholine), a valuable muscle relaxant used in surgery. When given intravenously in dosages of 20 to 40 mg., Anectine doesn't merely relax, it paralyzes.

Within 30 to 40 seconds paralysis begins to invade the small muscles of the fingers, toes, and eyes and then the intercostal muscles and the diaphragm. The heart slows down to about 60 beats per minute. This condition, together with respiratory arrest, sets in for as long as two to five minutes before the drug begins to wear off. But the individual remains fully conscious. At this point, while the prisoner is gasping for breath, the prison psychiatrist takes over as the negative reinforcer and begins to scold the prisoner, demanding that he mend his ways or face more of this punishment in the future.[31]

Describing their "exploratory study to determine the effectiveness of succinylcholine as an agent in behavior modification," three staff clinicians (Martin P. Reimringer, Sterling W. Morgan, and Paul F. Bramwell) reported having used the drug on 90 male patients, some of whom were "overtly psychotic, mentally retarded and sociopathic." Their verdict: "Succinylcholine offers an easily controlled, quickening, fear-producing experience during which the sensorium is intact and the patient rendered susceptible to suggestion."[32]

How did the prisoners feel about it? In a similar experiment with Anectine at the California Medical Facility at Vacaville on 64 prisoners, "sixteen likened it to dying. Three compared it to actual experiences in the past in which they had almost drowned. The majority described it as a terrible and scary experience."[33]

Dr. Arthur G. Nugent, chief psychiatrist at Vacaville, commenting on the efficacy of this "treatment" in influencing behavior, said "The prison grapevine works fast and even the toughest have come to fear and hate the drug. I don't blame them — I wouldn't have the treatment myself for the world."[34]

Arthur L. Mattocks and Charles S. Jew, who did an evaluative survey of the Vacaville experiment, refer to the group of prisoners as "angry young men," a reference used with ever greater frequency in describing inmates on whom aversive experimentation is performed. "Their average age was 25 years, with a mean time at the institution of 15 months."[35]

In Iowa, prison officials have injected the vomit-inducing drug apomorphine to "treat" noncooperative inmates. Prisoners found guilty of "not getting up on time, of giving cigarettes against orders . . . for talking, for swearing, or for lying" or of not greeting their guards formally were subjected to doses of this drug. According to testimony brought out in a trial, the injections were often given without specific authorization of the prison doctor. This treatment brought on uncontrollable vomiting that lasted from fifteen minutes to an hour, accompanied by a temporary cardiovascular effect involving "some change in blood pressure."[36]

Dr. Steven Fox, of the University of Iowa, testified that the use of apomorphine "is really punishment worse than a controlled beating since the one administering the drug can't control it after it is administered."[37] A three-man circuit court adjudged the "use of this unproven drug for this purpose on an involuntary basis . . . cruel and unusual punishment prohibited by the Eighth Amendment." But it did not forbid its use completely. It indicated certain guidelines such as getting consent from the inmate to accept such "treatment."[38]

Another "therapeutic" means designed to cow the intransigent prisoner or an emotionally ill individual is the electroshock (electroconvulsive treatment, or ECT). Prison authorities are able to get away with using it as a punishing method because it falls into the gray area of therapy. Ken Kesey's dramatization of its misuse in *One Flew over the Cuckoo's Nest* is by no means an exaggeration, in the view of those familiar with prisons and mental institutions.

Like most modalities, ECT is discussed from time to time in the specialty medical journals. But an evaluative article on its use on Vietnamese mental patients, which appeared in the *American Journal of Psychiatry* in July 1967,[39] seemed like an invitation to those shopping around for new methods to help maintain discipline in this country's corrective institutions. The article was by a California psychiatrist, Dr. Lloyd H. Cotter, about his work at the Bien Hoa Mental Hospital in South Vietnam. He reported on the "success" of operant conditioning* on hundreds of chronic mental patients, mostly schizophrenics, in that institution. The operant conditioning was accomplished through the means of a negative-reinforcement device, the electroconvulsive shock.

Dr. Cotter described the need for and the success of this action in view of the many problems he faced when he took over the 2000 patient facility in Vietnam. (These were allies, not North Vietnamese prisoners.) All these patients, in addition to being chronic schizophrenics, also suffered from TB, dysentery, malaria, and malnutrition because of food shortages. With a scarcity of tranquilizing drugs, a rapidly rising mortality rate, and unrelieved crowding, Dr. Cotter decided on a "mass treatment approach" to return them to their families.

Starting in a ward of 130 chronic male patients, Dr. Cotter announced that they could be discharged if they would shape up, begin working, and learn how to support themselves once they were on their own. His program called for their immediate participation in work details, which would continue for a three-month period on the hospital grounds, as proof of their readiness to return to normality.

When only ten of these patients agreed to go along, Dr. Cotter then warned that the rest would have to undergo special treatment so as to make them equally cooperative. The next day 120 of these patients were given unmodified electroshock three times a week. (The word "unmodified" means that the procedures were done without anesthesia, which ameliorates some of the accompanying distress.) "It can be seen," Dr. Cotter re-

*In the operant process, as originally conceived by Skinner, a motor response is reinforced by rewards, such as food or whatever other gratifications are likely to satisfy the person or animal undergoing behavioral manipulation. In time, the response will become a learned condition. In the case of Dr. Cotter and his electroshock administrations, behavioral modification was coerced by a negative, or aversive, operant influence.

ported, "that the ECT served as a negative reinforcement for
the response of work for those patients who chose to work rather
than to continue receiving ECT."

Dr. Cotter went on to compare this "treatment" to the administration of antibiotic injections forced on children ill with
pneumonia. "The injections hurt and even involve some slight
risk to the patient, but the damage without their use is potentially much greater. Inflicting a little discomfort to provide
motivation to move patients out of their zombi-like states of inac-
tivity, apathy, and withdrawal was, in our opinion, well justified."

Together with two Vietnamese psychiatrists, Dr. Cotter reported that he was "kept quite busy administering the several
thousands of shock treatments required as we started about one
new ward a week on the program." As a positive reinforcement
to encourage those who began working, the hospital began pay-
ing them at the rate of one piastre for each day's work. (A piastre
at that time was equivalent to one cent.) Dr. Cotter concluded his
report by indicating to his readers that the Bien Hoa Mental
Hospital experiment "offers a treatment which results in better
adjustment and probably in more rapid recovery for a very high
percentage of patients treated. It would appear to be most indicated for long-term patients who have failed to respond to other
treatment modalities. The use of effective reinforcements
should not be neglected due to a misguided idea of what constitutes kindness."

Aversive drugs, electroshock, psychosurgery — these treatments periodically have been prohibited by the courts and
criticized by congressional committees as unconstitutional, as
"cruel" punishment in violation of the Eighth Amendment or in
violation of other constitutional protections governing the principle of "informed consent" when prisoners are to undergo experimental procedures.

But do the court actions actually halt the infliction of such
punishing acts on prisoners, on the so-called criminally insane
and on youthful delinquents? Do government agencies such as
the Law Enforcement Assistance Administration (LEAA), a unit

of the Department of Justice, cut off funding for behavior-modification projects found to violate individual civil rights?

There is altogether too much evidence that this is not the case. There are too many loopholes that allow for an easy dodge or a bypass by prison wardens. Although the courts rung down the curtain on START, and have presumably inhibited the use of dangerous drugs in a few prisons, these decisions do not affect other institutions using similar programs.

Decisions are binding only on the specific program that is put before the court at a given time, and in the particular state or jurisdiction in which they are rendered. Even when a court has ruled that administration of a certain aversive drug, or a procedure, constitutes cruel and unusual punishment, it is still possible for a prison warden to get around the decision. All he has to do is to draft a program that involves either the same drug in a different dosage or a different form of administration (i.e., by mouth rather than intravenously) or use a different drug in the same manner.

Currently a law suit is under way in Michigan, in which a prison behavioral program strongly resembling START is being contested by the Michigan Legal Service of Detroit. Experts who have examined the details of this program are convinced that the techniques used in START are being used in the Michigan prison.

Another penitentiary under fire is the federal prison at Marion, Illinois, which helped to inspire START. It was built in 1962 to replace Alcatraz as this country's maximum security prison. About 80 percent of the inmates are black, Chicano, Puerto Rican, and Asian. Of its total population 25 percent are Black Muslims.[40]

About four years ago, at about the time START was initiated, Marion opened its segregation section after some 100 inmates protested the beating by a guard of a Chicano prisoner named Jesse Lopez. This division, called CARE (Control and Rehabilitation Effort) added a new twist to its isolation program, the so-called boxcar cells.

These are cubicles that are cut off from the rest of the penitentiary by two doors: a steel door to shut out the light and a covering plexiglass door to keep sound from coming in or out. A prisoner suddenly taken sick has no way of making it known, no matter how loudly he may be shouting for help. Ventilation is poor and one 6o-watt bulb supplies the light.

Fifty of the most outspoken inmates, some of whom were known to have communicated with their congressmen and news media protesting their plight, have been placed in the boxcars. Some have been there ever since.

The objective is the usual one: to make the prisoner submissive to whatever discipline is imposed upon him once he is released from the boxcar. Is this achievable? Dr. Bernard Rubin, a Chicago psychiatrist who toured the Marion prison doesn't think so. He found that the control unit so "dehumanizes, demeans and shapes behavior" that "violent behavior becomes the result rather than the cause. The unit produces frustration, rage and helplessness."[41] (Dr. Rubin's comments were included in the background information distributed by the National Committee to Support the Marion Brothers, St. Louis, Missouri.)

Eddie Sanchez, a long-time boxcar resident, was able to smuggle out a letter to a Washington newspaper in which he wrote: "It has been very hard not to lose hope. To tell the truth, I've just about lost hope. I feel I will be killed by my keepers. I really don't fear death. I've faced it often before. I do have one regret and that is that I've never been free. If I could be free for one week, I would be ready to die the next. Is it any wonder I don't believe in God? I can't picture a God as cruel as to deny a person even a passing memory of freedom."[42]

A legal battle has been under way for some time to close down the control units.

LEAA's loose control of the anticrime projects it subsidizes is tantamount to mammoth permissiveness of any number of abuses and monetary waste. One of former President Nixon's favorite programs, LEAA came into being in 1968, armed with an enormously swollen budget to help law enforcement agencies curb muggings, burglaries, and lawbreaking in general. From 1968 to 1975 the LEAA spent upward of $6 billion. (In this period, according to the FBI, the crime rate increased 32 percent and the rate of violent crime rose by 50 percent.)[43]

In keeping with Nixon's decentralization approach, the LEAA distributes its largesse to local law enforcement agencies, with practically no accounting as to how these funds are spent. When word got out that much of this funding was being used to experiment with aversive techniques, and possibly psychosurgery, a storm of protest began.

In January 1974, former Senator Sam J. Ervin, Jr. (who chaired the Senate Subcommittee on Constitutional Rights), wrote the head of LEAA raising questions concerning the ethical standards for behavior-modification projects that the LEAA had been financing. He doubted the propriety of federal spending for such projects in the absence of well-developed guidelines and research supervision for the protection of the human subjects.[44]

About a month later Donald E. Santarelli, then the head of the agency, issued a public announcement that the LEAA would no longer fund medical research in chemotherapy, psychosurgery, and behavior modification. But not because it had qualms about the ethics or constitutionality of these procedures: LEAA did not have the "technical skills on the staff to screen, evaluate or monitor such projects."[45] Despite this technical incapacity, the LEAA had subsidized 537 research projects dealing with human modification.[46]

Thus the United States government handed out blocks of money for experimentation with human beings with little or no supervision of the safety of the individuals involved or of the efficacy of these projects. Considering the dubious reputation of some of the law enforcement officers, particularly at the lowest levels, any one of these experiments may have been a basic violation of the Nuremberg Code, in which the international community of nations pledged to respect the basic human rights of captive populations such as prisoners and mental patients.

Senator Ervin's subcommittee declared, "The LEAA because of its law enforcement mission and large appropriations, attracted a wide variety of grant requests dealing with this type of research studies of violent behavior. Many of these research projects involved the study and use of coercive methods designed to deal with violence which appear to pose substantial threats to the privacy and self-determination of the individuals against whom the methods are directed."[47]

The subcommittee characterized the LEAA directive to discontinue further biomedical research as "ambiguous." On the one hand, the subcommittee declared, the LEAA stated its intent to discontinue financing such projects. On the other, a directive issued a while later allowed some of these projects to continue "as part of routine clinical care and physical therapy of mental disorders . . ."[48]

So once again it is not clear how far local prisons or law enforcement agencies are limited by using LEAA funding. Despite the LEAA's definitive statement that it would no longer support psychosurgical experimentation, word comes from the south indicating a strong possibility that psychosurgery is still being applied in certain state prisons.

Dr. L. A. Swan, a Fisk University sociologist specializing in criminal justice, believes it is conceivable that at least fifty psychosurgical operations were performed in 1975 at the Atmore State Prison in Birmingham, Alabama. Dr. Swan ran across this information while conducting an extensive interview project with relatives of black prisoners to find out what happens to the black family when the husband or father is sent to prison. The project is sponsored by the National Institute of Mental Health.

As Dr. Swan describes it,[49] some of the women interviewed complained bitterly that "They [the prison staff] were messing with my husband's brains"; or "the guard said my husband needed a brain operation."

In discussing his findings with me, Dr. Swan said that the women for the most part "did not know exactly what was happening to their husbands," but "they suspected that some kind of surgery was being done. Wives of the men who presumably underwent psychosurgery reported seeing dramatic changes in the appearance of their husbands. They found them lacking alertness, spark, and being slow in responsiveness. Commenting on a recent visit, a woman said, 'I went in there and I didn't even know him. I couldn't tell that this was my husband. He had become so passive, I couldn't believe it.'"

It is Dr. Swan's belief that those prisoners who were operated upon were politically active. Some of the wives indicated this possibility when talking with him. Other women, on hearing of these operations, pleaded with their husbands to avoid trouble. "Try and cooperate," they begged. "Stop agitating, keep your mouth shut."

Dr. Swan reports that in the south there is a rising tide of political consciousness among inmates in state and county prisons.

> They talk of their bank robberies as an act of survival . . . They define their crimes as survival acts in the sense that they were trying to get money to take care of their families because they couldn't find jobs. A lot of them are equating their public acts, such as robberies, to embezzlement and the kinds of rip-offs by public officials that were disclosed during the Watergate hearings.
>
> They see stealing as legitimate within the political context and they see their imprisonment in that context. Many describe themselves as convicts and not as criminals.
>
> And this attitude carries over into their behavior in prison. They demand better conditions and they organize resistance groups against the oppressive environment in which they find themselves.

For the prison authorities, Dr. Swan explains, this politicization represents a new wave that they cannot cope with or understand. The prison staff becomes edgy, panicky, ready to shoot from the hip. Every kind of device, possibly including psychosurgery, is flung into the battle to subdue the recalcitrants.

Atmore State Prison, in all likelihood, as all state prisons, receives part of its share of financial support from the block money grants that the LEAA distributes. But other government agencies besides LEAA carry on independently with no administrative restrictions.

The Ervin subcommittee discovered that the federal government has been financing behavior-modification research by such agencies as the Veterans' Administration, the Department of Labor, the National Science Foundation, and the Department of Defense.

The Veterans' Administration has openly declared that it uses psychosurgery as a treatment procedure and not as an experimental technique. Four of the VA hospitals are especially assigned to this task: in Durham, North Carolina; Long Beach, California; Minneapolis, Minnesota; and Syracuse, New York. Although officially its guidelines restrict the use of psychosurgery, the Veterans' Administration "indicated that it considered drug users and alcoholics as potentially violent patients, and therefore possible subjects for psychosurgery."[50]

The Ervin subcommittee learned that the Veterans' Administration's research was decentralized and "subject to no agency-wide coordination and control," and that many techniques which other federal departments and agencies consider "experimental," the VA employs routinely as "therapy." Even more startling was the fact that the VA "indicates that a patient could be subjected against his will to a process designed to alter his behavior." The VA's official statement to the committee was:

As to whether a patient might refuse psychotropic or behavioral modification programs or psychosurgery drugs, this must be determined by the same criteria that determines the patient's capacity to give informed consent for any treatment. Good professional practice seeks to find a way to engage the patient in doing those things which are likely to be beneficial to him, recognizing that at times the individual's capacity to form sound judgments for himself is seriously impaired. Under these latter circumstances, a variety of considerations must be reviewed by the physician with the conclusion, at times, that treatment must be insisted upon despite the patient's temporary objections. In many circumstances, it may be that a judgment will have to be made by a responsible person legally entitled to act on behalf of the patient.[51]

The Ervin subcommittee called for further investigation to determine whether the Veterans' Administration is violating the rights of individuals in its care.

Other agencies, such as the National Science Foundation (NSF), foot the bill for "a substantial amount of research dealing with 'understanding human behavior,'" but the Ervin subcommittee was unable to obtain information about these "understanding" projects. The subcommittee further charged that the NSF provision to safeguard the rights of human subjects in these experiments is extremely general. All told it consists of only one paragraph. The subcommittee report concluded with this comment:

> As experience with the Department of Justice and other agencies has demonstrated, there is wide variation in the understanding of what behavior modification is. One might expect each of the ten agencies to have difficulty in deciding which programs fell within the scope of the committee's inquiry. It is also reasonable to expect that other agencies besides the LEAA might have difficulty discovering all its pertinent projects. These considerations point to the need for an intensive legislative inquiry into behavior modification throughout the government.[52]

Notwithstanding this observation and the occasional public outcry when some of the more outlandish forms of behavior modification are brought into the limelight, another experimental establishment has made its debut, early in 1977: it is the Center for Correctional Research at Butner, North Carolina.

Long aborning, the federal facility at Butner has been at the center of controversy relating to prisoner experimentation for nearly fifteen years. Construction of the center began in the early sixties, then came to a halt because the funding ran out. It is now operative, $13,500,000 later. Initially, there was great suspicion that psychosurgery, among other techniques, was to be high on the program. This has been denied by the prison authorities. They insist their program will involve the newest techniques to develop methods "aimed at improving correctional effectiveness."[53]

In spite of these assurances, the facility's purpose remains mysterious. There is well-founded doubt that the prisoners to be experimented upon will be true volunteers; rather, that they will be individuals who will agree to undergo this "treatment" because of threats of reprisal from the prison officialdom. Repeated requests from Senator Ervin (until November 1974, when the subcommittee report was issued) for specific information on the mechanisms to be developed to guarantee informed consent brought vague responses from Dr. Martin Groder, a psychiatrist who was until recently the chief architect of the programs to be instituted at Butner. His explanation, apart from promises that the programs would adhere strictly to the nonpunitive, nondrug, and nonpsychosurgical protocols, was that the consent technicalities were still being formulated and would be issued shortly. The rules governing the experimental work and the nature of the review structures to oversee it are equally vague.[54]

Officially Dr. Groder projected a "multiple, integrated approach"[55] that will draw on a number of techniques, from the "Asklepieion," self-help transactional analysis, to psychodrama, a program involving role reversal in given life situations designed to strengthen and rebuild personality structures. Butner officials insist that their prime objective is to modify antisocial behavior so that a particular individual can become a useful and productive member of society, while critics charge that this super brain-refashioning institution more likely than not will resemble a house of horrors.

According to the Bureau of Prisons, the Butner Research Center will house 348 inmates. Of these, 140 will be assigned to mental health units for treatment and the remainder, composed of four correctional units, with 50 prisoners in each, will be devoted to different experimental treatment methods.[56]

Dr. Groder drew much of his inspiration from the theories of Dr. Edgar H. Schein, professor of organizational psychology at the Massachusetts Institute of Technology, a proclaimed American authority on "brainwashing" techniques reportedly used by the Chinese on GI prisoners of war during the Korean conflict.

Dr. Schein is on record as believing that successful changing of a prisoner's personality is dependent on a thorough shakeup of his environment and his thinking processes and a total destruction of social relationships with his peers. To begin with, he says, the jailer must sow mistrust of the person's fellow prisoners and "undermine ties to his home by the systematic withholding of mail." At the same time he should be placed "in a new and ambiguous situation for which the standards are unclear" and then have pressure brought to bear on him.

Dr. Schein puts it this way:

> In order to produce marked change of behavior and/or attitude, it is necessary to weaken, undermine or remove the supports to the old patterns of behavior and the old attitudes . . . This can be done either by removing the individual physically and preventing any communication with those whom he cares about, or by proving to him that those whom he respects are not worthy of it and, indeed, should be actively mistrusted. If at the same time the total environment inflexibly provides rewards and punishments only in terms of the new behavior and attitudes to be contained, and provides new contacts around which to build up relationships, it is highly likely that the desired new behavior and attitudes will be learned . . .[57]

Dr. Schein set forth this thesis at a symposium sponsored by the U.S. Bureau of Prisons in 1962 as part of a training program for associate wardens. "I would like to have you think of brainwashing not in terms of politics, ethics and morals," he told the wardens, "but in terms of the deliberate changing of behavior and attitudes by a group of men who have relatively complete control over the environment in which the captive population lives." Since that lecture, Dr. Schein's dictum has become a pervasive force in influencing many of the behavior-modification programs within the prison system.

According to ACLU attorney Saunders, the initial plans for Butner, when it was still known as the U.S. Behavioral Research Center, were based in great measure on Dr. Schein's approach — maximum psychological isolation of the inmate until he was brought to heel. Butner was also to become a major testing arena of the START behavioral techniques. Saunders stated that the START court hearings revealed that the START program was to be the forerunner for Butner. But most of the limelight was to be focused on Dr. Groder's own recipe for the remodeling of the recalcitrant prisoner. This was what he called the Asklepieion method (Greek for "Temple of Healing"), Saunders says.

Putting together bits and pieces of transactional analysis and Synanon "attack sessions," Groder added his own ingredients to a procedure that he tried out at the Marion penitentiary. When a prisoner entered this program, his behavioral and psychic characteristics were studied thoroughly, so as to pinpoint his more vulnerable areas, and then, Saunders said, the assault began. The inmate was interrogated, ridiculed, assailed for his real or imaginary crimes, furiously tossed about emotionally, threatened, and bullied.[58] After some months of being subjected to these pressures, and when the individual was reduced to human rubble, Saunders explained that the prisoner's reformation was now seen possible. A new, meek person would be in the making. With this total overhaul of behavior, prison wardens felt confident that much of this change would carry over into the nonprison world of the inmate once he was released.

It happened that in the fall of 1975, Dr. Groder's appointment to the post of warden for Butner was suddenly in doubt and in a fit of anger he resigned from the Bureau of Prisons altogether. This does not necessarily mean that his program will go out with him. "There has been no change in the basic mission of Butner,"[59] said Norman Carlson, the director of the Bureau of Prisons. The ACLU continues to fear that regardless of who heads Butner the program will be directed against "troublemakers" who protest prison conditions.

One highly qualified observer who has been following the Butner plans for years told me that if the various Groder, Schein, and other theories don't work out, there is still the other alternative close by geographically. One of the four hospitals designated by the Veterans' Administration to perform psychosurgery on patients considered violent is only a few miles away.

Since most of the prisoners are veterans, it would take only a minor clerical arrangement to effect a transfer.

Meanwhile, as the economic decline continues, accompanied by massive unemployment and a corresponding rise in crime, there has been a dramatic increase in the number of people going to jail. This is particularly true in the south, where the term "warehousing" has become the standard reference to the jammed penitentiary facilities. As an example, in Louisiana the prison population jumped by 34 percent, or from 4744 inmates in January 1976, to 6409 in January 1977. In the same period the number of those jailed in Montana rose by 33 percent, in Illinois by 23 percent, and in Delaware by 36 percent.[60]

This mass migration into prisons has brought behavior modification and experimentation on human subjects to a top priority. Prison Director Carlson, in recent testimony before a congressional committee, said plans are underway to build institutions similar to Butner on the West Coast and in the Midwest. It appears obvious that the spillover from the techniques developed in penitentiaries will affect Americans outside jails as as well.

By the year 2000 "the prison system will increasingly be valued and used as a laboratory and workshop for social change"[61] is the prediction of James V. Bennett, in his book, *I Chose Prison*. Mr. Bennett was director of the U.S. Bureau of Prisons for nearly thirty years.

6. Predicting the Violent among Us

ALONG WITH PSYCHOSURGERY, vomit-producing drugs, solitary confinement, and other "aversive-therapeutic" techniques to tame violence in the prisoner or the emotionally ill, there is yet another facet of the behavior-modification phenomenon. This is the newly launched "science" of predicting which of us may be "potentially violence-prone."

If you are a male, rather tall and generally oversized, the possessor of an extra Y chromosome and given to sulky moods — watch out. If government-sponsored researchers and certain law enforcement authorities have their way, you may fall into the "potentially violent" profile category — the "XYY" syndrome — thus becoming a candidate for "correctional" treatment, even if you've never committed a crime.

If you are a female whose menstrual cycle is associated with tempestuous ups and downs in mood and an irascibility approaching tantrum levels, you too may become a marked person. Your hormonal imbalances during menstruation, according to this theory, may trigger assaultive outbursts to justify your being restrained, or possibly institutionalized for the public good.

If the balky young Chicano, or the rebellious Black Panther prisoner, behind bars because of an altercation with police during a ghetto protest rally, continues to be defiant of authority, the prison psychiatrist may ponder: Is there something uncontrollably impulsive about this man? Is such recalcitrance possibly brought on by the malfunctioning of certain brain cells? Is he then a suitable subject for a brain-scanning procedure? If the answer is yes, then electrodes would be implanted to stimulate parts of the inner brain, and if the resulting electroencephalogram squiggles form a pattern that some would consider abnormal, then the prisoner could be regarded as a candidate for psychosurgery.

The implantation of the electrodes is itself fraught with danger. Nick a blood vessel and it's most likely that the outcome will be disastrous. There is very little, if anything, that can be done to stop a brain hemorrhage.[1] There is also a certain amount of damage to brain cells that get in the way of the electrodes as they are sunk deep into the brain through holes drilled in the skull; and brain cells, unlike other body cells, do not regenerate. As one scientist put it, "Once you intrude on a brain cell, it will not forget, nor forgive."

But what better way to cut down on crime than getting to the would-be lawbreaker by screening such deviants out of the population and setting him or her apart from the rest of society before this individual breaks out in a rash of felonies?

The development and acceptance of the idea of pinpointing those who may be potentially assaultive or crime-prone because of genetic, hormonal, or brain abnormality received major impetus during the Nixon administration. The Nixon general staff was determined to sweep away the "permissiveness" of the sixties, in which social and economic factors took center stage as the prime causes of crime and disquiet. Their view, at least as publicly stated, was that there was ample opportunity for everyone to "make it" socially and economically and that those failing to do so had something intrinsically wrong with them. "Shape up or be zapped" was to be the motto of the new generation.

This was also the Nixon attitude when dealing with the civil protest disorders that continued to break out immediately before and after the assassination of Martin Luther King, Jr. It was in this climate of heightening demands for a better deal by the minorities, on the one hand, and the law and order frenzy, on the other, that three Harvard professors, Dr. Sweet, Dr. Mark, and Dr. Ervin (as mentioned in Chapter 2) put forward the proposition that riots and civil disobedience may be sparked by individuals who unfortunately may be carriers of damaged brain cells. When under stress of such emotionally high-pitched confrontations as street demonstrations, these people will run amok, become assaultive, and precipitate acts of violence. The Harvard trio presented their view in a letter to the *Journal of the American Medical Association*, which appeared under the headline "Role of Brain Disease in Riots and Urban Violence." The letter, in part, follows:

> That poverty, unemployment, slum housing, and inadequate education underlie the nation's urban riots is well known, but the obviousness of these causes may have blinded us to the more subtle role of other possible factors, including brain dysfunction in the rioters who engaged in arson, sniping, and physical assault.
>
> It is important to realize that only a small number of the millions of slum dwellers have taken part in the riots, and that only a subfraction of these rioters have indulged in arson, sniping, and assault. Yet, if slum conditions alone determined and initiated riots, why are the vast majority of slum dwellers able to resist the temptations of unrestrained violence? Is there something peculiar about the violent slum dweller that differentiates him from his peaceful neighbor?
>
> There is evidence from several sources . . . that brain dysfunction related to a focal lesion plays a significant role in the violent and assaultive behavior of thoroughly studied patients. Individuals with electroencephalographic abnormalities in the temporal region have been found to have a much greater frequency of behavioral abnormalities (such as poor impulse control, assaultiveness, and psychosis) than is present in people with a normal brain wave pattern.[2]

These conclusions lead to a variety of questions: Is the activist just a violence-prone slum dweller? Is agitation for civil rights tantamount to impulsive pathological symptomatology? Is docility or acquiescence to slum conditions a sign of emotional health? Is this theory to serve as the scientific rationale to justify putting politically conscious ghetto protesters into the same category with muggers and murderers?

A vastly contrasting profile of a rioter was drawn by the Kerner Commission after interviewing 1200 persons in twenty cities in the course of its investigation of the causes of civil disorders. The commission was established by President Lyndon Johnson to study the disturbances that broke out immediately after the assassination of Dr. Martin Luther King, Jr. It was headed by the late Otto Kerner, then governor of Illinois, and former Mayor John V. Lindsay of New York. It included, among others, Charles B. Thornton, board chairman of Litton Industries; John L. Atwood, head of North American Rockwell Corporation; Walter E. Hoadley, senior vice president of Bank of America; Louis J. Polk, Jr., vice president of General Mills, Inc.; as well as mayors, congressmen, and senators. Nowhere in the 650-page account, *Report of the National Advisory Commission on Civil Rights*, is there a reference to the rioter being either emotionally sick or organically below par.

According to the commission, the typical rioter was:

> somewhat better educated than the average inner-city Negro, having attended at least high school for a time. Nevertheless, he was more likely to be working in a menial or low status job as an unskilled laborer.
>
> He feels strongly he deserves a better job and that he is barred from achieving it . . . because of discrimination by the employers . . . The rioter rejects the white bigot's stereotype of the Negro as ignorant and shiftless. He takes great pride in his race . . . He is substantially better informed about politics than Negroes who are not involved in riots. He is more likely to be actively engaged in civil rights efforts, etc.[3]

Soon after their letter to the *Journal of the American Medical Association*, Dr. Ervin and Dr. Mark published their book *Violence and the Brain*, which expanded their theory to include the possibility that there were as many as ten million Americans wandering around the country who "suffer from obvious brain disease" and an additional five million whose brains "have been subtly damaged." They thus provided "compelling" data for the need to start a program for mass screening of Americans.[4]

"Our greatest danger no longer comes from famine or communicable diseases," they asserted.

Our greatest danger lies in ourselves and in our fellow humans . . . we need to develop an "early warning test" of limbic brain function to detect those humans who have a low threshold for impulsive violence . . . Violence is a public health problem, and the major thrust of any program dealing with violence must be toward its prevention.[5]

In their book the two doctors urged, among other things, that funds be made available for further research into chromosomal abnormalities and psychosurgery, and that screening centers be established throughout the nation to monitor people with abnormal brain waves.[6]

Their pleas fell upon receptive ears. Under pressure from a group of congressmen, a reluctant National Institute of Mental Health found itself handing over $500,000 from its dwindling research funds to the three Boston physicians for further investigation into the use of psychosurgery as a weapon against violence.*

In the ensuing months the "violence and the brain" theory may not have produced much enthusiasm among the neuroscientists, but it made headway among important government officials. The Law Enforcement Assistance Administration became so intrigued with the psychosurgery idea that it awarded the Boston doctors a grant of $108,000. More money was on the horizon. The idea of stemming the growing crime rate by the simple expedient of lopping off a few defective brain cells to make the muggers more manageable spurred some members of Congress to even greater generosity. An additional $1 million was earmarked for Mark, Ervin, and Sweet to enlarge the scope of their investigations. But cooler heads prevailed. Thus this appropriation was voted down by Congress.

---

*This NIMH award caused a near scandal because many of the scientists on the institute staff found the project scientifically and socially untenable. According to *Science* (March 16, 1973), an NIMH-NINDS (National Institute of Neurological Diseases and Stroke) Ad Hoc Committee on Psychosurgery circulated petitions opposing the appropriation. The petition said: "Since psychosurgery can severely impair a person's intellectual and emotional capacities, the prospects for repression and social control are disturbing."

Whether wittingly or unwittingly, Michael Crichton, the young doctor-writer from Harvard, introduced the "violence and brain" theory to the general public. His sensational book, *The Terminal Man*, a fast-paced thriller, describes how a team of neurosurgeons attempted to regulate the behavior of a murder-bent paranoiac by having his brain controlled via a computer. Much of this material is based directly on the Mark-Ervin book, *Violence and the Brain*. No coincidence, Dr. Ervin told me. Crichton was his student at Harvard Medical School just a short while before.[7]

Some of Crichton's narrative reads as though quoted directly from *Violence and the Brain*. Dr. Ellis, the neurosurgeon in the Crichton novel, estimates that there are "ten million Americans who have obvious damage and five million more who have a subtle form of it . . . "

In the course of this statement Dr. Ellis adds: "Now that shoots down a lot of theories about poverty and discrimination and social injustice and social disorganization . . . you cannot correct physical brain damage with social remedies . . . "[8] Similar views are heard in the film based on Crichton's book. As in most instances involving highly technical developments, the public was strictly on the receiving end and was in no position to make a sound evaluation of this presentation.

A few months after the Crichton book was published, Dr. Sweet was testifying at the Senate Committee on Appropriations hearings (May 23, 1972), urging that diagnostic centers be established to sort out those of us who may imperil society because of extra chromosomes or damaged brain cells.[9]

One such center was being planned in California. The Center for the Study and Reduction of Violence was to be set up to develop "behavioral indicators, profiles, biological correlates," to assist "school administrators, law enforcement personnel and governmental departments" to detect and control "overt expression of life-threatening behavior by identifiable individuals and groups."[10] The proposed center was to be under the direction of the prestigious Neuropsychiatric Institute of the University of

California at Los Angeles, and it would be the prototype for other such facilities in different parts of the country. It was to be funded jointly by the State of California and the LEAA.

For the first time in the history of the United States, criteria were to be set up for the labeling (or stigmatizing) of individuals believed to be potentially criminal, even though they had committed no crime. It was also astonishing that the program was so blatantly rigged against those sections of society that were most vulnerable and least able to defend themselves: for those to be drawn upon for experimentation would be children, minority group members, and prisoners.

Formation of the UCLA Center was announced in September 1972 by Dr. Louis Jolyon West, director of the Neuropsychiatric Institute and chief architect of the overall plan. An affable, plumpish man in his early fifties, Dr. West is an adventurous psychiatrist who somehow appears in the headlines more often than most of his colleagues. Known as "Jolly" West, he came to considerable prominence as the very young director of the psychiatry department at the University of Oklahoma. It was there that he overdosed an elephant in the Oklahoma Zoo with LSD.*[11]

Ronald Reagan, then governor of California, hailed the Center for the Study and Reduction of Violence. He gave his official blessing in his January 1973 state of the state address. Reagan's secretary of health and welfare quickly made known that "more than one million dollars would be invested in the center in the fiscal year 1973–74."[12] Part of the subsidy was to come in the form of matching funds from the LEAA.

As stated in Dr. West's original proposal, "a major thrust of the center's work will move into the largely unexplained interface between biological and psychological aspects of violent be-

---

*There appears to be no connection between this zoo incident and the recent CIA revelations. But according to the *New York Times* (August 2, 1977), Dr. West was asked to make a study of LSD in relation to the CIA behavior-control experiments. The *New York Times* reported that Dr. West was paid by the Geschickter Foundation, an organization allegedly used by the CIA to disburse funds to finance behavior research.

havior," with the main lines of investigation focused on the genetic, biochemical, and neurophysiological factors.[13]

In the genetic studies, emphasis was to be placed on the relationship of violence and "a disorder in sex chromosomes (the
XYY defect) . . ." Two junior high schools would provide the
source material for this investigation, "one in a predominantly
black ethnic area; the other in a predominantly Chicano area."
The proposal made the assumption that a high incidence of violence was shown to be related to these factors: "sex (male), age
(youthful), ethnicity (black), and urbanicity."[14]

There are those who see the chromosome-crime approach as a
sort of return to the theories of Cesare Lombroso. This Italian
investigator, it will be recalled, created quite a sensation in the
late nineteenth century when he launched the theory that criminal types could be identified by certain physical features. Lombroso believed that individuals with head and skull peculiarities
or those with protruding large jaws, low foreheads, and small,
receding chins were destined to become dangerous outlaws.

For a number of years many criminologists held fast to Lombroso's speculation. As late as 1911, Lombroso's views received
serious consideration in the United States among some of the
most prominent lawyers, physicians, and law enforcement authorities. The theory began falling apart when Lombroso's own
students discovered that 63 percent of Italian soldiers shared
similar incriminating characteristics. It went into eclipse after an
English study involving 3000 prison inmates failed to confirm
Lombroso's conclusions.[15]

The genetic approach was revived some ten years ago by researchers who claimed to have noted a significant number of
oversized males with an extra Y chromosome among the criminally insane with a background of violence. The principal investigator associated with the discovery of the XYY chromosome
anomaly was Dr. Patricia Jacobs, whose findings came from a
study she conducted in a Scottish jail in 1965.[16]

Ordinarily most people carry 46 chromosomes, which house
the genes, or the basic genetic material. Two of these chromo-

somes determine the sex of the individual. Thus in the male it is generally 46 XY, and in the female it is 46 XX. Dr. Jacobs reported that in comparative studies of noncriminal groups she found a much lower incidence of the XYY phenomenon. But when scientists in England, France, Denmark, the United States, and other countries tried to replicate her work they were unsuccessful in backing up Dr. Jacob's theory. They began finding XYY males among such respectable types as priests and ministers, businessmen, factory workers, and others who had no background of violent or aggressive behavior.[17]

Dr. West's biochemical inquiry was to be based on the hypothesis "that hormones are an important determinant of aggressive behavior." Excessive secretion of testosterone in males "is thought to be related to uncontrolled aggression," the Center for the Study and Reduction of Violence proposal maintained. "The drugs which hold promise for diminishing violent outbursts . . . would be tested in the laboratory and then in prisons, mental hospitals and special community centers . . ."[18] The drug to be tested is cyproterone acetate, which is known to produce a castrating effect.

In evaluating women with emotional reactions associated with their premenstrual and menstrual periods, the center would employ hormonal monitoring to determine estrogen and progesterone levels in the plasma.

The most frightening part of the proposal dealt with brain screening. In this connection critics charged that Dr. West undoubtedly received a good deal of help from Dr. Ervin, who had moved from Harvard to Dr. West's Neuropsychiatric Institute at UCLA. The center prospectus listed Dr. Ervin as one of those who would be directly involved in the development of its program. In introducing this concept, Dr. West echoed the Mark-Ervin theory by stating that "approximately 5–10 percent of the population suffers from some impairment of brain function. The proportion is probably much higher among inmates of prisons and institutions for the criminally insane." He went on to say that "in some patients, outbursts of uncontrolled rage have definitely been linked to abnormal electrical activity in deeply buried areas of the brain . . . For many years, neurologists have measured the electrical activity of the brain with electrodes attached to the scalp . . . Now by implanting tiny electrodes deep within the brain, electrical activity can be followed in areas that cannot be measured from the surface of the scalp."

The future looked even more promising, Dr. West declared. "It is even possible to record bioelectrical changes in the brains of freely moving subjects, through the use of remote monitoring techniques. These methods now require elaborate preparation. They are not yet feasible for large-scale screening that might permit detection of violence predisposing brain disorders prior to the occurrence of a violent episode. *A major task of the center should be to devise such a test, perhaps sharpened in its predictive powers by correlated measures of psychological test results.*"[19]

Apart from the junior high schools where some of the chromosome research was to be done, most of the experimentation would involve prisoners from Atascadero State Hospital, Camarillo State Hospital, and the Vacaville facility.

As details of the plan began leaking out, opposition developed rapidly. Ironically, the Center for the *Reduction* of Violence became the lightning rod for a series of polemical sorties and violent encounters.

Professors were charging one another with misrepresentation of facts; students went back to the picket line for the first time since the Vietnam war protests; Bill Walton, then the UCLA basketball center, became an anti-center activist who, together with 5000 others on the campus, took part in a referendum in which 60 percent voted against the center; and the university's *Daily Bruin* became the arena for heated exchanges by the opposing sides.[20]

Soon the controversy spilled over beyond the campus and began involving lay organizations as well as scientific, community, and professional organizations. Joining the opposition were the ACLU, the NAACP, the Federation of American Scientists, the California Psychiatric Society, the Mexican-American Political Association, the National Organization for Women, the United Farmworkers' Organizing Committee, the Committee Opposed to Psychiatric Abuse of Prisoners, the California Mental Health Coordinating Council, the Black Panther Party, and others.

There were many questions about the center that troubled these organizations. But what they found most sinister was the possibility that medicine and psychiatry would be used to mask the development of methods to curb and police those Americans who might hold unorthodox political views.

A group of psychiatrists, lawyers, social workers, and other professionals, one of the most vocal in its criticism of the center, set itself up as the Committee Opposing Psychiatric Abuse of Prisoners (COPAP). It issued a statement warning that "in an age of rapidly advancing technology, when new methods of scientific control and behavior are becoming a reality, and when the cry for law and order at any cost is at its most shrill, it is necessary to be even more sensitive to the preservation of human dignity and fundamental principles of liberty and freedom . . . What is being proposed here [*the center*] is not just some work at UCLA but the beginning of a network of activities which would involve UCLA, the State prisons, the State mental hospitals and law enforcement agencies," Dr. Lee Coleman told a hearing of the California legislature. Because the center was to get its funding from the state and the LEAA, he went on, the control of research would be of a political character, rather than a scientific one. Dr. Coleman is a San Francisco psychiatrist who represented the views of COPAP.

"We are not opposed to law enforcement," he said, "but we are opposed to using medicine and psychiatry as a veneer for techniques which might and could be used for law enforcement, which at the same time raise very, very serious ethical, constitutional and legal questions . . ."[21]

The Southern California Psychiatric Society issued a special report following its task force study of the center in which it questioned the basic premise of the project. It said it couldn't go along with the center's program because of the many reservations it shared with the organizations opposing the center's objectives. Among other things, the Psychiatric Society expressed concern that prisoners would be used as "volunteer" subjects for experimentation. Such "volunteering" would be especially suspect in California because most state prisoners do not serve a fixed sentence. Release or parole is based on "good" behavior. The Psychiatric Society was also uneasy because the funding would be coming from law-enforcement agencies, thus impinging on the scientific integrity of those participating in the program.[22]

Other organizations opposing the center pointed out that much of the experimentation would have a racist quality since most California prisoners are black or Chicano.

The fact that Atascadero and Vacaville and Camarillo would be the principal sources of supply of human material for experimentation sent a shudder throughout the community. The names of these penitentiaries, especially Atascadero and Vacaville, had already become synonomous with some of the worst atrocities on the West Coast. In 1971, three years after the secret psychosurgery experiments in Vacaville, California authorities had tried to reinstate these on a much more extensive scale. But the revelation of secret documents and the public uproar that followed had forced the Department of Corrections and the University of California at San Francisco, which had also been involved, to drop the plan. Atascadero had its own history of torture, with Anectine and other aversive drugs. Now there was strong belief that plans for the use of psychosurgery would be revived through the center.

One of the most persistent critics of the center is Dr. Isidore Ziferstein, associate clinical professor of psychiatry at the Neuropsychiatric Institute, UCLA, who crossed swords with his boss, Dr. West, over its scientific and ethical concepts. Objecting to the basic aim of the proposed center, Dr. Ziferstein challenged the idea that by "studying a relatively small number of violent individuals, the proposed Center will help combat the rise of violence, and will reduce it . . . It is clear," he said, "that the increase in violence is not due to an increase in brain disease in individuals but is a social phenomenon which has social causes, which need to be examined and remedied."[23] Dr. Ziferstein is a Life Fellow of the American Psychiatric Association and widely known for his research into Pavlovian theory and transcultural psychiatry. He appeared before the California Council on Criminal Justice as the official representative of the Federation of American Scientists.

Dr. Ziferstein scorned the idea of "predicting" which people are potentially violent. "This means labeling persons as potential criminals, and involves a serious threat to civil liberties." Greatly concerned that psychosurgery might be employed to "correct" behavior at the center, he warned that "psychosurgery is a highly controversial experimental procedure" which should not be performed until more is known about the human brain.[24]

Considered by his colleagues a dedicated clinician and teacher, Dr. Ziferstein was ever more deeply involved in the center controversy as time went on. When I went to see him at his home in Los Angeles, in February 1974, when the debate over the center was at its height, the mild-mannered psychiatrist was in his study surrounded by bookshelves crowded with scientific and general literature. His desk was piled high with newspaper clippings and documents relating to the center. In his late fifties, Dr. Ziferstein looked like a man who would rather be engrossed in research than in a polemical exchange with some of his colleagues. He seemed tired but ready to elaborate on why he felt it important to stop the Center for the Study and Reduction of Violence from coming into being. As he talked he would gently lift down a Siamese cat that persistently jumped onto his lap or strolled across his desk, unheeding of his master's attempts to constrain its repeated intrusions.

"We have a new situation on our hands," he said. "Because of the intensifying economic decline it is inevitable that more and more jobless will go beyond the limits of the law to satisfy their needs. There are probably upwards of 30 percent of our population who are permanently impoverished, for lack of opportunity, for lack of retraining to newer industrial needs as old skills disappear because of automation. And once these 30 percent become convinced that the democratic process is not working for them, they become desperate and may resort to violent means.

"And when that happens nobody can remain secure. Even if you live in Beverly Hills, these kids from Watts, who are in despair, frustrated but mobile, can throw Molotov cocktails into the fanciest of homes. So it is really in our own self-interest to bring these people into the mainstream of society and to give them a stake in society. For a while, in the sixties, there was a kind of social optimism, there was a hope that if you directed enough skilled manpower and resources, money and so on, into certain areas, you could really produce a significant change for the better. But since Nixon all this has been swept away.

"And so our prison population is burgeoning with young and vigorous people. There is a rising radicalism in their midst and there is an uppitiness among the blacks and the Chicano prisoners which prison officials find intolerable.

"To subdue them, the authorities are using new methods. They're employing the psychiatric armamentarium and a new technological tool set — what has come to be known as psychotechnology. Under the guise of therapeutic behavior modification they're applying anything from Anectine and other aversive drugs to psychosurgery. The wardens do not differentiate between the pathologically violent prisoners and the political militants. In their view these prisoners are all the same — creatures who should be tranquilized at all costs. Depending upon who it is who sets the standards there is no end to which this approach could lead. Gradually you begin 'treating' large numbers of individuals as social deviants, even if they do not commit any crimes; if all they do is 'act sort of peculiar,' 'dress funny,' 'talk funny.'"

The psychiatrist scoffed at the idea of screening potential criminal suspects via EEG readings. "I've sent patients to three different encephalologists and gotten three different reports. This entire brain-wave measuring approach is frightening and primitive. Doctors Ervin, Sweet, and Mark talk about some ten million people with abnormal brain function, but I'm sure there are many times that number whose EEGs might register abnormally.

"When we are children we do a lot of running and a lot of falling and we hurt our heads fairly frequently. The possibility of pinpoint hemorrhages here and there in the brain, with a few cells being damaged, is very great. When you also consider that all of us are subject to childhood diseases, there again may be some brain involvement because of the many complications, mild or serious, that may follow.

"You know, every time you have a fever the brain is somewhat affected. Influenza, measles, and so many other ailments may leave their mark. I doubt whether there's anybody alive, walking, who has a perfectly functioning brain. But that doesn't mean that we're abnormal to the point where we need to have our defective brain cells zapped. There may even be people who, from time to time, lose control of themselves under certain conditions. We are all slightly neurotic, we all have certain fears, certain anxieties, depressive moments, and so on. But I would hate to see anybody assume the decision-making power to decree that on the basis of suspicious-looking brain waves certain individuals should undergo psychosurgery.

"The whole notion that there are certain centers in the brain that occasionally begin to malfunction and therefore require surgical correction, is probably incorrect. I believe that the brain is not structured in terms of areas, that is, geographically; it's more likely that it is structured functionally in terms of systems. The psychosurgeons focus on a few cells and claim that with the availability of sophisticated instrumentation they can now implant an electrode within a millimeter of the desired pinpointed area. But you see, the equipment is more sophisticated than the knowledge of what you're about. You may be impressing people with sophisticated technology but you really don't know what you're doing.

"You may think that you'll be removing aggession by destroying the amygdala, but that part of the limbic system also carries at least 29 other functions. So [by] working on the flimsy supposition of calming aggressive behavior you are also obliterating many other facets of the personality.

"Pavlov made reference to the fact that the advantage of the conditioned reflex approach to the study of behavior was that you were working with a whole person or a whole animal. He criticized those who sought to change the individual by removing or destroying a portion of the brain. He said that such a procedure is very much like taking a very delicate clock or watch and going at it with a chisel and hammer; the wrong way of finding out how the brain works."[25]

When I talked with Dr. Ervin, he seemed to be reacting to increasing criticism as to the validity of his theory advocating the destruction of defective cells in the amygdala to calm aggressive behavior, which he and Dr. Mark set out in *Violence and the Brain*. His statements to me, I think, could be fairly described as backtracking: "And if somehow the way I wrote the book made it sound like that's what I was talking about [destruction of cells to curb violent behavior], then I've written very badly," he told me in March 1974, during an afternoon cocktail break in the course of the Fifth Annual Cerebral Function Symposium, in San Diego.

I was also startled to hear him say that fewer than 10 percent of psychomotor [temporal lobe] epileptics have rage disorder. Most of the book is predicated on the claim that violence is usually associated with epileptic seizures, which they ascribe to diseased areas in the limbic region of the brain. It is from this premise that they extrapolated their theory of violence in general.*

---

* New data tends to disprove the belief that rage is part of the epilepsy syndrome. Dr. Ernst A. Rodin of the Lafayette Clinic and Epilepsy Center of Michigan has examined "several hundred patients with psychomotor seizures" over a period of fourteen years and found little to back up the traditional surmise that epileptic seizure triggered violence. Two studies on 150 patients revealed that few patients fell into the category of being deliberately aggressive. Similar observations were made at the Montreal Neurological Institute, one of the largest institutions concerned with the problem of epilepsy.[26]

"When I wrote the book" he said, "we didn't report on the epileptics without rage disorders because it wasn't a book about epilepsy. We were interested in the question of violence. We took about six or seven cases for the book, cases that happened to have the rage syndrome, and we focused on what we thought we understood about them. It was, you know, a potboiler; it was meant to be a semipopular book, it wasn't meant to be a technical volume.

"But we thought it was an important insight in noting that there are some individuals who have brain disease which is related to rage disorder . . . Now I don't think that I've ever said anything that is really stronger than that, although looking back at this, that, and the other, maybe it does come out sounding a little stronger. The implication to many people, who I assume have tried to read the book thoughtfully, is that surgery is a great thing for the patient with violence. Now you know we never said that. We never meant it."[27]

But a careful perusal of the book indicates many references to surgery as the answer to violence. As a matter of fact there is a chapter titled "The Surgery of Violence," in which Ervin and Mark summarize their views by stating that "there is a significant and growing body of clinical and especially surgical evidence to indicate that the production of small focal areas of destruction in parts of the limbic brain will often eliminate dangerous behavior in assaultive or violent patients."[28]

When he says that "no, in no way" did he and Dr. Mark contemplate the use of depth electrodes to screen potentially violent people, one is ready to accept his assurance. Dr. Ervin is anything but a Dr. Cyclops in appearance. His easy, informal manner, his casual dress — somewhat suggestive of hippy attire with heavy boots — and a lisp that is unexpected in a pipe-smoking man in his late forties, provide Dr. Ervin with a strange kind of charm, a disarming manner. One finds it difficult to doubt Dr. Ervin's word.

The book that he and Dr. Mark have written speaks differently. Outlining their proposed plan of investigation on people with "uncontrollable violent behavior," Dr. Mark and Dr. Ervin write that "these particular individuals, with implanted brain electrodes, offer an unusual opportunity to assess abnormalities in limbic brain function, and also represent the best chance we have to find out how to detect these abnormalities."[29]

The link between the Mark-Ervin book and the proposal for the center as outlined by Dr. West, was obvious.

As the debate began to heat up, the recriminations at UCLA took on greater political coloration. At the same time, however, Dr. West began to discard those features of his program that appeared most vulnerable to criticism. He began rewriting the proposal to try to stem the growing protest. But with each new version the credibility gap widened, and the center's aims became more eerily puzzling.

To meet the objection that the center failed to provide adequate safeguards to protect the constitutional rights of those who would be subjected to its research, Dr. West announced the formation of a "Section on Ethics and the Law," to be headed by Professor Richard H. Wasserstrom, an eminent specialist who is professor of philosophy and law at UCLA. But only a month later Dr. Wasserstrom withdrew, explaining that his decision to resign from the center was based on doubts "about the adequacy of the proposed safeguards against certain kinds of experimentation." He added that he also felt that "the creation of the Center may well be misused by those outside the University as confirmation of their view of what is the answer to the problem of violence in our culture."[30]

Dr. West's own chief-designate of Planning and Evaluation, John R. Seeley, a nationally known sociologist, stated that the "conceptualization of the project was inadequate, careless, and therefore dangerous, and a great number of the research proposals were rejected by the Center's own core staff as vague, intellectually or scientifically defective or inadequately safeguarded."[31] And he too defected. Somewhat earlier, LEAA's own John A. Gardiner, director of the Research Operations Division, declared that the researches on the proposed center showed "little evidence of established research ability of the kind or level necessary for a study of this scope."[32]

In subsequent versions of the proposal, Dr. West dropped all references to the Chicano and black neighborhood schools to be used in the screening for XYY boys. When public concern about the possibility of psychosurgical experiments grew in intensity, Dr. West denied that this was the intent of the program. In an interview in the UCLA *Daily Bruin* in January 1974, he stated that "human experimentation with psychosurgery was never proposed." But this contradicted what Dr. J. M. Stubblebine, director of the California State Department of Health, had said not long before: "There may be some psychosurgery on a selected basis."[33]

Similarly clashing statements were made regarding the use of "volunteer" prisoners for experiments from such places as Atascadero State Hospital, Camarillo State Hospital, and the Medical Facility at Vacaville.

Dr. West's increasingly frequent denials that psychosurgery or depth electrode screening would be employed by the center were further weakened by the disclosure that he had secretly written to Dr. Stubblebine about the opportunity to have much of the center's activities conducted in a former Nike missile base in the Santa Monica mountains. "It is accessible, but relatively remote," he wrote the California official. "The site is securely fenced. Comparative studies could be carried out there, in an isolated but convenient location, of experimental model programs, for the alteration of undesirable behavior."[34] Dr. West's clear desire to avoid public scrutiny of the center's activities intensified suspicions as to the intent and scope of the program. The critics' cries of shame grew into a roar.

In the meantime, it also became known that the university would not after all control the center. Succeeding drafts of West's proposal indicated that the operational control of the center would now rest with state officials. In short, as the Committee Opposed to Psychiatric Abuse of Prisoners put it, "This Center will be a laboratory for the Department of Corrections and law enforcement officials with the diaphanous veneer of UCLA used to make it appear to be a respectable University research facility."[35]

So the Nike letter, coupled with all the other charges against the center, finally forced the LEAA to announce a policy that would deny matching funds for the center. Officially the decision was based on the fact that, as the LEAA had told the Ervin Committee earlier, it was cutting off subsidies for all programs involving human experimentation because it didn't have enough competent staff to supervise such experiments.[36]

For the present, the UCLA Center for the Study and Reduction of Violence project is at a standstill. Dr. West is said to be rewriting yet another version of the proposal (the ninth) in the hope of getting the necessary funds. Regardless of the ultimate fate of the center, the very idea of setting up criteria to catalogue potential violence-prone individuals of the scope envisioned at UCLA is indicative of how seriously the concept of crime prediction is being considered by leaders at the highest levels of government (Reagan, Nixon), and medicine (Dr. Sweet, Dr. West), and by state and federal law-enforcement agencies. Despite LEAA's public pronouncements that it would no longer support psychosurgical or other experimentation on human subjects because it hasn't the staff to monitor such activities, there is little it could do to inhibit such practices on local and state levels precisely because of its lack of supervisory competence.

The chromosome studies, however, are still under way. An investigator was given a $250,000 grant in 1975 for research into "Gene-Environmental Interactions and Crime and Delinquency" and "Neurophysiological Behavior of 47, XYY and 47, XXY Males." A grant to another researcher amounted to nearly $27,000 to probe the XYY syndrome. Yet another grant, in excess of $100,000, was given to a child psychologist, Dr. Stanley Walzer, of the Harvard Medical School, for the study of "Sex Chromosome Abnormality and Behavioral Variation."[37]

This last study was partially halted following protests by a group of scientists in Boston. They charged that this genetic approach is another attempt at linking social deviance to biological causes, "thus distracting attention from the basic economic and social reasons that lead to crime." Moreover, this group declared that even though there is very little knowledge about the XYY phenomenon, the chromosome view has become so closely associated with criminality in the public's mind that, once tagged as "chromosomal deviates," individuals could be ruined for life. Schools, employers, and institutions, however little they know about the XYY factor, these scientists pointed out, may automatically regard them with suspicion and uneasiness. Even parents may begin looking at an XYY child with special reservations and anxiety, thus possibly leading to a self-fulfilling prophecy of the child's psychological insufficiency or disorder.[38]

Despite these protests, Dr. Walzer, as of July 1977, was still continuing with his research at the Boston Hospital for Women. A spokesman for the Center for the Study of Crime and Delinquency, the organization sponsoring this research, indicated there may be a possibility that similar chromosome investigations are being undertaken by other government agencies.

7. Eroding the Legal Protections

LOBOTOMY AND LATER psychosurgery have had an "on again" and "off again" controversial history for upward of forty years. Despite the devastating aftereffects suffered by thousands of lobotomized patients, and the rumblings of disquiet concerning psychosurgery, it is only in the past four or five years that the arguments have begun reaching the courts. Principally, the legal in-fighting focuses on whether psychosurgery is indeed of benefit in treating psychiatric ailments or whether it is still an experimental procedure that in many instances will permanently alter an individual's behavior and personality. The courts have also been asked to determine whether prisoners or institutionalized mental patients and children should be used for such experiments, particularly when their consent to such operations is in question.

The most significant developments in this connection were the Kaimowitz case, which wound up as a landmark opinion by three Michigan judges in July 1973, and the recent recommendations by a congressional commission that would pave the way to striking down this opinion.

The Kaimowitz case concerns a 35-year-old prisoner, who throughout the trial was referred to as John Doe and not by his real name in order to protect his privacy.[1] (Kaimowitz is the lawyer who filed the brief on Doe's behalf.) Doe had been confined to the Michigan Ionia State Hospital for nearly seventeen years as a criminal sex psychopath. About five years ago, he became eligible for release because of a new state law that repealed the Michigan statute under which Doe had been tried. Also in his favor for a speedy return to the outside world was the fact that since his commitment Doe had displayed little or no violent behavior, and toward the latter part of his confinement he became known as a model inmate. Because of his steady improvement in self-control, he was considered to be safe and no longer posing an "unreasonable danger" to the community.

In the fall of 1972, about a year before his term was up, Doe was visited by a rather distinguished personage, no less than Dr. E. G. Yudashkin, director of the State Department of Mental Health. Dr. Yudashkin's very presence was an extraordinary happening for John Doe. But Doe was even more nonplussed when Dr. Yudashkin discussed with him a highly sophisticated proposal for a research project designed to control impulsive sexuality, and asked him whether he wanted to participate in such a scientific adventure.[2]

In a facility such as Ionia, with prisoners living in what the court described as an "inherently coercive institutional environment," few decisions are left to the inmates. During the entire length of Doe's stay at this prison nearly every important aspect of his life was decided without his participation. The kind of clothes he wore, the kind of bed he slept on, the food he ate, and certainly the prison policies were matters on which his opinions were not sought. Yet suddenly he was confronted by a top state health authority with a project in which he was to be one of the chief participants. Theoretically he could have rejected this offer, but as the court hearing later revealed, this was almost impossible to do "because of the inherent inequality" in the positions of Doe and Yudashkin. Quite obviously Yudashkin personified the prison authority that Doe felt he would have to cater to if he wanted to be released.

Dr. Yudashkin told Doe that the project was designed to compare the results of two approaches to the problem. The first, involving twelve prisoner candidates, called for the Mark-Ervin procedure: implantation of depth electrodes into various brain structures of the limbic system; monitoring brain-wave activity;

stimulating the different sections of the limbic system; and finally psychosurgery if the electric discharges indicated that defective brain cells were implicated in aggression. In the second approach, an equal number of prisoners would be treated with the drug cyproterone acetate to depress testosterone output, on the theory that the presence of the excess male hormone led to a variety of impulsive sexual offenses. (The drug, developed in West Germany, reportedly produces a permanent castrating effect.)[3]

Doe held back. After all, his liberation was at hand, as Dr. Yudashkin himself had indicated. But the pressure was unremitting. The mental health director tried to persuade Doe to take part in the experiment if only to help pass the time, which would be hanging heavily upon him, as it was bound to do in the last lap of a long-term sentence. When Dr. Yudashkin finally prevailed, Doe agreed to be a subject in the psychosurgical part of the study. He was given reassurances by Dr. Yudashkin and other staff members. His parents, as his guardians, were notified to come and cosign the consent form.

Expectation that John Doe would understand what he was doing when he agreed to permit the doctors to experiment with his brain opens up a veritable Pandora's box of doubts as to the validity of the principle of informed consent within a prison setting. Was it likely that Doe, incarcerated these many years and scarcely exposed to formal education, would understand the meaning of the document that he signed? Was he in a position to know anything about the intricacies of the limbic system or what intracranial disturbances might follow in the wake of a psychosurgical procedure?

The consent document speaks of his acceptance of the idea that if the electrode probings pinpointed the areas of his brain believed to be responsible for his sexual aggressiveness, the doctors would "destroy this part of the brain with an electrical current." And "if the abnormality comes from a larger part of the brain," the document went on, "I agree that it should be surgically removed, if the doctors determine that it can be done so without risk of side effects." What must the prisoner have thought of this "agreement" when the very next paragraph stated,

I realize that any operation on the brain carries a number of risks which may be slight, but could be potentially serious. These risks include infection, bleeding, temporary or permanent weakness or paralysis of one or more of my legs or arms, difficulties with speech and thinking, as well as the ability to feel, touch, pain and temperature. Under extraordinary circumstances, it is also possible that I might not survive the operation.[4]

It is interesting that none of the medical staff bothered to talk to the parents about the surgery. They received their explanations from Doe, and as it turned out, Doe himself inferred, presumably from the doctors' verbal assurances, that the operation would consist of depth-electrode exploration only, not the actual destruction of brain cells. But as sometimes happens with the best laid plans, this project not only failed in being carried out, it also became a celebrated court case culminating in a landmark decision centering on certain basic constitutional rights, especially those covered by the First, Fourth, Fifth, and Eighth Amendments.

The plan to evaluate the effectiveness of psychosurgery in calming sexually violence-prone individuals originated with two Detroit physicians on the staff of the Lafayette Clinic, a research institute financially supported by the state of Michigan. Dr. Ernst Rodin, chief of neurology, and Dr. J. S. Gottlieb, the director of the clinic, read *Violence and the Brain* and became convinced that some of the procedures advocated by Dr. Mark and Dr. Ervin could be applied to patients with impulsive sexual aggressiveness.[5] They soon persuaded their colleagues at the clinic as well as the oversight committee in the state legislature of the desirability of this experiment.

Both the Human and Animal Experimentation Committee and the Human Rights Review Committee of the Lafayette Clinic, as well as the state senate — which approved a budget request of $164,000 for this project — gave the "go ahead" signal with scarcely a token consideration of what was involved.[6] The scientific basis for the undertaking was not only meager and vague but even distorted: Dr. Rodin later admitted to having misunderstood the surgical criteria outlined by Mark and Ervin. Before deciding to go ahead with John Doe's psychosurgery, Dr. Rodin had consulted Dr. Mark, who cautioned him to proceed only if the patient had evidence of temporal lobe epilepsy. In the Mark-Ervin theory, temporal lobe epilepsy is usually associated with aggression and violent behavior and is related to abnormal electrical activity of the amygdala region. In the case of John Doe there was no evidence of epilepsy. The epilepsy-aggression theory is now under serious question if not total rejection by many neurophysiologists, as mentioned in Chapter 6.[7]

What made the whole project even less justifiable scientifically was the fact that many of the other prisoners selected to take part as subjects or controls were released (because of the repeal of the criminal sex psychopath statute) before it got underway, so that the entire experiment was to hinge on the results with John Doe alone. It would appear that for Dr. Rodin the idea of correcting undesirable behavior by surgical or medical means had become a matter of dedication. "Get down to cold-blooded medical research dealing with individuals rather than masses,"[8] he once demanded of his colleagues in an address at a scientific conference. He scorns sociological considerations when analyzing emotional rebelliousness and denounces expenditures for the funding of what he calls "ill-conceived do-good projects." Dr. Rodin prepared to proceed with the implantation of the electrodes into John Doe's brain in January 1973.

Early that month a doctor at the Lafayette Clinic heard about the impending experiment and suspected that something not quite ethical was in the making. He leaked this information to Gabe Kaimowitz, a senior staff attorney for the Michigan Medical Committee for Human Rights.[9] Kaimowitz in turn got in touch with the *Detroit Free Press*, which published a front page story questioning the proposed procedure on John Doe.[10] The publicity that resulted from the story, combined with

Kaimowitz's filing of a petition and complaint in court on behalf of John Doe made the would-be experimenters back away. Dr. Yudashkin withdrew the funds for the project and Dr. Rodin and Dr. Gottlieb dropped all further plans to proceed with the psychosurgery.

In spite of this retreat, the three-judge Circuit Court for Wayne County, Michigan, decided to take up the case in order to render an opinion on some of its implicit constitutional questions. First, the court released John Doe from further imprisonment because of the recent revision of the Michigan statutes and also because the court's psychiatrist felt that it was now safe to return him to society. The court then focused its consideration on two questions, which, though especially related to the psychosurgery attempt on John Doe, have much broader ramifications.

The first question: Could "legally adequate consent be obtained from adults involuntarily confined in the State mental health system for experimental or innovative procedures on the brain to ameliorate behavior?" Second: Should the state "allow such experimentation on human subjects to proceed?"[11]

On the issue of consent, the court declared that "under a free government, one of a person's greatest rights is the right to inviolability of his person, and it is axiomatic that this right necessarily forbids the physician or surgeon from violating, without permission, the bodily integrity of his patient." The court referred to the Nuremberg Code, declaring that the involuntarily detained person must be in a position "to be able to exercise free power of choice without any element of force, fraud, deceit, duress, overreaching, or other ulterior form of restraint or coercion. He must have sufficient knowledge and comprehension of the subject matter to enable him to make an understanding decision. The decision must be a totally voluntary one on his part."[12]

The Nuremberg Code is an international agreement subscribed to by the United States and other countries that fought against Nazi Germany. It is considered one of the most solemn

documents growing out of World War II. At the time of its signing, it represented a visceral outcry against one of history's most
terrifying obscenities — the concentration camps where, among
other things, the captive population was subjected to some of the
most heinous experiments by German scientists and doctors. In
the Nuremberg Judgment, which denounced all those participating in the concentration camp "research," the entire world
was put on notice that hereafter persons held in prisons or mental institutions, regardless of their crimes or sickness, were never
again to be forced into experiments without their consent or
knowledge of what these experiments were all about.

In the Michigan case, the court said the very nature of John
Doe's incarceration diminished his ability to consent to psychosurgery. In the court's view, "the fact of institutional confinement has special force in undermining the capacity of the mental
patient to make a competent decision on this issue, even though
he be intellectually competent to do so. In the routine of institutional life, most decisions are made for the patients." It pointed
out that institutionalization "tends to strip the individual of the
supports which permit him to maintain his sense of self-worth
and the value of his own physical and mental integrity."

As subsequent testimony disclosed, John Doe went along
partly because he wanted to show the doctors that he was a
cooperative patient. Even Dr. Yudashkin stated that "involuntarily confined patients tend to tell their doctors what the patient
thinks these people want to hear."

The court stressed that the individual must be "protected
from invasion into his body and personality not voluntarily
agreed to." It further added that "consent is not an idle or sym-
bolic act; it is a fundamental requirement for the protection of
the individual's integrity." And it concluded that "involuntarily
detained mental patients cannot give informed and adequate
consent to experimental psychosurgical procedures on the
brain."[13]

The court raised yet another objection to such "corrective"
brain surgery. The judges believed that performance of such an

operation would violate the provisions of the First Amendment, which, among other things, "protects the dissemination of ideas and the expression of thoughts . . . and equally protects the individual's right to generate ideas." In support the court cited opinions by several Supreme Court Justices, including Justice Cardozo's statement that

> We are free only if we know, and so in proportion to our knowledge. There is no freedom without choice, and there is no choice without knowledge . . . Implicit, therefore, in the very notion of liberty is the liberty of the mind to absorb and beget . . . The mind is in chains when it is without the opportunity to choose. One may argue, if one please, that opportunity to choice is more an evil than a good. One is guilty of a contradiction if one says that the opportunity can be denied, and liberty subsist. At the root of all liberty is the liberty to know . . .
>
> Experimentation there may be in many things of deep concern, but not in setting boundaries to thought, for thought freely communicated is the indispensable condition of intelligent experimentation, the one test of its validity.[14]

But how can a person be in a position to "generate ideas" following psychosurgery, the court asked. Since experimental psychosurgery "is irreversible and intrusive, often leads to the blunting of emotions, the deadening of memory, the reduction of affect, and limits the ability to generate new ideas," it "can impinge upon the right of the individual to be free from interference with his mental processes."[15] The court then went on to assert that regardless of the state's interest in performing psychosurgery, it "must bow to the First Amendment, which protects the generation and free flow of ideas from unwarranted interference with one's mental processes."[16]

The court also invoked the constitutional concept of the right of privacy as guaranteed by the Bill of Rights. It referred to Justice Brandeis's opinion in a case dating back to 1928, when he said:

> The makers of our Constitution undertook to secure conditions favorable to the pursuit of happiness. They recognized the significance of man's spiritual nature, of his feelings and of his intellect.

They knew that only a part of the pain, pleasure and satisfaction of life are to be found in material things. They sought to protect Americans in their beliefs, their thoughts, their emotions and their sensations. They conferred, as against the Government, the right to be let alone — the most comprehensive of rights and the right most valued by civilized men.[17]

The Michigan case helped underscore yet again the constitutional protection of basic rights that are increasingly challenged and eroded by psychological and physical intrusions upon the individual to manage or mold his or her thoughts, feelings, and actions. Some believe this situation is nearing the acute stage because of the proliferation and effectiveness of behavior-modification techniques.

The Kaimowitz-Michigan case was a constitutional triumph. But alas, the John Doe case is the exception. Far more often the courts turn the other way when basic constitutional rights for prisoners or other institutionally confined persons are in question.

For every such court restraint, it is safe to say that hundreds of prison officials are inflicting "cruel and unusual punishment" or committing other unconstitutional acts and getting away with it because they do not fall within the jurisdiction of the few courts that have rendered definitive opinions on these matters. Of course, the one court that could force all the American institutions in which people are incarcerated to obey the Constitution is the Supreme Court. It is astonishing, however, how seldom it has condemned any kind of physical punishment within the framework of the Eighth Amendment.[18] [19] [20]

Though the scope of its judicial authority was limited, the Michigan ruling was a precedent that prisoner advocates could have seized upon to try to stop psychosurgery experiments in other institutions. But now even this possibility seems doomed. A congressionally mandated body — the National Commission for the Protection of Human Subjects of Biomedical and Behavioral Research — has come up with a set of guidelines for the performance of psychosurgery that, in effect, rebuts the Michigan court decision. As the commission itself declares, its conclusions are "at variance" with those of the Michigan court. In light of new data it has gathered, the commission maintains that "psychosurgical procedures are less hazardous than previously thought and potentially of significant therapeutic value,"[21] and, therefore, the constitutional questions raised by the Kaimowitz case no longer apply.

The commission came into being with the signing of the National Research Act on July 2, 1974. It was charged with the task of probing the overall question of experimentation of human beings (men, women, and children) in American prisons, mental institutions, and by federal agencies, and to come up with appropriate recommendations. In addition, it was directed "to investigate and to recommend policies that should govern the use of psychosurgery."[22]

The psychosurgery assignment, according to the commission, was "in response to widespread public concern" based on the fear that a lobotomylike operation was making a comeback and that it might be used as a "behavior control" technique to repress political and social dissidents. A variety of developments reflected this anxiety. Among these: a two-year study beginning in 1972 by the Senate Subcommittee on Constitutional Rights chaired by former Senator Sam Ervin, which expressed dismay at the extent and nature of federal involvement in behavior modification and psychosurgery; a proposal by Senator J. Glenn Beall, Maryland (which he was later persuaded to drop), for Congress to declare a two-year moratorium on psychosurgery so that an objective, scientific evaluation could be made of psychosurgical operations performed during a previous five-year period; and, of course, the Kaimowitz case.

In addition, the scientific community became aroused and this eventually led to an evaluative review of psychosurgery prepared jointly by the National Institute of Neurological Diseases and Stroke (NINDS) and the NIMH. Their report, issued in January 1974, declared that "psychosurgery should be regarded as an experimental therapy at the present time. As such, it should not be considered to be a form of therapy which can be made available to the public because of the peculiar nature of the procedure and of the problems with which it deals."[23]

The ethical and legal aspects of psychosurgery, as well as the scientific validity of the procedure, troubled several professional organizations. In August 1973, a unit of the American Psychological Association debated these issues in a symposium. Four months later, these questions were taken up in a multidisciplinary conference by the Boston University Center for Law and Health Sciences. At about the same time, the American Psychiatric Association appointed a task force to study the issues involved.

Among the first to attack psychosurgery was Harvard-trained psychiatrist Peter Breggin of Washington, D.C. In what amounted to a single-handed crusade against psychosurgery advocates, Dr. Breggin began publishing articles in the medical and lay press. He charged that a rise in the number of psychosurgical operations in the middle sixties was unwarranted. He claimed these operations were undertaken without scientific justification or proper evaluation. He also pointed to possible political implications associated with this type of surgery, particularly in relation to the theory of Mark, Sweet, and Ervin concerning so-called brain dysfunction and urban riots. In March 1972, Dr. Breggin's exhaustive critique on psychosurgery was entered in the *Congressional Record*,[24] stirring concern among a number of congressmen that psychosurgery may indeed be an instrument for potential brain-control schemes.

Another early critic of psychosurgery was Dr. Stephan Chorover, a neurophysiologist at the Massachusetts Institute of Technology. He, too, was alarmed at the high risks of psychosurgery, particularly because it leads to irreversible conditions, and because the existing data on the effects of surgical intrusion on the brain are inconclusive and often contradictory.[25]

By the time the National Commission for the Protection of Human Subjects of Biomedical and Behavioral Research was set up, much had been written and argued about psychosurgery but "relatively little was known about the nature and extent of its use, the kinds of patients receiving operations, or the safety and efficacy of the various procedures."[26]

The commission consists of eleven members: three physicians, two behavioral psychologists, two bioethicists, three lawyers (two are professors and one is a practicing attorney), and one representative of a national women's group. They were appointed by Caspar Weinberger, secretary of HEW during the Nixon administration.

For nearly two years, mostly weekends, the eleven commissioners deliberated the issues in keeping with the congressional mandate requiring that:

> The Commission shall conduct an investigation and study of the use of psychosurgery in the United States during the five-year period ending December 31, 1972. The Commission shall determine the appropriateness of its use, evaluate the need for it, and recommend to the Secretary policies defining the circumstances (if any) under which its use may be appropriate.[27]

Psychosurgery was defined as brain surgery on

> (1) normal brain tissue of an individual who does not suffer from any physical disease, for the purpose of changing or controlling the behavior or emotions of such individual, or (2) diseased brain tissue of an individual, if the sole object of the performance of such surgery is to control, change, or affect any behavioral or emotional disturbance of such individual. Such term does not include brain surgery designed to cure or ameliorate the effects of epilepsy and [sic] electric shock treatments.[28]

The commission expanded the definition by replacing the word "sole" with "primary" to read:

> Psychosurgery means brain surgery on (1) normal brain tissue . . . or (2) diseased brain tissue of an individual, if the primary object is to control behavioral or emotional disturbance.

It further explained that psychosurgery included "implantation of electrodes, destruction or direct stimulation of brain tissue by any means (e.g., ultrasound, laser beams) and the direct application of substances to the brain, when the primary purpose of such intervention is to alter mood or behavior."[29] Brain surgery to relieve anguish from persistent pain would fall within this definition, but an operation to remove physical causes of pain or to control movement disorders (such as in Parkinsonism) would not be covered by the definition.

The commission's recommendations, published in the *Federal Register*, May 23, 1977,[30] unless modified by Joseph A. Califano, Jr., the current secretary of HEW, will constitute the criteria for the use of psychosurgery in all federal agencies under HEW authority and in hospitals getting government subsidies. These recommendations were also offered to Congress for application to agencies over which its jurisdiction resides.

The proposed regulations, however, will not inhibit surgeons who operate in private institutions and hospitals that are not dependent on financial assistance from the government. Even if such procedures are done without the commission's recommended safeguards for the protection of the patient, there would be nothing in the law to restrain the private surgeon from going ahead with the operation, once his or her patient agrees to submit to it. There will be no peer review to assess his diagnostic workup, the surgical procedure that he would employ, or the consequences of such surgery.

"Neither the tone nor the content of the Commission's report on psychosurgery in August 1976, was anticipated," Professor George J. Annas commented in the April 1977 issue of the *Hastings Center Report*,[31] published by the Institute of Society, Ethics and the Life Sciences. Most observers expected the commission to recommend banning the procedure or at least to declare a moratorium on its use until considerably more animal experimentation had taken place.

Instead, the commission came out with a kind of ringing endorsement when it recommended that the secretary of HEW be "encouraged to conduct and support studies to evaluate the safety of specific psychosurgical procedures and the efficacy of such procedures in relieving specific psychiatric symptoms and disorders . . ." On the basis of two studies especially prepared for it, the commission declared that "there is at least tentative evidence that some forms of psychosurgery can be of significant therapeutic value in the treatment of certain disorders or in relief of certain symptoms." Thus, the commission proposed that the operation should be extended to prisoners, to institutionalized mental patients, and even to emotionally ill children. Though in the context of its guidelines the surgery would be done with research protocols in mind, it was not to be viewed as "experimental," even though by its own admission "the safety and efficacy of specific psychosurgical procedures . . . have not been demonstrated to the degree that would permit such procedures to be considered 'accepted practice.' "[32]

The commission, it would appear, seemed hopeful of moving psychosurgery into therapeutic respectability by not labeling it "experimental," thereby absolving surgeons of charges that they are tampering with patients' brains on a trial-and-error basis. But there is more to it than respectability; the procedure, in the view of the commissioners, takes on the character of a curative blessing that should not be withheld from anyone: "It seems unfair to exclude prisoners or involuntarily confined patients from the opportunity to seek benefits from new therapies,"[33] the commission contended.

Considering the near purgatorial conditions in which so many prisoners and the institutionalized mentally ill find themselves, and the dread with which many of them regard psychosurgery, it seems odd that this procedure should be put so high in the order of priorities designed to make the lives of these people more endurable. The commission assures HEW and Congress that the legal constraints it has formulated with regard to psychosurgery (discussed later in this chapter) are so foolproof that its use as a punishing measure would be almost impossible.

The optimism with which the commission announced its recommendations in the summer of 1976, as noted by Professor Annas, stirred surprise and misgivings in certain sectors of public opinion. (He cited articles in *Science*[34] and the *Nation*.)[35] Somewhat taken aback at this reaction, the commission began reconsidering some facets of its position for another six months. Basically, however, the thrust of its recommendations remained the same. Thus, when in March 1977 it voted its final draft, Commissioner Patricia King, associate professor of law, Georgetown University, submitted a dissenting statement in which she said, "I accept . . . the criticism of some that the Commission's report might be viewed as a more enthusiastic endorsement of psychosurgery than we intended."[36]

Indeed, the commission's "endorsement" contrasted sharply with the testimony from scientists and others at the hearings conducted before it acted on its final recommendations. Neuroscientists, psychologists, psychiatrists, prisoner advocates, civil libertarians, and others warned that at best the procedure is experimental and a long way from being a standard treatment for anything. Again and again they pointed to inconclusive experiments with animals. At times intervention into the limbic system would tame the animal, some of the witnesses told the hearing; at other times the very same technique would bring out even greater viciousness. But even when successful, when animal experimentation proved promising, application of such a procedure on the brain of a human might be premature. How can one extrapolate from the behavior of a monkey's brain to that of the higher functions of the human brain? It would scarcely seem possible to compare the impact of psychosurgery on animal intelligence and recall to the consequences of this operation on human sensitivity and cultural and intellectual heritage. Can one correlate the social behavior of rhesus monkeys, or of a cat or a dog, with the subtleties of human interpersonal relations?

It is the lack of answers to these and other questions that prompted many of the scientists to plead for caution.

At an open hearing held by the commission in June 1976, Richard F. Thompson, Ph.D., and John P. Flynn, M.D., testifying for the Division of Comparative and Physiological Psychiatry of the American Psychological Association, contended that as yet the human clinical literature does not provide "compelling evidence" for the use of psychosurgery as an accepted medical procedure. Nor, for that matter, do animal research data provide convincing support of psychosurgery, they said. The two scientists urged that psychosurgery be labeled an experimental procedure and that it be regulated by a variety of safeguards before it is applied to any patients.[37] In a similar vein, Dr. Kenneth Heilman, representing the International Neurological Society, also urged that psychosurgery should be put into the experimental category. He pleaded that psychosurgery not be performed on prisoners, saying that criminality should not be considered a sickness.[38]

Representative Louis Stokes (D–Ohio) called for the prohibition of psychosurgery in federally supported health facilities. He questioned the therapeutic value of this procedure since indications for it do not depend on the presence of identifiable brain pathology. He charged that psychosurgery has the potential of becoming a means for the social and political repression of minority groups, political dissenters, and the poor.[39] Representative Stokes does not believe that the practice of psychosurgery is amenable to effective regulation either by the doctors themselves or by the public, and he has drafted a bill to bar psychosurgery in all federally funded institutions.

But even those who saw promise in psychosurgery for certain emotional ailments that resist drug or psychoanalytic therapies advocated that it be done only as a "treatment of last resort." Dr. John Donnolly, of the American Psychiatric Association, was among several who advocated this view. He felt, however, that this operation should not be done "on minors and prisoners, if in the case of the latter, the purpose is to alter their criminal behavior."[40] The National Association for Mental Health also urged that psychosurgery be used experimentally and only as a last resort.[41]

Dr. Ernest A. Bates, a black neurosurgeon on the faculty of the University of California Medical School in San Francisco, conceded that "in certain cases psychosurgery can relieve suffering, or make a bad situation better — for both the patient and his social milieu." He thought it might be useful in alleviating certain mental disorders. But he strongly criticized those physicians who have adopted the rationale that psychosurgery may be the answer to individuals prone to violence and aggression, adding that surgery for aggression and violence is experimental.

"Much of this experimental surgery is close to worthless from a broad scientific point of view, as well as being of dubious therapeutic value in some cases," Dr. Bates declared. "We are a long way from the time when psychosurgery may be considered a 'cure' for violent behavior in human beings." He made a special point of urging that "psychosurgery should not be performed on any prisoner" nor on children. Dr. Bates admonished his colleagues "not to become the tool of social and political institutions that are the root of our violent society . . ." The neurosurgeon, he added, "must not become the dupe of those who are looking for a quick and easy solution, or seeking medical answers to social and political problems."[42]

It is ironic that discussion of psychosurgery as the answer to violence via the destruction of sections of the amygdala area of the brain, as proposed by Dr. Mark, Dr. Ervin, and others, is completely omitted in the commission report. After all, this is what spurred consideration of the psychosurgery question by the commission in the first place, especially because of charges that the procedure could be used punitively to subdue nonconformist elements of society.

Only a few years back, Dr. Bertram S. Brown, director of the National Institute of Mental Health, when testifying before a Senate hearing on the possibilities of psychosurgery being used as an instrument of mass behavioral control, declared, "Yes . . . I can picture scenarios under certain kinds of authoritarian situations where it could be used for such purposes. I think it would be dreadful — and un-American."[43]

In its initial draft of the report in the summer of 1976 the commission made only one reference to this matter. It stated:

Whether destruction of a portion of the amygdala would . . . reduce aggressivity may not be clear, but the possibility of benefits to be derived from other psychosurgical procedures with respect to a variety of psychiatric symptoms have been demonstrated to the satisfaction of the Commission.[44]

It would seem that the door was left open to the notion that the amygdala may be strongly implicated in the soaring crime wave in the United States. Now, in its final draft, there is no mention of this question at all. Some observers have suggested that the commission preferred to soft-pedal the issue for the present and first have the public become receptive to psychosurgery as a new psychiatric therapy.

What has led the commission to adopt a euphoric, upbeat attitude toward psychosurgery and at the same time to rebut the Michigan court opinion, were two studies contracted for by the commission. One study team, headed by Dr. Allan F. Mirsky and Dr. Maressa H. Orzack, neuropsychologists at Boston University, involved twenty-seven patients who had undergone surgery and were referred to Mirsky by three surgeons who had performed the operations.[45] This retrospective approach made it impossible to provide a convincing comparison of the patient's postsurgical and presurgical conditions. As the commission itself pointed out:

> The examination of patients was proposed notwithstanding the acknowledged limitations of a retrospective study: that there would be no preoperative evaluation of the patients, performed by the same team, against which to measure gains or losses of function clearly attributable to the surgical intervention. Such preoperative data as would exist might be uneven both in quantity and in quality, since the data would be obtainable only through medical records provided by psychiatrists and surgeons directly responsible for the patients' care.[46]

Evaluation of psychosurgery effectiveness in treating patients' disorders (mostly diagnosed as symptoms of depression or of obsessive-compulsive conditions) was done through psychological and neurological testing and interviews. Dr. Mirsky reported that fourteen of the twenty-seven patients were considered to have had "very favorable outcomes" and the remainder had results that ranged from "only moderate improvement" to "worsening of their conditions."[47]

Since the Mirsky researchers depended on the files of the doctors who performed the operations to contact the patients for the interviews, there is a nagging suspicion among some observers that these patients represent a biased sampling. As one neurosurgeon put it when commenting on psychosurgical results in general, "Human nature is such that most surgeons probably do not want to acknowledge post-surgical deficit in their patients, even though such findings would advance our knowledge of brain function."

In the other study, the team of researchers was headed by Professor Hans-Lukas Teuber, Ph.D., of the Massachusetts Institute of Technology, and included Suzanne Corkin, Ph.D., and Thomas Twitchell, M.D.[48] They examined a total of thirty-four patients who had undergone cingulotomies (one of the variants of the psychosurgery procedure), eleven for relief of pain and depression and twenty-three for treatment of "other psychiatric disorders." All the operations were done by the same surgeon, and in some cases the patients went through the procedure more than once. Professor Teuber's examinations took place relatively soon after the surgeries were done (from four to eighteen months), so that long-term results are yet to be ascertained.

Dr. Teuber was impressed with his finding that the patients he examined showed no serious neurological consequences. Teuber, and for that matter Mirsky, did report, however, that some patients (one in Mirsky's group and two in Teuber's) developed seizures following surgery, although they had no history of convulsive disorders.

Teuber's interviews with the thirty-four patients revealed very mixed reactions. More than half continued to complain of various pains, memory losses, and other conditions which were far from resolved. For instance, several of the patients indicated they were still suicidal, still angry, still suffering from depression. One woman who complained of having "irresistible thoughts about various ways of hurting people, by stabbing them, putting poison into their food, etc.," claimed not to have had even temporary alleviation of her troubles. Another woman reported improvement only because of the fact that whereas before surgery she would hear voices which she could not control, since her surgery she could tell the voices to "shut up." Yet another patient, who underwent two cingulotomies following a suicide attempt, said that he was not sure the third operation was any more successful in lifting his depression. He still thinks of suicide and he had taken an overdose of drugs only recently. Professor Teuber describes this man as grimacing, with tremors, giving the impression "of being at the end of his rope," and yet praising the operation nonetheless.[49]

Professor Teuber himself has raised a fundamental question about the integrity of this procedure. Was it the surgery that led to improvement of some patients or was it the placebo effect of a reassuring surgeon? It happens that the patients in Teuber's study were under the care of a solicitous and deeply religious physician whose empathetic involvement may have produced the therapeutic effect rather than the surgery.

"As our analyses of personal interviews with the patients and with members of their family indicate," Teuber reported, "the vast majority of this particular surgeon's patients speak of him with expressions of deep gratitude, and often reverence." Teuber reflected on the possibility that "the same surgical procedure, in other hands, or in other clinical settings, may have somewhat different outcomes." With an uninterested surgeon, he felt, the results could be less impressive. Thus, he added, the extent to which the benefit is directly attributable to the surgery itself remains conjectural.[50]

Commenting on the Mirsky-Teuber studies, one of the commissioners, Dr. Donald Wayne Seldin, professor and chairman, Department of Internal Medicine, University of Texas, said that while psychosurgery appears to alleviate certain types of pain and anxiety, "there is absolutely no proof . . . that this is a direct result of the surgical procedure rather than other things than the surgery. No one, to my knowledge, has done a control study in which issues such as suggestion, loyalty to the physician, and complex other factors are involved . . . Now that doesn't mean that surgery may not be responsible for it, but by the same token, it may be that surgery isn't responsible for it, that certain other things connected with the surgery are. And Teuber himself admitted this . . . the evidence is not compelling, to say the least."[51]

To some extent Dr. Seldin's view was buttressed by still another study contracted by the commission. This was a survey of medical literature dealing with psychosurgery since 1971.[52] Conducted by Elliot Valenstein, professor of psychology at the University of Michigan, the survey revealed that 56 percent of the published articles in the United States indicated that no objective tests were used by surgeons in evaluating the usefulness of this procedure.

Most surgeons performing psychosurgery, Dr. Valenstein said, did not report their results: at best only about 27 percent of this group published articles on the outcome of these operations. All told, the Michigan University investigator observed, "the great majority of the psychosurgical literature has no scientific value and little validity. The possibility that a significant part of the improvement seen after surgery can be attributed to biased selection of patients and 'placebo' effects cannot be ruled out." However, he added, the claim that some patients receive "significant improvement from psychosurgery" cannot be ignored altogether.

Dr. Valenstein noted considerable disagreement among surgeons as to which patients are most likely to benefit from this procedure. While some felt that psychosurgery was ineffective for schizophrenic patients, others insisted that the results were good. He pointed out that there was also disagreement in the literature as to whether criminals, psychopaths, sexual offenders, and aggressive individuals lacking clear evidence of brain damage improved with psychosurgery.[53]

Even granting that the Mirsky-Teuber findings show that psychosurgery's therapeutic possibilities are to be taken seriously, the question remains: Why the hard stand of the commission in backing this procedure and removing it from the experimental category? The documentation in the Mirsky-Teuber studies would scarcely overwhelm many in the medical community who are accustomed to weighing a new procedure on the basis of results involving dozens of patients with a good deal more convincing "before and after" objective data than that presented by the two studies.

The commission's effort to drum up enthusiasm for large-scale psychosurgical research is dismaying enough for those who see insufficient scientific justification for such a move at this time. But the commission's decision to proceed with psychosurgery on prisoners is a rejection of the views of minority leaders whose opinions it sought at the National Minority Conference, which it cosponsored with the National Urban Coalition early in 1976.[54] The conference was held in recognition of the fact that the prison population is overweighted with blacks, Chicanos, and Puerto Ricans. Some 250 individuals took part in about a dozen different workshops on issues directly connected with the agenda of the National Commission.

Basically, what emerged from the conference was the consensus that all experimentation, whether drug testing before the product is released to the consumer, or innovative procedures to alter the mind, is largely carried out on members of minority groups. Dr. L. Alex Swan, chairman of the sociology department at Fisk University, said:

> There is no question in my mind that most scientific research in America is politically determined, controlled and manipulated in order to repress healthy dissent and legitimate disagreement in a society which has used violence to solve its problems and only condemns it when others resort to it.[55]

The conference as a whole urged that psychosurgery not be performed on prisoners and others "involuntarily confined in institutions, sexual deviants, political deviants, or social deviants."[56]

Now it is true that the data gathered by Dr. Valenstein and others indicate that in the past several years the overwhelming majority of those undergoing psychosurgery were private, white patients. The objective was therapeutic, to find relief from emotional difficulties that proved refractory to drugs, psychoanalysis, electroshock therapy, or other treatments. But this information did not allay the fears of minority spokesmen, who are aware that the surgery can be used to punish and subdue those voicing very legitimate grievances against the steadily deteriorating conditions of the prison system. The use of psychosurgery on recalcitrant prisoners in California and Michigan penitentiaries a few years back is still fresh and searing in the minds of those who recall it was done under the guise of therapy to rid these men of uncontrollable, impulsive aggressivity.

In formulating its stand on psychosurgery, the National Minority Conference viewed the issue as yet another instance in which blacks or Hispanics would be used as research material. The "social context of institutionalized racism in this country," it declared, "insures the use of the least powerful as the major source of subjects in human experimentation." It went on to say that

> Procedures such as psychosurgery have been and can be misused by those in power against the powerless in society. With this constant fear in mind, we have approached the issue of psychosurgery . . . in a very cautious manner, fearing that the door to further abuse from the people in power may be opening wider.[57]

The conference report stated that:

> The moral issue in psychosurgery is compelling. We believe that anything as irreparable, as final, as psychosurgery must be restrained in its use . . . It appears that the major effect of psychosurgery is to subdue the subject. Side effects of the "quieting" can include lowered attention span and vegetable-like behavior.[58]

Despite its strong opposition to the use of psychosurgery on prisoners and those involuntarily confined in institutions, the conference would not ban psychosurgical experimentation completely, provided it is done after all other alternatives have been exhausted. The conference called, however, for minority representation on the review boards concerned with the selection of candidates for the operation and the supervision of the experiments.

Among other things, the conference recommended that the National Commission continue on a permanent basis but with the inclusion of a substantial number of minority representatives. It added that conference participants were apprehensive — on the basis of "conference discussions" and "off the record" comments — that the commission as presently constituted is "another 'white paper' committee."[59] (Curiously enough, this Minority Conference observation was not mentioned in the commission report.)

The conference seems to have had little influence on what finally came out as the commission's recommendations to HEW and the Congress. When I asked Dr. Kenneth John Ryan, the chairman of the commission, whether these recommendations did in fact amount to a rejection of the National Minority Conference views, he looked somewhat annoyed and said, "You can't satisfy everybody."

The paucity of hard, fully dependable scientific data concerning psychosurgical methodology and efficacy troubled some of the commissioners even months after the commission had announced its decision to back the use of these operations on children and prisoners. One of the commissioners, Patricia King, told me that she was unhappy about the recommendations and would try to reopen the question. She had been absent from the session at which the final vote was taken. A few months later, when the full commission reconvened to make final decisions on wording of the recommendations, Professor King raised the question whether present-day knowledge — including the Mirsky-Teuber studies — warranted psychosurgery on minors. Commissioner King stated:

> I think I should let everybody know that, after much soul searching, I do not feel that I can support psychosurgical procedures on children,

at this time. I think the Commission recognizes that in its comments, but in thinking about it, I don't think this Commission is going to have the last word on psychosurgery. There will be others that will succeed us, and my own feeling is that, at this time, I don't think that there is anything to warrant the suggestion that we should do it.

I know that this is a position that is in disagreement with most members of the Commission. I thought, that if we were to suggest that it could be permitted, that we should have adequate safeguards, and I am satisfied that we have adequate safeguards, now, if we should go on. I just am reviewing everything that we have before us, and I don't see any reason at this point for even suggesting that we might want to permit it.[60]

Another commissioner, Mr. Robert H. Turtle (practicing attorney, Washington, D.C.) had similar reservations:

I have much the same problem that Pat does, especially with regard to the children. I think I basically view the psychosurgical situation at the present time to be a very large research program. . . I just feel, instinctively, that I would not like to see that program carried out on children, or prisoners, at the present time . . .

Now it can be argued from the other side that I am, therefore, in favor of depriving children and prisoners of their right to obtain a form of treatment. I admit to that, quite frankly . . . I would be willing to withhold that right, or privilege, until such time as a particular procedure became generally accepted therapy . . .

I have in mind a particular situation which occurred in a D.C. jail, when I was in court one day . . . Two prisoners took over the entire cellblock, in the basement, and created quite a state of siege, and basically they did it because they were being transferred from one institution to another, to Springfield, Missouri, where they thought that — and I am not supporting their allegations — they were going to be subjected to psychosurgical procedures. I think that we could give prisoners, in this country, people who are involved in prison reform in this country, a considerable easing of their state of mind, if we were to, at the present time, quite clearly state that psychosurgery should not be carried out on prisoners.

Mr. Turtle added:

In the absence of any evidence in regard to safety and efficacy on children, I am prepared to say that I would say "no" [to psychosurgery] at the present time. I think that the evidence that we have received on adults is so close, in terms of the chances you take versus the benefits that you might receive. Unless the evidence on children were significantly better . . . I would say that it would be inappropriate for children.[61]

Commissioner Albert R. Jonsen, associate professor of bioethics, University of California, San Francisco, also joined those with second thoughts about psychosurgery for children. He said that the commission should explain that even though it has taken a position favoring psychosurgery because of the Mirsky-Teuber investigation, "those studies gave us no information about children; and therefore, at the present time, we have no evidence to be permissive, relative to children."[62]

Dr. Ryan, chairman of the commission, conceded that there was little to justify doing psychosurgery on children. He said: "We're not aware of any medical basis, in the literature, or any justification for doing the procedure at the present time."[63]

But even in this instance, when commission members openly admitted that the scientific grounds for psychosurgery on children are nonexistent, the commission would not recommend banning it, or even declare it experimental. Rather, it recommended that there should be no obstacles to using psychosurgery on children once a National Psychosurgery Advisory Board* concluded that such a procedure "will benefit" them.

Strangely enough, the board's determination would hinge on the very type of data that the commission felt would not justify psychosurgery on children at the present time, namely "evidence from animal and adult human studies." The commission feels confident that the legal safeguards built into its guidelines will go a very long way in protecting children, prisoners, and mental patients from abuse or from being forced to undergo psychosurgery against their will. To begin with, every hospital offering psychosurgical service would have an Institutional Review Board (IRB) that would examine the technical aspects of

---

* As described by a commission staff member, this board is envisioned as a sort of top level "think tank" of leading experts in the field who would assess all available data and determine appropriate psychosocial procedures for children as well as for adults who have specific psychiatric disorders.

the proposed procedure and also decide on the competence of the surgeon performing it. The IRB, consisting of a psychiatrist, a neurologist, a neurosurgeon, and a psychologist, would review the diagnosis and decide on whether or not there is absolute need for the patient to undergo this type of surgery.

It is on the matter of informed consent, that is, whether the child, prisoner, or involuntarily confined mental patient agrees to submit to psychosurgery, that the waters become muddy. At first glance, the commission's recommendations appear to guarantee that individuals, in each of these categories, would have the final word. It is only when one gets down to the fine print, as it were, that things begin to look different.

In the case of children, the commission "intends that the IRB take into consideration the reported feelings that a child may have expressed with respect to psychosurgery." Moreover, that "such feelings of a 'mature minor', that is, child with a certain capacity for rational judgment should be controlling."[64]

In view of the fact that in certain instances a child, as young as six years of age, may be a candidate for psychosurgery, it is rather unlikely that he would be in a position to influence the doctors towering over him on whether they should or should not burn out a part of his limbic system. Even in the case of a "mature minor" the commission does not define what "mature" means, or what "rational judgment" signifies, particularly when the patient is recommended for brain surgery precisely because he may not be rational or because he is suffering from a disabling psychiatric condition.

As though admitting to the weaknesses of this proposal, the commission adds that it recognizes "the limited capacity of children to consent to psychosurgery" and therefore directs that there be a court review of the individual case. It does not specify whether there would be a jury trial.

With respect to prisoners or patients in mental hospitals whose conditions have so deteriorated that their decision making becomes impossible, the commission would nonetheless allow the operation providing "the patient's guardian . . . has given informed consent and the *patient does not object*, and a court in which the patient has legal representation has approved the performance of the operation."[65]

When questioned about this provision, a commission staff member tried to explain that even though the commission's phrasing "was somewhat fluid," it was still possible that some of the patients tagged for psychosurgery would be in a position to indicate "that they would not object" to undergo the procedure.

Interestingly enough, the commission failed to extend even this "protective" shield — the court hearing — to persons who have voluntarily committed themselves to mental institutions. Commissioner King, in her dissenting statement, pointed out that this could jeopardize their consent privilege since they would have no judicial recourse to air their complaints should pressure from institutional authorities develop. Commissioner King criticized the commission for assuming that voluntarily committed persons were necessarily institutionalized through "voluntary" admission processes, particularly since these procedures might differ from state to state. She explained that "it is conceivable, for example, that as part of the 'plea bargaining' process in our criminal justice system that some persons 'agree' to voluntarily commit themselves to mental institutions in exchange for reduced or dropped charges."[66]

Recognizing the possibility that some of these voluntarily committed would be incapable of giving valid consent, the commission decided to have the IRB make the final judgment. This, Commissioner King declared, "is outrageous in my opinion." She did not feel that the IRB should be saddled with the responsibility of such a decision "with respect to those residing in institutions." The impact of institutionalization alone, she maintained, "as discussed in 'Kaimowitz' is significant enough to warrant treating those inside institutions different from those outside." She went on to say:

> Were I a member of an IRB operating under the Commission's recommendations, I would always vote for court review of the IRB determination at least until such time as we know more about the safety

and efficacy of specific psychosurgical procedures, and the law re
garding informed consent is more settled.[67]

With this dissenting note from Commissioner King, the commission's deliberations on psychosurgery have come to a close.
Next on the agenda are the decisions from the secretary of HEW
and from Congress on how many of the commission's recommendations they should accept or modify.

8. Surveillance Machines and Brain Control

THE MAN SITTING next to you at a lunch counter may to all intents and purposes share the anonymity of the others in the coffee shop. He is munching on a sandwich as he scans a newspaper, and he reveals nothing that would set him apart from those around him. But this man is different. He is a recently released prisoner and is now on parole. And he is under constant surveillance — 24 hours a day — even though there is no policeman outside eying him through the window and no informant huddling in a doorway ready to shadow him the moment he leaves the restaurant. His every move within a radius of twenty miles is known to the authorities. And a lot more than that is known to them: for instance, his respiration rate, his adrenal output, his heart rate. Thanks to the latest developments relating to psychosurgery, even his brain wave activity can be monitored by remote control.

This combined intelligence, when relayed to a central computer, will enable it to weigh the possibilities of whether the parolee at any given moment is up to no good. Should he be strolling about in an attractive shopping area and the programmed computer begins getting signals that the wares on display might be tempting, his whereabouts are automatically flashed to the computer. If at the same time his heart begins to beat faster and his adrenal output increases as his brain waves (electroencephalograms) register a spiking pattern (considered by some to be indicative of excitement leading to violence), the computer may decide that his general behavior profile points to possible mischief. The computer will then alert the police closest to where the parolee is and/or send out a signal to inhibit or distract him.

All this is not yet a fact. But the technology is here and the possibility of implementing such surveillance is at hand. As far back as nine years ago, a dress rehearsal of sorts, on a very limited basis, was tried in Boston with sixteen volunteers, several of them borderline juvenile delinquents.[1] Each was equipped with two boxes, roughly the size and shape of a paperback book, which were strapped to their chests underneath their shirts. One box contained a set of batteries and the other a transmitter that sent out signals coded to each individual wearer.

Repeater stations on rooftops or in places where these volunteers were employed picked up the signals, which were conveyed to a central console at a frequency range from 90 seconds to half an hour or more. Each signal, visualized on a televisionlike screen, indicated the exact location of one of the volunteers. Most of the group soon found it hard on the nerves and dropped out. Of the two who carried on, one was an ex-convict who stayed with the program for 40 days. The other, a mental patient, hung on for 167 days.

The concept of tracking parolees via telemetry basically originates with Dr. Ralph K. Schwitzgebel, who designed the Boston experiment and who has devoted much of his adult life to the study of behavior technology aimed at regulating the criminal offender. He has taught at Harvard Law School, but he also holds a degree in psychology and is currently teaching that subject at California Lutheran College. He is also a part-time inventor and has written a number of monographs on crime deterrence for the Center for Studies of Crime and Delinquency, a unit of the National Institute of Mental Health.

Dr. Schwitzgebel sees his surveillance proposal as humane and just. After all, he explained to me in a phone interview, the idea is to release the prisoner from incarceration and wean him back to society by a scheme that would, at the same time, protect society against his committing another crime. "My project," he said, "is not an attempt to turn the world into a prison."[2]

Electronic rehabilitation systems "may reduce the need for imprisonment and at the same time protect the public from future offenses more surely than present procedures," Dr. Schwitzgebel declared in an article in the *Law and Society Review*.[3] "Technology may make it possible to regain some measure of freedom to walk the streets and enjoy the parks in safety, and to greet the stranger as a friend rather than as one to be feared." For the average citizen this idea is extremely appealing at first glance. It sounds humane and seems to point to a solution of the crime epidemic. For the parolee, as unattractive as the prospect is — being under constant vigil, with the police monitoring his every breath and thought — Dr. Schwitzgebel contends that it is still a more desirable alternative than confinement in what are admittedly some of the worst prisons in the world.

Dr. Schwitzgebel concedes that the danger that telemetric surveillance could be abused is always present. For instance, he says, this approach could be extended to "involuntary surveillance of groups not generally incarcerated." He acknowledges that "some administrators may wish, for example, to control certain behaviors of high-risk probationers, suspects in gang war activity, Communist Party members, or government employees." Individuals belonging to these groups might be "committed on minor violations for the purpose of later releasing them under surveillance."[4]

It is therefore entirely conceivable that political dissidents, such as the 12,000 protesters against the Vietnam war who were arrested during a Washington demonstration in May 1971, could be outfitted with monitoring devices and then locked into a surveillance system for as long as the authorities wish. These devices would no longer be as cumbersome as those used in Dr. Schwitzgebel's early experiments in Boston. As he explains it, his patents cover the development of a "low-power transmitter" that is worn on the wrist. It is lightweight and nonremovable. "You can't remove the wrist transmitter without having the alarm go off, because you break the circuit to remove it."[5]

Dr. Schwitzgebel expects many rapid changes in our social mores because of the extraordinary character of the new technologies about us, and he thinks that the faster society wakes up to this phenomenon the better off it will be. "A new field of study may be emerging, variously known as behavioral engineering or behavioral instrumentation, that focuses upon the use of electro-mechanical devices for the modification of behavior."[6]

Another surveillance enthusiast is J. A. Meyer, a defense department computer expert who has come up with a similar scenario that he calls the "Crime Deterrent Transponder System." These radio signaling units "would be attached to criminal recidivists, parolees and bailees to identify them and detect their whereabouts."[7] Meyer goes on to describe in detail how the system could be set up, the costs, and the way it would operate.

Meyer visualizes his system as being used on a large scale. He talks of long-term surveillance. Meyer suggests that to make the plan work effectively, and at the same time make sense on a cost-accounting basis, it should be used to monitor hundreds of thousands of people all over the country, even though inevitably hundreds of thousands more, people who are not targets of police interest, would also come under scrutiny. Some of the costs would be defrayed by the parolees (whom Meyer euphemistically refers to as "subscribers"), who would be obligated to purchase these devices and contribute to their maintenance by a weekly charge of $5.

Meyer pictures a typical network:

> In New York City, the Harlem region between 110th Street and 155th Street, bounded by 8th Avenue on the west and the East and Harlem Rivers on the east, is a high crime area. It contains about one-quarter million people, concentrated in approximately 400 city blocks. Transceivers at one-block intervals would be strung along 110th Street, 114th, 118th, etc., from 8th Avenue to the river.
>
> A system of about 250 transceivers in this topology is capable of monitoring the whole region on a street-by-street basis.[8]

Although freed of the relentless torpor and squalid existence of the prison, the parolee, as profiled by Meyer, would be ceaselessly under rigid control:

> Most of the subscribers [parolees] will do ordinary things like get up in the morning and go to work. At night they will stay close to home, to avoid being implicated in crimes. At their place of work, a human surveillance system will operate. Low-power transceivers in their domiciles can monitor them indoors. Alarm transceivers in banks, stores, and other buildings would warn security personnel of their approach.[9]

In comparison to the steadily soaring costs for prison maintenance, Meyer sees great savings in the surveillance system. He calculates that on a mass-production basis each transponder would cost some ten to twenty dollars. The cost of each control unit, mounted on apartment and office buildings, would be several hundred dollars. In a city like New York the cost for a system of 20,000 transceivers and several computers would be in the range of $25 million annually. The current police budget is nearly one billion dollars a year.

Meyer says he is aware of the many pitfalls in such a scheme and the miscarriages of justice that might occur. But why not give it a try, he asks. He concedes that criminal acts are frequently "a response to the facts of the social and economic system" and he agrees that most of those arrested and convicted are the poverty-stricken, usually from the minority groups. Moreover, because the population in the big cities is increasing faster than the number of available jobs, poverty will steadily intensify and provide the breeding ground for more crime. As Meyer puts it, "the poor and uneducated urban dweller is *fundamentally unnecessary* to the economy of the city, and he is soon made aware of this." Therefore, he adds, as long as the problem of "the unwanted people" continues, so will crime continue. Since the present system has nothing to offer by which to counteract this phenomenon, he feels that the transponder or electronic surveillance proposal may be the answer.[10]

Neither Schwitzgebel nor Meyer talk in terms of doing anything about the conditions that give rise to crime, the original sin, as it were. Both seem to accept the causes as though they were put there by God or by nature. Thus each turns to methods of controlling crime rather than dealing with the cause of crime.

Operating on this premise, Schwitzgebel, in a brochure prepared for the National Institute of Mental Health, sees the need to keep a section of the population strait-jacketed because no basic solution is in sight. He declared, "Ultimately, most offenders will have to live in an environment similar to the one that produced, or at least did not successfully inhibit, their illegal behaviors."[11] Meyer defines the criminal as one who "by middle-class standards, lacks strong inner controls, and seldom experiences guilt."[12] Since the usual forms of punishment via prison have, if anything, warped the inmate's life, Meyer believes that his methods would be a lot more effective:

> A transponder surveillance system can surround the criminal with a kind of externalized conscience — an electronic substitute for the social conditioning, group pressures, and inner motivation which most of the society lives with.[13]

Meyer rejects criticism of the electronic surveillance system as a step closer to the creation of a police state. Detractors, he says, could probably say the same thing about prisons, the judicial system, taxes, and other state institutions.

Meyer's proposal and certainly that of Schwitzgebel have hit a sympathetic chord with a number of criminologists and behaviorists who see telemetric control of crime as part of the wave of the near future. For a half dozen years criminologists and law professors have been debating the Schwitzgebel proposal. Others see additional applications of the techniques. For instance, Dr. D. N. Michael, testifying before a congressional subcommittee investigating the perils of "Computer Invasion of Privacy," envisaged a surveillance system that would control mental patients when released from an institution:

> It is not impossible to imagine that parolees will check in and be monitored by transmitters embedded in their flesh, reporting their whereabouts in code and automatically as they pass receiving stations

(perhaps like fireboxes) systematically deployed over the country as part of one computer-monitored network. We may well reach the point where it will be permissible to allow some emotionally ill people the freedom of the streets, providing they are effectively "defused" through chemical agents. The task, then, for the computer-linked sensors would be to telemeter, not their emotional states, but simply the sufficiency of concentration of the chemical agent to insure an acceptable emotional state . . . I am not prepared to speculate whether such a situation would increase or decrease the personal freedom of the emotionally ill person.[14]

The most far-reaching proposals for surveillance and behavior control may come out of the laboratories of such neurophysiologists as Dr. José M. R. Delgado, for many years professor of physiology at Yale.*

Dr. Delgado, some of whose accomplishments were touched on earlier, is now involved in the development of so-called brain pacemakers that on radio command will stimulate certain sections of the brain to bring about a predetermined pattern of behavior. The implications of this development dwarf anything contemplated by Schwitzgebel and Meyer.

A handsome man in his middle fifties, dressed in a conservative blue suit with a Savile-Row look, Dr. Delgado has the easy manner of a diplomat conferring with fellow delegates at the United Nations. The famous neurophysiologist, who is frequently at the center of controversy because of his somewhat sensational ideas for the manipulation of brain function and his innovative electronic instruments with which to do the manipulation, spoke with quiet conviction as he pointed to a small object in the palm of his right hand. The size of a thick, fifty-cent piece, it was imprinted with purplish red circuitry. He describes the device as a "radio link for wireless communication between the brain and a computer."[15] He named it "stimoceiver" because it can stimulate certain sections of the brain when it receives radio signals of what the targets should be.

* Recently he returned to his native Spain. Shortly before Franco's death, he accepted an offer of the post of director of the Medical Faculty, Autonomous University, Madrid.

He told me that once the stimoceiver is embedded under the scalp, with tiny electrodes extending from it into the limbic system of the brain, it will go into action on radio command. This device, he said, now has four channels, which means that it could reach out to that many sections of the brain. "Sometime soon," he said, "we shall have maybe twenty such channels." Eventually "these appliances could remain implanted in the person's head forever — he could carry this instrument for life, if necessary."[16] The energy to activate this device would be supplied by radio frequency externally and therefore there would be no need for batteries.

The purpose of all this? Dr. Delgado feels this development represents a great breakthrough in the treatment of a variety of conditions, such as pain, emotional illness, and epilepsy. It is based on the principle of having one section of the brain "counter" the activity of another section. "We know that perception, decision making, learning, and other activities may be accompanied by detectable electrical phenomena," he recently wrote. "We also know that electrical stimulation of the brain may induce or modify a variety of autonomic, somatic and mental manifestations."[17] So why not apply this knowledge in controlling brain phenomena at will? By way of example, Delgado cites a situation in which an epileptic attack is about to begin. A spindling pattern of electroencephalograms is fired off by a defective amygdala nucleus of the brain, presumed to be the augury for such an attack. These EEG signals are picked up by the in-dwelling electrodes and fed into the stimoceiver, which in turn signals the programmed computer. The computer then orders the stimoceiver to stimulate the anterior lobe of the cerebellum, which apparently inhibits such an attack. All this takes place within fractions of seconds.

Following this logic, and accepting the technological feasibility of programming behavioral patterns, it becomes entirely possible for the computer to be used to stymie any kind of behavior not consistent with norms set by legislators or law-enforcement authorities. As Dr. Delgado explained in an article in 1975,

"Long term, repeated excitation of the brain permits the application of programs of stimulation to suitable structures, to induce autonomic, somatic and behavioral responses . . . and also to influence inhibitory systems."[18]

Inhibition and dampening of self-assertiveness are the underlying reasons why some prison administrators look to psychosurgery as an answer to the troublesome inmate, especially if destruction of portions of the amygdala is involved. (The psychosurgery studies done for the commission, discussed in Chapter 7, were based for the most part on surgery on the cingulum region of the limbic system.) Once the amygdala is operated upon, this prisoner is not likely ever again to have the wherewithal, the dynamism, to organize discontented fellow inmates. It is fair to infer that the emotional and intellectual deterioration of the individual following the destruction of the amygdala would shatter any further thoughts of defiance among the other prisoners.

Dr. Delgado cited an experiment with a chimpanzee, in which the spontaneous bursts of EEG spindles from the amygdala of the animal were telemetered and identified by a computer that was programmed to trigger radio stimulation of "negative reinforcing" points in the brain each time it detected spindling activity. As the amygdala is generally related to aggressivity, the suppression of its activity would reduce the likelihood of spontaneous, impulsive outbursts of rage. He reports that after two hours of this "feed-back contingent stimulation" the spindling was reduced by 50 percent, and that after six "stimulations" of two hours a day, the chimpanzee "showed diminished attention and motivation."[19]

An equally significant observation was that after two weeks of such "repeated feedback radio stimulation" the specific EEG pattern was finally suppressed and, in effect, the animal was able to learn a new pattern of behavior by means of "direct electrical stimulation of a cerebral area."

Dr. Delgado is optimistic that with

the increasing sophistication and miniaturization of electronics, it may be possible to compress the necessary circuitry for a small computer into a chip that is implantable subcutaneously. In this way, the new self-contained instrument could be devised, capable of receiving, analyzing and sending back information to the brain, establishing artificial links between unrelated cerebral areas, functional feedbacks, and programs of stimulation contingent on the appearance of predetermined wave patterns.[20]

"Detection of brain activity, processing of this information, and the automatic triggering of a stimulator," he points out, "could be of critical therapeutic value" and could be used only when needed. "This is the way I foresee psychiatry within five or ten years," he predicted, "when it would begin depending upon the implantation of little computers to deal with emotional illness."[21]

Even if we take these scientists' word that such uses of telemetry have compassionate motives (as in the case of Dr. Schwitzgebel's parolee surveillance plan), or therapeutic ones (as with Dr. Delgado), the inescapable fact is that electronic techniques aimed at behavioral control are edging steadily toward becoming a daily reality among people who are neither lawbreakers nor criminal suspects.

The former Supreme Court Justice William O. Douglas gave a strong early warning of this possibility:

> We are rapidly entering the age of no privacy, where there are no secrets from government. The aggressive breaches of privacy by the government increase by geometric proportions. Wiretapping and "bugging" run rampant, without effective judicial or legislative control . . . The time may come when no one can be sure whether his words are being recorded for use at some future time; when everyone will fear that his most secret thoughts are no longer his own, but belong to the government; when the most confidential and intimate conversations are always open to eager prying ears. When that time comes, privacy, and with it liberty, will be gone.
>
> If a man's privacy can be invaded at will, who can say he is free? If his every association is known and recorded, if the conversations with his associates are purloined who can say he enjoys freedom of association? When such conditions obtain, our citizens will be afraid to utter any but the safest and most orthodox thoughts; afraid to associate with any but the most acceptable people. Freedom as the Constitution envisages will have vanished.[22]

The concern expressed by Justice Douglas and others reflects the fear that these developments are on a direct collision course with certain rights guaranteed by the Constitution, specifically as they apply to privacy.

The First, Fourth, and Fifth Amendments are supposed to protect against scrutiny of one's thinking or beliefs; it would seem that they preclude the use of surveillance or depth-electrode screening of individuals suspected of criminal tendencies. In practice, however, the courts have allowed the privacy principle to be bypassed in innumerable ways, including such expedients as the use of semantics, describing a snooping operation as an act of "observation" rather than "search,"[23] which the Fourth Amendment specifically prohibits, unless a warrant is issued for reasons supported by sworn statements. The Fifth Amendment, which declares that "no person . . . shall be compelled in any criminal case to be a witness against himself . . . " can also be straddled.

Historically the Fifth Amendment has been applied only in criminal actions and not in civil cases. Since Schwitzgebel sees his surveillance program in the context of prevention rather than criminal pursuit, the Fifth Amendment would be a very soft reed on which to lean when resisting electronic oversight through the courts. Indeed, the Schwitzgebel proposal discusses the possibility that the two-way radio communication system would permit a parole officer or therapist at the central control room to guide or steer the parolee away from temptation whenever his transmitter emits such electrical beeps as would indicate an emotional crisis that might be interpreted as leading to a criminal act.

The steady stream of information pouring out of the transmitter concerning the parolee's emotional and physical state would be tantamount to a forfeiture of the protection guaranteed by the Fifth Amendment against divulging information that might prove self-incriminating. Certainly with respect to Delgado's stimoceiver there would be no question of a violation of the Bill of Rights; for Delgado's claim is that this procedure is strictly therapeutic and in no way to be considered an imposition of brain control per se.

Up to now there has been no comprehensive or unifying legal declaration of what privacy encompasses. The courts have not been clear on this issue, although from time to time constitutional scholars have tried to clarify certain principles common to the concept of privacy. Professor Alan Westin of Columbia University feels that the Fourth Amendment is there to protect personal autonomy, individual choice, and independent thought. Privacy, he feels, should be understood as the "claim of individuals, groups, or institutions to determine for themselves when, how and to what extent information about themselves is communicated to others."[24]

Interestingly enough, Professor Charles Fried of Yale Law School comes to similar conclusions about the constitutional sense of privacy. He has written that privacy can promote intimacy, friendship, and trust by permitting an individual to control whatever it is he wants to communicate about himself to others.[25]

Needless to say, neither the surveillance proposals nor such mass screening programs as the one planned by the UCLA Center for the Study and Reduction of Violence are instances in which the information to be gathered is under the direct and sole control of the individual. Nor are they designed to generate trust between the individual under surveillance and people with whom she or he would like to develop a friendship.

Commenting on the Schwitzgebel and other proposed systems of surveillance, Professor Fried contends that privacy is not "just a defensive right . . . it is not just an absence of information abroad about ourselves." The concept of privacy requires "a sense of control and a justified, acknowledged power to control aspects of one's environment . . . it is a feeling of security in control over information about ourselves." He questions whether rehabilitative results could be expected from electronically monitored surveillance of ex-convicts. If privacy "forms the necessary context for the intimate relations of love and friend-ship," he asks, how can a parolee develop such attitudes when he is forced to be constantly on guard, constantly apprehensive that any natural gesture or extension of himself might be misinter-preted or distorted by that "unseen audience" — the authorities who are keeping vigil over him?

Monitoring, Professor Fried argues, makes it virtually impos-sible to enter into personal relationships of trust. The parolee is also "denied the sense of self-respect inherent in being trusted by the government which has released him."[26]

If an employer is aware of the arrangements under which the parolee is operating, he will probably be reluctant to either hire him or to trust him with any important information. In some ways being on the "outside" may create deeper psychological and emotional problems for the parolee than when he was be-hind bars. In prison he was at least free of the pressure of the make-believe that he was really like everybody else. But on the outside, as Professor Fried says, "the subject *appears* free to per-form the same actions as others and to enter the same relations, but in fact an important element of autonomy, of control over his environment is missing: he cannot be private."

Fried points out that a person subject to monitoring is ex-pected by people he deals with to have certain responses, certain interpersonal relations, and at times to indicate certain in-timacies with individuals with whom he works or wants to de-velop a friendship. People expect some of these amenities from him. Yet because he is constantly aware that whatever he says will be scrutinized by those monitoring him, the likelihood is that he will choose to withdraw and cut himself off from social con-tacts as much as possible. And so by such action, "he would risk seeming cold, unnatural, odd, inhuman to the very people whose esteem and affection he craves."[27]

There is another aspect to electronic monitoring which inten-sifies the insidiousness of this technique — it forces an individual to betray others with whom he or she may become intimate. Un-aware of the continuous surveillance, they may find themselves confiding in the parolee certain information about themselves which automatically becomes part of the police record, once again in violation of constitutional safeguards to privacy.

But much of the debate as to the interpretation of the Fourth and Fifth Amendments could become irrelevant; for should the government invoke the principle of "compelling state interest" it could simply jettison the constitutional safeguards. With the general rise in crime in the city streets, the authorities' inability to control the situation under the existing socioeconomic conditions, and the public clamor for action, the federal government, through either Congress or the courts, could declare that social defense and crime prevention required mass screening or any other type of surveillance without regard to constitutional restrictions.

A number of court cases have set precedents for such federal action, and certainly there are continuing practices based strictly on the theory of the nation's self-protection that could exclude the application of the Fourth or Fifth Amendment to surveillance. For instance, federal agents have the authority to search foreigners and Americans alike when they cross territorial borders from Mexico and Canada, or arrive from overseas; no warrant is necessary and persons and/or property as well as automobiles are scrutinized to protect the United States from aliens and contraband. On the same basis the government could justify the Schwitzgebel proposal by stating that it is in the national interest to prevent "infiltration" of society by criminals.

The recent airport antihijacking regulation is even more to the point. With no warrant on hand, federal agents force people to undergo frisking and body searches and have their luggage examined by magnetometers. Notwithstanding frequent suits against the searches, the courts have so far maintained that the passengers' interest is so compelling that mass screening must be used to protect it.

While laudable for its effectiveness in controlling hijacking, the suspension of constitutional provisions lays the basis for the erosion of some of the most valuable protections that the Constitution provides for the citizenry. Certainly this can become a precedent to meet the compelling-interest test for the installation of a national surveillance program. It would obviously violate the basic moral principles that underlie Anglo-American criminal justice. As Peter Northrop Brown points out in the *Southern California Law Review*, it would set up a precedent for mass intrusions into personal autonomy on the basis of one's "mentation" alone, that is, a frame of mind assumed to tend to violent behavior.

Brown says that the government could contend that "the interests of the entire society in the reduction of crime and the clear benefits that would flow from such reduction would outweigh the interest of the individual, however substantial, in his or her personal autonomy."[28] This approach would seek justification from the presumption that crime would be reduced. The indignation of citizens over intrusion into one's private life would appear speculative and not convincing in the eyes of the courts.

Brown points to the danger that acceptance of a surveillance program would pave the way to its use on individuals and groups that are not criminals, groups that may have minority views or advocate antiestablishment programs. He says:

> The effectiveness of such physical surveillance, once the precedent is established, would argue for surveillance of other dissident or minority groups threatening to the majority. We must therefore assume the high probability of a society in which surveillance of certain groups is well known and surveillance of any nonconformist . . . activity is suspected.

J. A. Meyer has similar apprehensions about the possibility of misuse of his transponders. There is, for instance, the prospect of "prophylactic arrest, just to induce a transponder assignment, after which the case can be stalled for years while an arrestee carries the stigma of surveillance." Similarly, he says, these devices could be used for punitive measures in noncriminal cases, "e.g. for arrests following riots or confrontations." [29] He feels that the very threat of the use of transponders for minor offenses would have an intimidating effect on suspects.

Intimidation has a dramatic and far-reaching bearing not only on the individual but on society as a whole. The fear of becoming a suspect, of being under the prying eyes of officials authorized to probe one's political objectives and associations has become known as the "chill" factor, which in effect frustrates the privilege and even the obligation of the citizen to participate in the political life of his country.

Professor Frank Askin, of Rutgers University Law School, examines this question against the backdrop of the witch hunts of the McCarthy period of the 1950s. In that era many people began to shy away from groups that were labeled subversive even though they were engaged in legitimate political activity. "Guilt by association" was an omnipresent monster that could not be confronted directly, since one could not be certain of exactly how it operated. A person fearful of being tainted by his association with friends belonging to suspect groups begins to redefine "legitimate political activities as illegitimate and is therefore reluctant to act on his political beliefs."[30]

Askin cites the work of two investigators, who questioned seventy professors in government service and fifteen university faculty members, all in the Washington, D.C., area, about their attitudes during the McCarthy era. They reported that fear of federal investigation had forced many of these people to change their behavior drastically. They severed membership in organizations on the attorney general's list and they became extremely cautious in political conversations with strangers.[31]

"Since the key to political democracy is not that citizens be always active (i.e., acting politically) but that they be 'potentially active,'" Professor Askin says, "the public's reactions to various political experiences, such as surveillance, are of the utmost importance . . . The dynamic of potential activity is in this way eliminated, and the psychological precondition needed for a participative political system is absent. A frightening aspect of this situation," he adds, "is that individuals or groups who are only curious bystanders can also be stigmatized, by being indiscriminately included in the lists of those present at the activity surveilled."[32]

Schwitzgebel has also expressed some concern that his surveillance scheme could be misused. He is confident, however, that appropriate government regulations and strict controls would minimize the possibility that surveillance would filter into the lives of the noncriminal sector of society. One critic of electronic surveillance, Professor Bernard Beck of Northwestern University, questions Schwitzgebel's reassurances. "The history of our age," he says, "is not very reassuring about the power of enlightened, humane thinking to limit or guide the implementation of powerful technological advances." Schwitzgebel, he says, "gives us only injunctions, 'we must,' 'they must,' but we get no help if we can't and they will not. Can we expect that sometime the same technical cleverness that devises systems like this will devise strategies for insuring the responsibility of adopting agencies? Or would that be one more gift from Pandora's box?"[33]

Such doubts about the Schwitzgebel-Meyer expedients might readily disappear if the authorities were to veer in the direction of the Delgado formula. The adoption of methods to reshape behavior via Delgado's depth-electrode technique would definitely fall into the category of therapy, as presently defined, and would therefore be free of criticism that it would inhibit political self-expression. The central, and growing, danger is that nonconformism of all types — social, sexual, or political — can be associated with and interpreted as deviance of a neuropsychiatric nature. If this is accomplished, the psychiatric establishment and the neurosurgeons can begin playing a much more important role in policing unacceptable behavior of any kind (street violence, political dissidence, etc.). If all of these begin to be treated as ailments, it may increasingly become the psychologist-psychiatrist rather than the magistrate who decides whether a violation of the law is "treatable" by means of electronic brain stimulation.

Thus the question of privacy, the matter of transgression of the First, Fourth, and Fifth Amendments, might no longer be considered relevant. And, of course, what could happen to the governmental structure of the United States as more and more of its citizens dropped out from participation in political activity, is another matter.

9. It's Not Just Theory

AT ANOTHER TIME critics might have said "too hasty" of the endorsement of psychosurgery by the National Commission for the Protection of Human Subjects of Biomedical and Behavioral Research and let it go at that. In the ensuing months and years, if the outcome did not meet the desired expectations, the procedure would have been chalked up as yet another in a series of medicine's "magic bullets" that failed to produce the overnight cure. After all, the catalogue of such failures is impressive.

In some instances, years of continuous damage was done to thousands of patients (who, incidentally, were also made to foot the bills for the indignities and pain they suffered) before some of these operations or drugs were conceded to be useless. Tonsillectomies, which Dr. Francis B. Moore, surgeon-in-chief at Peter Bent Brigham Hospital, Boston, characterizes as "unnecessary and unwise,"[1] and which other specialists have come to deplore, are still being performed — some one million such operations a year. "Gastric freezing," a procedure very popular in the early 1960s to control ulcer disease, has also gone into eclipse — but again, not before a multitude of patients had submitted to a painful experience at great financial loss.

But the government's countenancing of psychosurgery and its willingness to extend the application of such surgery to prisoners and others involuntarily institutionalized, takes on a political significance. However much members of the commission argue that medical and legal safeguards will prevent abuses, evidence points to the contrary — for example, consider the well-known abuses in antibiotics, nuclear energy, and pesticides. As one scientist pointed out, "once psychosurgery gets under way the possible side effects and dangers, as was in the case of pesticides, would be relegated to the footnotes," and the various restrictions and constraints will be looked upon as "interference by those pushing for the extended use of psychosurgery."[2]

It is more than likely that a rationale would be developed to justify the application of the curative powers of psychosurgery to homosexuals, hot-tempered individuals, and political dissidents — something a number of psychosurgeons have been advocating for years.[3] Certainly there would be mounting pressure to deal with violent muggers and rebellious prisoners by utilizing psychosurgery. Such an expedient would find ready acceptance by a substantial section of the population that is desperate for a short-cut remedy for crime, since no major plan is yet in sight to resolve this crisis.

Unemployment continues to spiral, particularly hitting the minority populations (45–50 percent of the 18- to 25-year-age group, according to official figures), with the resulting rise in burglaries and crimes in the city streets. Solutions such as a massive economic crash program along the lines of the Marshall Plan, which was suggested as far back as 1968 by President Johnson's Kerner Commission, have been sidestepped by every administration since the economy began to decline. Instead, those at the controls seem to insist on examining the crime phenomenon from the wrong end of the telescope, as it were, and to focus exclusively on the physiological and psychological make-up of the wayward individual.

Needless to say, such an approach is not going to lead to the abatement of the crime wave; on the contrary, it will continue to rise. For instance, the New York City 1976 crime record was at an all-time high. Felonies were committed at the rate of 75 every hour, or 1798 crimes in an average day. All told, there were 658,147 serious crimes for the year.[4] (And New York City is only about the fourth most crime-ridden metropolis in the United States.) It is significant to note that there was "a relatively small" rise in violent crime, but an upsurge in burglaries. As reported in the *New York Times*, "Many high police officials and field commanders attributed the large increases in burglaries and thefts to the city's depressed economy and high unemployment." According to Deputy Chief Joseph C. Hoffman, "Each time we have a downturn in the economy, we get an increase in property crimes." So far as violent crime is concerned, the police said that there was a decrease in murders and most of these "involved persons who knew each other,"[5] thus suggesting that in a fit of temper murder might be committed because of the ready availability of the handgun rather than because of calculated motivation.

A recent report, especially prepared for the Joint Economic Committee of the U.S. Congress, for the first time traces the long-term effects of unemployment on "stressful situations" leading to criminal aggression as well as to physical and mental illness. Conducted by Professor M. Harvey Brenner, of Johns Hopkins University, the study reveals among other things that even a relatively small increase in unemployment will cast a long damaging shadow for years to come. For instance, Brenner reports that "a 1% increase in unemployment . . . creates a legacy of stress, of aggression and of illness affecting society long into the future. In just the subsequent five years [unemployment] has a multiplier effect far exceeding the relative size of the unemployment rise." He suggests that a 1.4 percent rise in unemployment during 1970 "is directly responsible for some 51,570 deaths including 1,740 additional homicides, for 1,540 suicides, and for 5,520 additional mental hospitalizations."

Aggravating the situation, Brenner's study declared, is the deterioration of the quality of life of the majority of the inner-city residents (the minorities), which, at the very least, "has not kept up with the general trend of national prosperity." He pointed out that "this problem of recent urban decline has been particularly serious for younger persons and for ethnic minorities."[6]

The Johns Hopkins study in all likelihood will meet the same fate as that of the other studies; it will be examined and routinely shelved. At the same time, a call for action to deal with crime is becoming ever more shrill and strident. With the prodding of the media, which is hooked on sensationalizing crime rather than explaining its causes, the public finds itself demanding that the victim of the economic condition should behave, should accept the unacceptable, or face maximum punishment. Even if prosperity returns, those living a marginal existence will hardly continue to accept docilely their exclusion from the better things that the economy can offer.

A foretaste of what lies ahead is the looting that struck New York on the night of the blackout (July 13, 1977). Thousands of people, mostly teenagers and young adults, romped through the darkened streets of the ghetto areas — Harlem, the Bedford-Stuyvesant section of Brooklyn, and the South Bronx — and helped themselves to whatever they could lay their hands on. Without question this made for a new national record: the largest transfer of goods to the "have not" section of a city population in the history of the United States. An estimated one billion dollars worth of products changed hands overnight. It was "Christmas in July," as one Brooklyn resident described the occasion. It was also curtains for some 2000 small-time shopowners.

The city was stunned, and the nation pondered whether the same catastrophe could hit other localities. Understandably there was sympathy for the expropriated storeowners; and predictably the cry went up for the prosecution of some 3700 suspects "to the fullest extent of the law," as Mayor Abraham Beame demanded. The *New York Times* commented editorially a few days later (July 17th):

> If these are the only lessons that President Carter and Mayor Beame . . . and the rest of us carry away from last week's anguish, we are in much worse trouble than we thought in the ugly hours, before dawn on Thursday [the day the lights began coming back on]. . . . We may continue to ignore the terrible problems of poverty and race, but we must do so aware of the risks to both justice and peace.

Riots, apparently, have been anticipated by government authorities for some time, because of the declining economy. But their solution or containment was conceived in terms of police tactics and not in measures that will lead to employment, thereby defusing the tensions of the ghetto streets. Only four months prior to the New York City outbursts, in March 1977, a government group, the National Advisory Committee on Criminal Justice Standards and Goals, had issued a report in which it urged the police everywhere to prepare for such developments. "The present tranquility is deceptive," the report declared, urging the police to guard against complacency. Prepared by a special task force lead by Jerry V. Wilson, a former Washington, D.C., police chief, the 660-page report outlines one hundred different ways on how to deal with mass disorders, including tactics to institute mass arrests.[7]

While the nation's police forces are preparing to do battle in the streets, the public is being psychologically conditioned to demand ever greater punitive sanctions for those out of step with the law. Harsher imprisonment conditions and longer sentences are among the remedies advocated in dealing with the crises of the cities.*

Perhaps even more ominous are the theories being ground out by academicians that are used to provide the scientific validity for the need to track down the "aberrant" individual while excusing the society that created him. As though orchestrated by design, geneticists and behaviorists alike, whether at the University of California at Los Angeles or at Berkeley, Stanford, Harvard, the University of Michigan at Ann Arbor, or at the University of Pittsburgh, are pouring out their treatises which, in effect, obfuscate social and political realities with the fog of pseudoscience.

Misuse and misdirection of the sciences are nothing new. They

*The public is also being urged to deal with the crime situation by taking the law into its own hands. A new publication, *Vigilante — The Magazine of Personal Security*, encourages its readers to become "vicious themselves" when handling intruders, even when such action may border on "deadly force, perhaps even violating the law."[8]

have provided justification of the status quo or for the adoption of chauvinist policies well before Nazi Germany. In this country, when the power structure has been threatened, whether by an economic crunch or because certain institutions, such as slavery, were facing disestablishment, all kinds of "logical" rationales or myths were hatched to repel and deflect questioning so as to reinforce the continuity of things as they were.

As far back as the turn of the century, a number of important American industrialists subsidized the eugenics movement, aimed at "improving mankind" by the application of certain genetic principles. Positive eugenics would encourage the reproduction of the "fit" individual; and negative eugenics would reduce the number of the "unfit" types within the population. Basically it was a racist concept that was intended to keep blacks separated from whites at a time when trade unionism began to take hold across the nation.

With the introduction of the IQ tests, the eugenics movement was bolstered by new "proof" that certain segments of the population (such as blacks and East Europeans) were genetically predisposed to become feeble-minded or criminal or sexually promiscuous or degenerate.[9] Madison Grant, the author of a best seller of that period, *The Passing of the Great Race*,[10] published in 1916, began sounding the alarm that the increasing number of foreign immigrants was threatening the Anglo-Saxon purity and "Nordic civilization" in America.

And Professor C. C. Brigham of Princeton, another eugenicist, declared:

> The Nordics are . . . rulers, organizers, and aristocrats . . . individualistic, self-reliant, and jealous of their personal freedom . . . as a result they are usually Protestants . . . The Alpine race is always and everywhere a race of peasants . . . The Alpine is the perfect slave, the ideal serf . . . the unstable temperament and the lack of coordinating and reasoning powers so often found among the Irish.[11]

For his part, Professor Nathaniel Hirsch, who had held a National Research Council Fellowship in Psychology at Harvard, was warning the nation about the pernicious effects of Mexican and French Canadian migration into the United States.[12]

Eugenics was the basis for the formulation of the Johnson Act in 1924, barring most of the immigration from Eastern Europe and from the Mediterranean countries in an attempt to inhibit further radicalization of the labor unions. The eugenicists were able to pave the way for the adoption of the miscegenation laws that proscribed interracial marriage in some thirty states. Twenty-four states passed legislation for the sterilization of social "misfits," a category that took in anybody who might be adjudged as mentally retarded, insane, an epileptic, or of criminal disposition, depending on how that term was defined. By 1928 the study of eugenics was introduced to most of the American colleges and involved some 20,000 students.[13]

It is interesting that those active in the development of the theory of eugenics were some of the most eminent scientists, such as W. E. Castle. They were academicians on the faculties of the most prestigious American universities and were members of the National Academy of Sciences. It is true that years later a few of these scientists had second thoughts about the validity of their theories. W. E. Castle, for instance, tried to recant after having contended for many years that interracial marriage would lead to the same type of misfit hybrid as "a cross between a thoroughbred and a drafthorse."[14]

Because of World War II, promotion of racism became somewhat embarrassing, particularly as the Nazi concentration camp obscenities became front-page news. The moratorium on eugenic theories didn't last very long, however, once the war was over. The emergence of the Jensen-Shockley thesis that a hereditary factor was at the root of the inability of blacks to reach the IQ levels of the white population was welcome reinforcement for the segregationist position. Critics of the theory, such as Nobel Prize winning geneticist Joshua Lederberg, challenged its scientific validity and decried its divisive effect on the nation. He said:

> Jensen feeds Shockley and Shockley feeds the racists — people who are impatient about making a significant investment in improving the

conditions of blacks, and would welcome any excuse to be off-loaded with it.[15]

The Jensen-Shockley approach also came under fire from many distinguished anthropologists, such as Ashley Montagu and Margaret Mead.[16]

Now, however, the genetic approach has been revitalized with the launching of sociobiology, a concept originating with Professor E. O. Wilson, of Harvard, author of *Sociobiology, the New Synthesis*. Wilson's contention is that it is the genes and not cultural evolution or socioeconomics or political environment that are responsible for human behavior. Drawing upon his study of ants, bees, monkeys, and birds, the Harvard geneticist sees their behavior to be analogous with that of the human being. He states: ". . . a single strong thread does indeed run from the conduct of termite colonies and turkey brotherhoods to the social behavior of man."[17]

Continuing from this premise he sees aggressiveness, male dominance, military discipline, and even genocide as basic mechanisms of human nature about which little can be done to effect a change. Wilson has been acclaimed in many quarters as breaking new ground in the analysis of the various social problems confronting this society. In a front-page story regarding the publication of Wilson's book, the *New York Times* said:

> Sociobiology carries with it the revolutionary implication that much of man's behavior toward his fellows . . . may be as much a product of evolution as is the structure of the hand or the size of the brain.[18]

Sociobiology courses are now being given at a number of universities. Even high schools are being circularized with special study materials based on Wilson's text. Concerned that sociobiology essentially is the latest attempt to make the Jensen-Shockley ideology more respectable by dressing it in new vestments, a group of scientists, professors, and researchers from Harvard, M.I.T., Boston University, and other academic centers in the Boston-Cambridge area have formed a Sociobiology Study Group, which has published a number of analytical articles in scientific journals taking issue with Wilson's theories. Among other things, this group accuses Wilson of confusing the lay public when he uses metaphors from human societies to describe characteristics of animal society. For instance:

> In insect populations, Wilson applies the traditional metaphors of "slavery" and "caste," "specialists" and "generalists" and "elites" in order to establish a descriptive framework. Thus, he promotes the similarity between human and animal societies and leads one to believe that behavior patterns in the two have the same basis. Oppressive institutions seen in human societies are made to seem natural because of their "universal" existence in the animal kingdom. But metaphor is no substitute for logical connections.
>
> Wilson also establishes specific genes for various human social behaviors by simply stating them to be true, without providing any data.[19]

According to the Sociobiology Study Group, Wilson

> has taken human behavior in modern industrialized society, as he sees it, and by analogy to animal behavior, by irresponsible use of language, and elastic arguments, he has portrayed this behavior as universal, genetic, adaptive "human nature." The political implications are clear. For if our behavior is genetically determined, then efforts to alleviate social problems resulting from that behavior must fail. Genes are beyond our control.[20]

Two members of the Sociobiology Study Group, Professor Richard Levins and Professor Richard Lewontin of Harvard, both noted geneticists and population experts, further elaborated on Wilson's thinking in brief interviews with this writer. Dr. Levins explained that what the sociobiologists do "is to take a prevailing pattern of behavior and then decide that there must be a hereditary basis for it. They further assume that if something is hereditary it is therefore not amenable to very much environmental modification." This type of thinking, he believes "stems from social and philosophical biases present in our society." He continued:

> We generally find that biological determinist theories are more popular in periods of conservatism. Where there is a lot of biological knowledge and only a little social knowledge, the biology can swamp

the social knowledge. Sociobiology is a powerful movement because it provides a very congenial result. It tells you that things are the way they are because they really couldn't be much different. You can't buck 400 million years of evolution overnight. And then sociobiologists look for their analogs in different groups. Since Wilson's own area of speciality is with insect behavior, he tends to define it most broadly as properties of behavior in general.

Dr. Levins pointed out that "although Wilson is not suggesting public policy based on his sociobiological observations, he is developing the fear from which policies might be made." The Harvard geneticist further explained that "Wilson himself saw his work as a piece of scientific scholarship, notwithstanding that his prejudices are exposed through it. He didn't visualize it as a political act, which indeed it is."[21]

Dr. Lewontin sees sociobiology as having a great deal in common with Skinnerian philosophy, in terms of determinism, even though seemingly both are opposed to each other.

I think they both suffer from a confusion about social behavior. Sociobiology attempts to explain human social behavior and social organization on the basis of evolutionary principles about the selection of individuals and how individuals behave.

And the prime error it makes, he argues, "is to confuse the properties of individuals with the properties of collections of individuals." Sociobiology, he emphasized

makes the mistake in assuming that important aspects of human social organization could be understood by seeing how natural selection has favored one kind of individual behavior over another.

Skinner makes the same error in a different way, Dr. Lewontin maintains.

Skinner doesn't talk about genes. He talks about a different kind of determinism which presupposes that if one could control all the inputs into a person from the time of birth his behavior could be fully controlled; you can create his behavior. But the error lies in the supposition that that is a way of understanding social organization and social behavior as well as human history and human economic activity.[22]

In connection with violence, the so-called senseless violence and muggings, Dr. Lewontin feels that for the most part these also cannot be evaluated unless they are considered against the sociopolitical background of the particular circumstances. He strongly criticized the view of Dr. Mark and Dr. Ervin that violence may be sparked by "brain dysfunction," having nothing to do with the social environment. Dr. Lewontin added:

The argument, in their words, was "Look, everybody in the ghettos didn't burn down buildings . . . only some. Therefore the ones who did must be crazy." Not crazy, but aberrant. Suppose it were true that the only people who would burn down a store in a black ghetto were people with certain neuron subnormal connections. That doesn't speak to the causes of burning down a store, and that's the error they make. It could be true that only crazy people will be violent, that is, what we call violent. But that is not the cause of the violence. That only says that some people will react in one way and some people in another to a form of social oppression. Of course there are many sick people who might be involved in aberrant or violent action. But I claim that many such actions are socially determined.[23]

For Mark and Ervin to say that people who perform so-called violent acts do so because they are mentally aberrant, Dr. Lewontin contended "is to misunderstand the notion of causation. There is an assumption that either the cause is social or the cause is neurophysiological, and this leaves no possibility that there may be an interaction between these two kinds of causation, namely, that in some social situations some people have a lower threshold for violence than other people."

Dr. Lewontin then raised the question of the solution to this dilemma. Obviously, he declared, "the cure is not in getting rid of the people with a lower threshold." Of course, he pointed out,

It is a cure if your main objective is to keep stores from burning down. Then all cures are equally good. As a matter of fact, psychosurgery is a very inefficient way of dealing with such people. There is an even quicker way of dealing with it and that is to kill them.[24]

Acceptance of the genetic determinist approach, as set forth by Lorenz, Jensen, and Shockley, or as updated by Wilson, leads to a number of conclusions with a rather chilling implication. Most important of these is the idea that some of our critical problems will not be solved by the alteration of our national priorities or the reorganization of our institutions. Their solution will depend on methods designed to multiply the number of people with good genes and to reduce the number of individuals with genes that lead to criminality, rebelliousness, laziness, or any other category of behavior generally frowned upon by those who set the criteria.

In such a Kafkaesque scenario, the proposal by the government advisory group mentioned earlier for the beefing up of the police forces when confronting possible civil disorders, might result in a situation in which rioters (obviously motivated by bad genes) clamoring for more jobs would be mowed down by machine guns and thus the proportion of people with good genes would automatically rise.

There is also a somewhat less dramatic method to reach the same objective — one that would omit the sound and fury of battle and yet be as effective — sterilization. The latter procedure is no stranger to the United States, as mentioned earlier.

While the sociobiologists may fire the imagination of genetically oriented industrialists, government leaders, and law-enforcement officials with ideas on how to improve the genetic reservoir of mankind, the environmental determinists, marching under the banner of Professor Skinner, have their eyes fixed on behavior modification as the method to right whatever ails us. In fact, hundreds of such behavioral engineers are swarming in the prisons, in mental hospitals, and children's homes, devising programs that would make people conform to whatever regulations and standards are designed for them. Behavior modification is "in."

On a theoretical basis, Skinner, the high priest of the behaviorist movement, personifies the antithesis to genetic determinism. So far as he is concerned, it is all environment. "What has happened experimentally is the discovery of the extraordinary range of action of the environment in determining behavior,"[25] he told me in the course of an hour long interview at the William James Building, Harvard.

Now seventy-three years old, of a very spare build but agile, and moving about in a quick, birdlike fashion, Professor Skinner talked in machine-gun bursts, although frequently his thin, reedy voice would drift away to a whisper. Ready to respond to any question in a genteel, New England manner of a period long gone, he would at times show annoyance at comments that would presume to differ with some of his interpretations.

Most astonishing was that this man, enjoying a world reputation for having pioneered techniques in redirecting people's behavior on the basis of patterns that he used in training pigeons to play Ping-Pong, seemed at times to resort either to evasion or unbelievable naiveté when dealing with some of his basic philosophical principles in relation to the problems confronting the United States.

"People are beginning to recognize the importance of the consequences of environment and behavior," he said. "If you want to change behavior, change consequences." By way of illustration he referred to a news report that Charles L. Schultze, the Chairman of the Council of Economic Advisors, was proposing special legislation for the control of river pollution. Professor Skinner felt that this indeed represented a move forward in the sensible application of behaviorism, since the objective would be accomplished without the need of imprisoning the directors of industrial corporations who are responsible for such pollution.

> Instead of passing laws about polluting rivers and so on, and then punishing companies or throwing their officers in jail, Schultze will simply charge for pollution. If you want to dump a certain kind of pollutant into the river, you pay so much per gallon to do this and you put the price very high and before very long the company's going to figure out something else to do. They're not going to pay that price. Which is just nothing but changing the consequences of behavior. Which is precisely what we do in the laboratory.[26]

Considering the gravity of the consequences resulting from water contamination in terms of public health and destruction of marine life, Professor Skinner's reaction seemed somewhat overstated and his attitude toward industrial river poisoning rather mild. In contrast, Professor Skinner was considerably more demanding for harsher treatment for juvenile delinquents involved in car stealing. He conceded that the rise in the number of youthful offenders was a direct "byproduct of a very poorly arranged social system. I'd improve the system," he said.

> I don't know how to step in and stop violence. But we know some of the conditions under which organisms become aggressive toward other organisms. And I'd like to change those conditions with people. If life isn't going well, that's when you're going to attack people. I'd just like to build a world in which people's lives go well; that's the problem. Not punishing them for attacking, but to give them no reason to be attacking.[27]

But for the present it seems that Professor Skinner would go back on his own original premise, namely that of using positive reinforcement (rewards for desired type of behavior); for the immediate future he was foursquare for punishment. As he put it:

> I'm inclined to say that right now we would have to maintain punitive sanctions. We cannot simply drop punitive sanctions and be permissive. That's not the solution. That's what wrecked the American school system. I think you have to maintain punitive sanctions until you have something else to take its place. Right now in Massachusetts they've closed down all reform schools for juvenile delinquents. No place to put them after they've stolen a car. It's a nice, open, easy racket, stealing cars . . . One of the reasons the prisons are crowded is we have built up in young people the disposition to commit crimes, by letting them get away with it. The young people today can commit crimes and they don't suffer. They're still free to do it over again. And when they become adults they've learned that this is the way of life, to be criminal.[28]

Professor Skinner felt that once in reformatory schools the young thief would benefit from behavior-modification techniques to instill discipline and working habits. He mentioned the National Training School for Boys in Washington, D.C., by way of example. He said that with the use of behavioral procedures the juvenile delinquents there learned a great deal, certainly a good deal more than before their imprisonment. He thought that the results were good because only 25 percent of them were back in jail as compared to about 85 percent from another group that did not undergo behavioral training. He did admit that within a three-year period, even those who benefitted from behavior modification were back "in the bad world." Most of these young people, he added, were blacks, Chicanos, and Puerto Ricans.

When questioned as to the usefulness of behavioral training of youthful offenders considering the fact that on their release from prison most of them would go right back where they started from — to unemployment, Professor Skinner said that he really didn't think this question was within his purview. "You shouldn't be talking about that with me. I have no way of changing the overseas trade balance to stop the economic adversity. You should be talking to an economist."

When asked about the means by which society as a whole could be redirected in terms of the commonweal, Professor Skinner felt that it would depend primarily on the people themselves to effect a change.

It all depends on who runs things and how . . . and if we are aware of this, we are likely, if we are interested in the future and our way of life, to do things the right way. Some cultures will emerge, and I should hope that ours is one, in which we're in a position to design the environment in which people will be healthy, happy, productive, imaginative, creative, ongoing and so on.

I'd like to see the kind of thing like Walden II promoted. Lots of small utopias. I'd like to see the small town built up. I think face to face control is much better than delegating control to an authority, like the police or economic entrepreneurs and so on. I like face to face control in small communities. A lot can be done.[29]

An inkling of what it might mean to redesign the environment on Skinner's lines is provided by an experimental community center, known as the Huntsville–Madison County Mental Health Center in Alabama. This facility is run by the state and is operating on a grant from the National Institute of Mental Health. Its purpose is frankly stated: "To investigate the feasibility of employing behavior modification techniques in all its activities" with respect to the community about it.[30]

Alan W. Heldman, a member of the American Bar Association, some time ago did an in-depth study of this center and described his findings in the *Cumberland-Samford Law Review*, published by the Cumberland School of Law of Samford University, Birmingham, Alabama. Here are some of the highlights of Heldman's findings:

The director of the center, Dr. A. Jack Turner, feels "operant conditioning procedures that have proven effective in working with lower animals and subsequent application with humans offer promise in dealing with the general public or the community at large." The center is operated on the basic premise of behavior modification and it extends its services to a variety of conventional facilities, such as those for alcoholism treatment and the care of hospitalized psychiatric patients. But, according to Heldman, the center also operates an outpatient service for the inhabitants of a poor and mostly black section, known as the "Model Neighborhood Area." Its task there is to get people to participate in "educational and group therapy sessions designed for lower socio-economic groups." But its main thrust is to "shape" or "modify" child management and family counseling. According to Heldman, the main idea is to get this "model" community to send the "mothers out of the home and into the job market, and the children into controlled day care centers." Heldman feels this "serves the purpose of increasing the community's labor supply, reducing maternal influences on the child, and putting the child into the care of people who have been trained in behavior modification techniques."

One of the goals with respect to the model community is to develop "an ability to accept supervision and follow directions." Heldman says that the orientation of the model neighborhood program is clear: "These people are to be shaped by psychological techniques into patterns which will be more useful 'to the establishment.'" He adds that they will be made into "happy" obedient workers who have peer relationships that are "acceptable" to behaviorists.

When Heldman asked Dr. Turner who would judge what constitutes "appropriate social behavior," which the center was attempting to create, Turner replied, "We . . . reinforce those behaviors which society asks us to reinforce." And when pressed how "society" communicates its requests, he declared:

> We have a board of ten men, who are noted citizens in our community, and if we get to the point where we are having difficulty . . . deciding on a democratic basis whether this behavior is sufficiently aberrant to warrant change although it is not a public or illegal act, . . . we would go for advice to our board and to our professional advisory board and our citizens' advisory board and ask them . . . what we are trying to say [is] that at times the law as written is in conflict with the community's norms . . . and we then adhere to . . . the prevailing norm.

Heldman felt that Dr. Turner's board of ten "noted citizens" were essentially interested in "increasing the supply of pliant, industrious workers and in imposing middle class social values (as they see them) upon the more disadvantaged elements of the community."

As to the ethics of having behaviorists take over the decisions regarding community goals that are traditionally determined by legislation or by private groups and by the individual, Turner explained:

> I would contend that the people with the best data about the best decisions to be made at this time are the behavioral scientists, not the government . . .[31]

Among those championing the most extreme form of behavioral modification is neurophysiologist José M. R. Delgado. For nearly thirty years (mostly at Yale), this Spanish scientist has been involved in a variety of dramatic but controversial experiments in which he uses electrical brain stimulation to alter or direct the behavior of animals as well as human beings. His philosophy is spelled out in the book *Physical Control of the Mind* in which he foresees a "psychocivilized society" in which people will become wiser and happier because of better developed brains, thanks to advances in neurophysiology and such techniques as electro-brain stimulation.[32]

Although he was among the first to be associated with Dr. John Fulton, a pioneer in lobotomy research in the United States in the middle thirties, Delgado felt that it began too early and that he was "a little disturbed by the thought that so many frontal lobes were being destroyed, knowing that the brain does not regenerate." It is for this reason, he told me in an interview, that he veered toward electro-brain stimulation (EBS), which he described as a more conservative methodology. "That is why I started implanting electrodes in the brain, a procedure which, from the traumatic point of view, could be considered minor surgery."[33]

Implantation of depth electrodes, whether for EBS or for burning out tissue, has been considered by many neurophysiologists as another form of psychosurgery. The National Commission, which recently approved the use of psychosurgery to be done in a research context, very definitely states that psychosurgery includes "brain surgery, implantation of electrodes, destruction or direct stimulation of brain tissue by any means . . ."[34]

Delgado has called for massive governmental investments for increasing research and development of methods of "conquering the human mind." This, he said, "could be a central theme for international cooperation and understanding because its aim is to know the mechanisms of the brain, which make all men behave and misbehave, which give us pleasure and suffering, which promote love and hate."[35]

Delgado would have us believe that it is the absence of sweet reason secreted in the gulleys and crevices of the billions of neurons that make up the human brain, and not the social or political antagonisms within a nation or between nations that may be at the root of class warfare, atomic rivalries, or other troubles that beset and buffet society. In support of this view, Delgado says:

When atomic energy was discovered, its destructive capabilities were developed much faster than its constructive applications, and the blame for this tragedy must be placed on the lack of human reason — on the functional inadequacy of our little brains which have not yet learned to solve their behavioral conflicts reasonably. The danger of atomic misuse may, hopefully, be solved by new ideas produced by better brains to come.[36]

Delgado sees the human being as a biological machine whose functions, if properly understood and manipulated, would allow the individual the maximum fulfillment of potential. He feels that the principle that "all men are born free and equal," enunciated by the founders of the American Constitution, may be "commendable as an ideal of human rights." However, he says, "If we analyze its biological basis . . . we realize that freedom of the newborn is only wishful thinking, and that literal acceptance of this fallacy may cause frustrations and conflicts." We ought to realize, he suggests, "that liberty is not a natural, inborn characteristic of human expression,"[37] but something that would be dependent upon intelligent thinking and conscious effort. To accomplish this he would prescribe the fuller extension of the human brain capacity via electrical stimulation.

Delgado's belief that man's brain can be manipulated in any direction is derived from his investigative research on monkeys and animals in general. He recounts how the application of electrical current to a specific area in the brain of a small cat would drive it to do battle with a much larger cat. As long as the stimulation continued, the small cat would charge the larger animal, even though it was constantly overpowered. Alternatively, when the brain of the small cat was stimulated in another part, it would turn into a purring, cuddly animal.

In similar fashion, Delgado describes an experiment with rhesus monkeys, which are usually dangerous and will snap at anything, including the hands of the experimenter. But once electricity was allowed to flow to the caudate nucleus of the brain, the monkey's expressions of rage disappeared, and its attitude toward the experimenter became playful. Just as soon as this electrical flow was interrupted, the monkey once again became aggressive.[38]

In another instance, Delgado was able to make a monkey yawn, grimace, or eat repeatedly — all on electrical command to the brain. With humans, he claimed, not only was he able to bring about a calming of aggressive reaction by way of electrical stimulation, but in some instances he was able to elicit "expressions with sexual content" and an enthusiastic friendliness from a person who was generally either sulky or erruptively hostile. He states categorically that "humanity behaves in general no more intelligently than animals would under the same circumstances."[39]

Delgado calls for "experimental investigation of the cerebral structures responsible for aggressive behavior as an essential counterpart of social studies." He contends that this should be recognized by sociologists as well as biologists. He deplores the fact that social upheavals are usually associated with "economic, ideological, social and political factors . . . while the essential link in the central nervous system is often forgotten." Like his colleagues at Harvard, Dr. Frank Ervin and Dr. Vernon H. Mark, who tied the civil disorders of the late sixties to individuals who suffered from brain damage, Delgado declares that this realization should play a role when investigating the causes of a riot. It would be an error "to ignore the fact . . . that determined neuronal groups" in the brain of a rioter "are reacting to sensory inputs and are subsequently producing the behavioral expression of violence."[40]

Delgado feels that the human brain lends itself to easy manipulation in whatever direction, once the exact cerebral foci are accurately located. On this assumption, one would conjure the possibility of simply pushing the proper brain button to stimulate a generous streak in a Fifth Avenue tycoon, so that he would be eager to share his apartment with a Harlem resident; or by stimulating a specific point in the brain of a prime minister or president, that official would redirect his country's international policy to be in keeping with the economic interests of disadvantaged countries rather than with those of the political power groups that installed him into office. As Delgado put it:

> Human behavior, happiness, good and evil are, after all, products of cerebral physiology. In my opinion, it is necessary to shift the center of scientific research from the study and control of natural elements to the analysis and patterning of mental activities.[41]

The one question that Delgado continues to skirt, just as much as Professor Skinner does (a man whom Delgado obviously holds in high regard), is whether a psychocivilized society would indeed create an earthly paradise, or would it pave the way to an era of brain control? Delgado feels that even though the latter entails certain dangers, it is still worth the risk. Scientific discoveries and technology cannot be shelved because of real or imaginary dangers, Dr. Delgado believes. "It may certainly be predicted that the evolution of physical control of the brain and the acquisition of knowledge derived from it," he declares, "will continue at an accelerated pace." This, he added, points "hopefully toward the development of a more intelligent and peaceful mind of the species without loss of individual identity, and toward the exploitation of the most suitable kind of feedback mechanism: the human brain studying the human brain."[42]

The pivotal question remains: Who will be at the controls in programming education and supervising brain stimulation leading to acceptable modes of behavior? But this question, Delgado, very much like Skinner, evades completely.

When I talked to him in New York a few years ago on the same issue, he said,

> J.M.R.D. : We are only the blind product of a blind evolution, without human purpose. What I'm proposing is to give a human purpose to man himself. We need to think about the future, we need planning. How are we going to plan the consumption of energy? If our planning is not very good, then we have an energy crisis like we have now. And we are also going to have overpopulation throughout the world. If our planning is not good, then millions of people will die of hunger.
>
> S.C.: But who's going to do the planning?

J.M.R.D.:   Man himself.

S.C.:   But you seem to bypass the special power groups that frequently interfere with proper planning.

J.M.R.D. :   It is true that there is a conflict of interest among different kinds of people. But that is because we are dealing with economics. But when we think about man himself, then there is no such conflict. What I think we should have is social planning in agreement with biological ideas.[43]

10. Complicity

THE WORLD OF scientific research into which the United States government is ready to plunge psychosurgery experiments is a murky one. It is convulsed by frenzied competition for grants from the government and from private foundations whose funds are becoming depleted. There is mounting evidence that some scientists, desperate to build their images as important investigators so that they can renew their grants, will deliberately falsify data and will readily tailor their purported findings to comply with the biases of those who sponsor them.

But even more ominous is the fact that federal agencies that are supposed to act as watchdogs in the public interest have also become involved in bizarre experiments with human beings that violate basic ethical standards or constitutional human rights. And just like individual investigators, these agencies are also in hot pursuit of funds, and thus are equally ready to promote programs that are astonishingly out of character with the original purposes for which they were founded. In the process, not only is scientific integrity sacrificed but also the welfare of many thousands of this country's poor who make up the reservoir of experimental subjects: whether in the penitentiaries, the mental institutions, or as free individuals in the hospital wards. (According to Dr. Harry W. Foster of the Meharry Medical College, Nashville, Tennessee ". . . 80% of all human experimentation . . . in this country involved the poor . . . they are the functionally illiterate, the senile . . . and certainly the mentally incompetent.")[1]

It is true that psychosurgical research, as envisioned in the recommendation of the congressional commission, would have a variety of legal safeguards to prevent abuse. In the recommendations much is said about observance of the principle of informed consent by anybody being operated upon in an experimental setting. Unfortunately, the history of some of the medical research programs to date gives little cause for optimism with psychosurgery. The question of informed consent is regarded as a joke, particularly for those behind bars. All too frequently the wording of the consent form is beyond the comprehension of the illiterate or the semiliterate. For those in prison, consent may mean 25 cents a day, and possibly better living conditions for the duration of the experiment. For the noncriminal poor confined to hospital wards, there is no recompense when entering an experiment. They acquiesce in blind obedience, because the doctor represents authority and it is to him they look for the cure of whatever ails them.

Occasionally, investigative reporting and congressional hearings over the past decade have led to a series of disclosures that such government agencies as the U.S. Public Health Service, the CIA, the Justice Department, and even HEW have been engaged in deceptive practices aimed at people they were charged with protecting. A few examples:

For about forty years the U.S. Public Health Service conducted a syphilis study in Tuskegee, Alabama, in which over 400 "poor, uneducated, rural blacks" were deliberately deprived of therapy.[2] Some died from illnesses associated with unarrested syphilis. The purpose of the study was to get an in-depth evaluation of what happens to the human body as it undergoes the ravages of this venereal disease.

The study got under way in 1932, ten years before the discovery that penicillin cured syphilis, though there were other cures even then. Notices were mailed to farm laborers and also posted in black churches and schools announcing a new health program and urging black males to get a free physical examination. The men were given blood tests and some were told that they suffered from "bad blood" but were never told about syphilis. To insure the continuation of the project, public health officials used deceit as well as such inducements as free hot lunches on the days that these farm workers were brought into town to undergo periodic examinations.

A few of the participants received a one-time payment of $25 and a twenty-five-year certificate of appreciation. Most were never paid anything. Some families were cajoled into allowing autopsies on the bodies of the men who succumbed to syphilis and were then given $25 to $100 for burial expenses, depending on the length of time the man had been in the experiment.

Peter J. Buxton, an investigator for the Public Health Service, came upon the Tuskegee data in the course of his work and brought the matter to the attention of his immediate superiors. He subsequently left the Public Health Service and went on to law school. In this interim he had continued to communicate with public health officials who generally brushed aside his entreaties to stop the project. It wasn't until he broke the story through a friend on the Associated Press that the Tuskegee study came to a halt in 1972 — six years after Buxton made his initial report.

In testimony before a Senate subcommittee, chaired by Edward Kennedy in 1973, Buxton charged that the Tuskegee project "could be compared to the German medical experiments at Dachau . . . what was being done was very close to murder and was, if you will, an institutionalized form of murder . . ."[3]

Dr. V. G. Cave, a venereal disease specialist, who was brought in by the government to investigate the Tuskegee incident said, "I think the study accomplished nothing that could not have been accomplished by other means. The basic knowledge was not advanced by the study . . ."[4]

Fred Gray, a member of the Alabama legislature, who represented a group of Tuskegee project participants before the Kennedy hearings, pointed to the fact that the penicillin cure was known and available for thirty years but was deliberately denied to the experimental subjects. He charged that it was a racially motivated study . . . for 40 years the life and death of these participants have been determined by white Americans who had little or no concern for the well-being of black . . . Alabamans. Others directed their lives as to whether they would live or die . . . whether they would live long or die young.[5]

Another instance in which government officials abdicated their responsibilities in protecting the public was revealed in the course of congressional hearings by the same Senate subcommittee that learned of the Tuskegee incident. The officials, it was disclosed, were connected with the Department of Health, Education, and Welfare.

It appears that 150 Chicano women went to a San Antonio clinic to obtain contraceptives to prevent further pregnancies. The clinic was involved in a study to evaluate the psychological and physiological effects of the "pill," however, and the women were duped into becoming experimental subjects. None was told of the experiment and none was asked for authorization to be included in it. The supervising physician gave half of the women the contraceptive pill and the other half a placebo. A short time later some of those who were taking the placebo became pregnant. (There was further indignity: on learning of their condition, a number of the women asked for abortions, but this was denied them because of state prohibition of the procedure.)[6]

In the course of the hearings, Vice President Mondale, then a senator and a member of the subcommittee conducting the investigation, learned from Dr. Henry K. Beecher, Harvard Medical School, who was reporting on the case, that the HEW and a pharmaceutical company were involved in the "pill" research. The Harvard physician also touched on the callousness of certain sections of the medical profession with regard to this incident.

When Mondale asked about the reaction of the medical profession, Dr. Beecher replied,

It has been dreadful. The local medical society, I am informed, in San Antonio, issued a great vote of confidence in the doctor, and defended this experiment in very glowing terms as a fine, upstanding job.

Beecher then went on to say:

> Another serious question raised by this study is: Why were Mexican-American financially poor individuals dominant in the group under investigation? Would the investigators' wives have participated? Why are people too poor to pay for medical care utilized in this way?[7]

Even when the principle of informed consent is observed, the circumstances under which it is obtained become darkened by suspicion, particularly when applied in a prison setting. Dr. Beecher cited an experiment supported by the National Institutes of Health, which subjected a group of men, twenty-four to forty-two years of age, to testicular biopsies for a study of the spermatogenic process in man:

"It is most unusual for normal healthy young males to allow their testicles to be harmed, injected and incised," he told the subcommittee. "But this was done in prison . . . one can only wonder what the coercive force was on the prisoners. Threats? The use of men for the procedures stated indicates that some powerful factors must have been employed."[8]

The procedure called for an incision into the scrotal skin and tunica with the "testicular tissue separated from the tunica by lateral undercuts . . ." Dr. Beecher explained that in one phase of the study "radioactive thymidine $-H^3$ was injected into the testicles and the sites marked with a black thread 'so that the exact area could be relocated for subsequent biopsies.'" Eight previously vasectomized inmates "volunteered" for the procedure.[9]

Experts in the field of human research ethics have tried to assess the reasons for the frequent disregard, if not contempt, for the poor by so many of those involved in medical investigation. Professor J. Katz, Yale University, author of what has become a classic source book, *Experimentation with Human Beings*, feels that one of the reasons is that the researchers

> who generally come from a higher social class, have an impaired capacity to identify with the poor. This psychosocial fact contributes greatly to the ease with which the poor are chosen for participation in research . . . If we wished to take greater care in obtaining a more representative sample of the population for research purposes, we could do so. Computer technology has given us the tools to accomplish that objective.

But, he adds, "for a more sophisticated group of patients," the researcher would be compelled to provide more information on the experiment that was to involve the patient. Since the researcher would rather do as little explaining as possible, he would prefer using the poor, who, he feels, "do not understand anyway . . . Why bother to explain?"[10]

Sociologist Bernard Barber agrees with Katz. He has found that the most dangerous studies "were almost twice as likely to be done on ward or clinic patients . . . since they [the patients] are less knowledgeable . . . and least likely to know how to protect themselves."[11] Professor Barber, of Columbia University, had made an attitudinal survey of various investigators, finding that only 13 percent of the investigators were given as much as one seminar on ethics related to human research while in training. About 57 percent of the researchers failed to mention a single reference to the ethical aspects involved in experimentation.

Barber asked the investigators to name a set of three characteristics they considered important in potential research collaborators: 86 percent mentioned "scientific ability," 45 percent said "hard work," and 43 percent mentioned "personality." But only 6 percent made reference to "ethical concern for the research subjects."[12] This group of physician-investigators was at work on 424 different studies involving human subjects. While the outcome was generally unpredictable as to the benefit that would accrue to these patients, the investigators did concede that at least 18 percent of the experiments carried more risk than benefit for the subjects.

The popular image of a medical researcher bent over a microscope, absorbed in the task of running down a bacterial clue to an infectious calamity, oblivious to the worldly temptations about her or him, does not always coincide with reality. The drives and incentives in research, as is true with other professions, may stem more from an attractive monetary recompense than from a burning dedication to save lives, or from a compelling scientific and intellectual curiosity. It may be somewhat dismaying to learn that drug and medical research will often take a particular direction simply because there is more grant money available in certain areas of government or pharmaceutical interest.

For a time the emphasis might be on studies to evaluate tranquilizing drugs; at another time it might be on chromosomes; currently a good deal of stress is put on the overall question of violence and crime from a psychological and genetic point of view. If the word comes down the line that psychosurgery research is the latest thing on the research hit parade, some medical investigators will have little trouble with their conscience as they jettison their ethical principles and cast their nets in the direction where optimum funding will be found.

The same is true of government agencies. This was dramatically illustrated several years ago by one of the most prestigious scientific organizations in this country, the National Institute of Mental Health. This is one of a group of scientific institutes under the umbrella name of the National Institutes of Health — all of which employ thousands of researchers, technicians, and scientists whose task is that of tracking down some of the country's worst scourges: heart disease, cancer, and mental illness, among others. During the Nixon administration, these institutes were forced to retrench and even abandon some of their programs because of the executive decision to reorder the nation's priorities, one of which was to create a society in keeping with Nixon's notion of law and order. Thus a good deal of the emphasis was shifted from tracking down disease to tracking down law violators.

The NIMH was called on to do its part. In the process it became a bedfellow of the Department of Justice. At a meeting held in Colorado Springs in 1970, Dr. Bertram Brown, director of the NIMH, joined with Nixon, Attorney General John Mitchell, John Ehrlichman, H. R. Haldeman, and other key members of the White House staff to work out plans for close collaborative efforts between the NIMH and the newly organized Law Enforcement Assistance Administration. Dr. Brown was greatly moved by this experience; after the meeting he sent a memorandum to all state and territorial mental health authorities in which he said:

> An important new note was struck at this meeting — a note of cooperation and collaboration between governments, departments, and disciplines. It was in the spirit of collaboration that I was invited to address the conference, and it is in that same spirit that I am writing to apprise you of the areas for future joint ventures involving the mental health and law enforcement systems.[13]

A variety of programs were discussed in which the NIMH was to provide the technical assistance in campaigns having to do with drug addiction, alcoholism, and juvenile crime.

In this memorandum, Dr. Brown ordered his staff to give its utmost cooperation. "Know your state criminal justice planning agency," he declared. Dr. Brown was enthusiastic about the cooperative possibilities between the two government agencies and that they would lead to "joint program planning; exchange of state plans; joint training efforts; sharing of information, statistics, and epidemiologic data; and joint funding of projects."

It was the matter of funding that was the most influential factor for making the NIMH knuckle under and become a partner of the LEAA, an agency whose treasury was swollen with hundreds of millions of dollars, which it distributes to law-enforcement groups and to those doing crime research. In a relatively short while, the LEAA was subsidizing some 350 projects involving experimentation with medical procedures, behavior modification, and drugs — all within the context of delinquency control. Many of these projects were not even reviewed by NIMH as to their scientific merit.[15]

In reporting this development, *Psychiatric News*, the official organ of the American Psychiatric Association, cited a researcher who complained that "while Nixon was slashing mental health research funds . . . NIMH was pledging cooperation with an agency that reflects the government's obsession with law and order."[16]

When a *Psychiatric News* editor telephoned Dr. Brown for his comments, the NIMH director said that he saw no conflict of interest in using criminal justice money for mental health projects or vice versa. He added, "There are many areas of mutual concern between the agencies, and many ways that cooperation could facilitate the job we have to do." He then stated:

> It's not so much a question of mental health money being diverted into criminal justice; we just realized that criminal justice had so many millions of dollars, and rather than see it go into more guns and helicopters and tear gas for local law enforcement agencies, we thought it would be worth our while to get some of these funds for human services. We wanted to alert our local commissioners that criminal justice money was available for juvenile delinquency studies, forensic services on psychiatric wards, counseling and correctional programs, drug abuse, and more.[17]

It soon became increasingly apparent that in this affiliation the role of the NIMH began to erode, and its consultative opinions were taking second place. Scientists began to be answerable for their research directly to the LEAA and not to the NIMH. It is not surprising that the nature and form of some of the research projects seemed to bolster the prevailing philosophy that much of crime may have pathological origins. The LEAA began funding studies designed to associate fingerprints as well as chromosomal distinctions with violent behavior.

As revealed by *Psychiatric News*, one researcher, Dr. Lawrence Razavi of Massachusetts General Hospital, Boston, who was awarded an $80,000 grant, is reported to have said he found significant differences between fingerprint patterns of criminal and noncriminal groups, as well as between races. This information was passed on to law enforcement agencies in various states for their guidance.[18]

Another project typical of this trend was that of psychosurgical research, previously discussed. In this instance, the NIMH allocated $500,000 to Dr. Sweet, Dr. Mark, and Dr. Ervin in Boston. Yet another program was to have been the Center for the Reduction of Violence at the University of California, Los Angeles, into which the LEAA was ready to pump $750,000 for the initial stages of research.[19] As has been reported earlier, in Chapter 6, the LEAA was forced to cancel its involvement because of statewide protests against such a center.

In this instance, just as in the case of Dr. Brown of NIMH, money played a crucial role in the attempt to set up the center. Dr. West, director of the Neuropsychiatric Institute, told *Psychiatric News*: "I will admit that psychiatric aspects of violence are not the most influential in terms of numbers, but we . . . are responsible for those disturbed individuals and we have to find out what's behind it." He said that the Neuropsychiatric Institute went to the LEAA for money "because CCCJ [California Council on Criminal Justice] is getting over $50 million a year for state block grant money, and I think we should get some of it. If we don't get it, then it will go into more vans, police cars, dogs, and tear gas. NIMH has fewer funds to disperse in this area, so we had to go to LEAA."[20]

A unit of the NIMH, the Center for the Study of Crime and Delinquency, has maintained an especially close relationship with the LEAA, and an even stronger tie with the National Institute of Law Enforcement and Criminal Justice. For criminal research programs, the staff of the center has provided its expertise and technical assistance to both these organizations. The ever-growing collaboration between NIMH and the LEAA is seen by some as paving the way for the psychologist and psychiatrist to become more directly associated with the aims of law-enforcement agencies across the land. This is reflected in such undertakings as workshops organized jointly by the LEAA and NIMH. One of these had as its main topic "The Role of Psychologists in the Criminal Justice System."

Given the prevailing social and political climate, and the readiness of scientists and scientific institutions to participate in programs of dubious integrity, the appropriateness of launching psychosurgery research becomes questionable. Is it possible that the national commission approval backing psychosurgical research might lead to "half-truth" findings that in time might also turn into a half-fraud, with harrowing consequences for those caught in the experiments?

Fraud is not a stranger to the world of scientific research. Perhaps the most sensational case of deceit was that of the alleged discovery of the prehistoric Piltdown Man by the British anthropologist Charles Dawson. It took forty-five years; not until 1953 were scientists able to verify that Dawson's claim was a hoax, that the skull was that of a modern man and the jaw that of an ape — doctored to give them the appearance of antiquity. Fraudulent "discoveries" take on far more serious ramifications, of course, when they take place in medicine or the social sciences, such as education. According to some authorities, such as microbiologist Dr. Ernest Borek, University of Colorado, "faked data" in scientific journals is on the rise. Dr. Borek told the *New York Times* that "by fabricating nonexistent phenomena for their advantage, the miscreants are attempting to counterfeit a small part of nature itself."[21] Dr. Richard W. Roberts, chief of the National Bureau of Standards, asserts that perhaps more than half of the numerical data included in published scientific articles is of no value because of the faulty measurement procedures employed by the investigators.[22]

Recently the famed cancer research and therapeutic center — the Sloan Kettering Institute, New York, was thrown into confusion and embarrassment when one of its researchers announced that for the first time he has been able to develop a method of grafting skin between non-twins, a significant medical advance. It was subsequently revealed that on doing the transplant from the dark mouse to a white mouse the researcher was "caught coloring" the grafted patch on the body of the white mouse to make it appear that the graft took.[23] There is a series of similar faked discoveries, some being exposed to public scrutiny but most remaining in relative obscurity.

Leaders in scientific research feel that the trend to falsify data will increase because of the pressing need for scientists to prove their worth when competing for funds. Yet another development is the proliferation of "intentional bias" and therefore distortion in designing and interpreting research. Dr. Ian St. James-Roberts of the University of London has raised the question of impartiality of scientific investigators in an article titled "Are Researchers Trustworthy?" in the *New Scientist*. He contends that a good deal of cheating may be going on because of intrusion of special interests or biases that color the interpretations.[24]

One of the most startling examples of intentional bias was unveiled before the world with the exposé of a towering figure in educational psychology, the late Dr. Cyril Burt, who had claimed that most intelligence potential is related to heredity. It appears that Dr. Burt had fabricated data to prove his point and to satisfy his bigotry — something that went unnoticed for many years until it was first laid bare by psychologist Dr. Leon Kamin, of Princeton, in 1972, who later elaborated on his discovery in the book *The Science and Politics of I.Q.*[25] More recently, fall of 1976, the medical correspondent of the London *Sunday Times* unearthed additional information corroborating Dr. Kamin's findings of extensive fakery by Dr. Burt. These revelations are of prime significance because until a few years ago Burt was largely responsible for the character of the educational system in England. Based on Burt's contention that intelligence was determined at birth, England's children were given an IQ test at the age of eleven, and depending on the results were forever separated into different categories of schooling. Children considered to have lesser intellectual propensities were sent to trade schools and were not eligible to enter institutes that would lead them to higher education in the liberal arts or the sciences.*

The idea that IQ testing may be a measure of a child's intellectual environment rather than of his innate developmental potential, was brushed aside. Burt once referred to a child under his supervision as a "typical slum monkey with the muzzle of a paleface chimpanzee."[26] He argued that ghetto children were less intelligent than those of well-to-do families, and that the Jews and the Irish were far below the intelligence level of the English. He also had a word for women, whom he described as inferior in intelligence to men. He was the first psychologist to be knighted and he received a top award in the United States when the American Psychological Association gave him its Thorndike Prize.[27]

Currently there is a hue and cry for the reorganization of England's approach to education. In the meantime, however it will take years to undo the harm and deprivation to thousands of people because of a fraud perpetrated by an individual who successfully passed himself off as a super educational psychologist even though he made his prejudices blatantly public. Needless to say, it was not entirely a one-man, Cyril Burt crusade. Obviously there was substantial backing from the entrenched interests — the Tory elite who sought to fortify and perpetuate their status within the British class system.

Despite such revelations, and today despite the tenuous scientific scaffolding on which the theory of psychosurgery rests, some surgeons will feel that they now have clear sailing for experimentation into the limbic system of the brain with the full backing of the congressional commission. Proponents of this action see a new dawn for heroic surgical remedies in the treatment of psychiatric disorders. But the commission's decision overrides the caution of those scientists who for years have been at the center of these developments and who have come away

*It was only in the late sixties, and then especially with the change of government in 1974, that steps were taken to broaden the so-called comprehensive school plan. This was designed to make academic training available to a greater number of students.

with the feeling that the evidence for the justification of this procedure is insubstantial.

"After 25 years of reports on psychosurgery, most of us in the neurosciences remain skeptical of its efficacy," Dr. Herbert Lansdell told an international scientific meeting in Geneva, late in 1973.[28] Dr. Lansdell is a staff member of the Fundamental Neurosciences Program of the National Institutes of Health. He cited a psychosurgery study at the Institute to treat intractable pain which resulted in serious memory deficits, intellectual damage, and bizarre behavior for the individuals involved in the experiment. Cingulotomy, a psychosurgical variant, was employed in the experiment, the same procedure that was used in most of the cases that were reviewed for the commission, and which provided the basis for the commission's optimistic approval of psychosurgery.

Dr. Lansdell reported that "one poor result occurred with a man who had superior intelligence and a superb memory . . . after surgery he could not complete our tests. Another case did not get beyond the ventriculogram which caused a hemorrhage and noticeable drops in intellectual scores. Another was a clergyman who after surgery frequently masturbated and exposed himself to nurses. His postoperative scores on personality questionnaires were more neurotic than before surgery. These unfortunate cases paid a higher price than others did for a few months of not demanding analgesics for their pain."

As for the use of psychosurgery to treat violence-prone individuals, Dr. Lansdell told the Geneva meeting, "The physiological differences between the brain of a mugger and the brain of a demonstrator cannot be meaningfully investigated with present techniques."[29]

Yet the build-up of pressures to extend the use of psychosurgery for the "treatment" of violence and other so-called aberrant behaviors (political dissidence, homosexuality, etc.) is something that appears inevitable. And it's a sure guess that a respectable enough scientific institute will come up with a rationale to justify its involvement in such a program.

Experimenting on a convict's brain with the hope of finding the cure for criminality, many will argue, is a very small price to pay in terms of societal morality when compared with some of the draconian measures currently being aired. For instance, there was a proposal to declare open season on burglars and prowlers, with the offer of a $200 bounty to those who shoot and kill their alleged assailants. The offer came from the president of New York City's federation of 135 pistol and rifle clubs, with a membership of 5000.[30] In addition to this group there are about 25,000 others in New York who are licensed to carry weapons because of their jobs as guards or employees of security and protection agencies. It is somewhat awesome to consider the consequences when an army of 30,000 gun-toting individuals is offered monetary incentives to go out and kill.

It is entirely conceivable that once the psychosurgical alternative becomes publicized, demand for its application will come not only from people desperately in need of protection, but also from those individuals who are outraged at the sky-rocketing increases in the budgets that are being allocated to curb crime. In the ten years of its existence, the Law Enforcement Assistance Administration has spent billions of dollars, most of it in block grants to police departments across the country for the purchase of arsenals of gadgetry designed to apprehend and kill lawbreakers.[31]

But expenditures related to crime control are expected to jump to even higher levels. The prevailing cry, reaching a furious crescendo, is for harsher punishment and longer jail sentences for law offenders; and this demand is not confined to the Archie Bunkers who are boiling over with the spirit of vigilantism. It is getting vigorous support from the nation's leadership, whether from Gerald Ford or from President Carter. To accommodate the expanding prison population, which is multiplying at a staggering rate, new penitentiaries will have to be built.

There is a veritable prison building boom already under way. The government's appropriation just for federal penitentiary construction for 1977 was $57 million, more than twice the average for the past four years. This is exclusive of plans to enlarge the capacities of state and county jails. Congress is now considering ways to expand the federal prison system. According to *Corrections Magazine*, there are reportedly "over 860 penal facilities (including local jails)" that are being "proposed or under construction at a cost of several billions of dollars."[32]

But even these heroic financial outlays are unlikely to stem the housing demands of the soaring prison population. Over the past two years there has been a 25 percent jump in the number of Americans behind bars. Currently there are 283,000 in state and federal institutions and 200,000 in county and city jails. Over a period of a year there are upward of one million Americans who spend some of their time in prison. *Corrections Magazine* reports that on the basis of the population census there are 131 Americans in prison for every 100,000 citizens — "more than in any other democratic nation." North Carolina leads all fifty states with 283 persons in its state prisons for every 100,000 of its citizens.[33]

The Congressional Budget Office report of January 1977 sees this situation as being directly related to the economic slump. It says that unemployment figures and federal prison admissions have followed strikingly similar patterns, both moving sharply upward between 1974–1976; a disproportionate number of those jailed are from the minorities. On a national basis (all age groups) some authorities estimate that approximately one third are blacks, Chicanos, and Hispanics. Others believe the number to be twice that of the whites. Regionally the disproportion may become even more lopsided. In the northern industrial areas, as for instance New York State, 75 per cent of the prisoners are blacks and Hispanics. In the south, blacks make up more than 60 percent of the prison population.[34]

With the public demand for speedier solutions to the crime wave, coupled with a burning desire for a tighter national budget so as to lower the tax bite, such alternatives as psychosurgery or other drastic means of dealing with law offenders become ever more attractive. The operation may be expensive to perform in its initial stages of development. But Dr. Breggin, the psychiatrist who has been among the most vocal opponents of psychosurgery, predicts that with advances in electronics and technology in general, the procedure would probably be speeded up, made more simple, and less costly.[35] Thus the threat of its application on a mass basis may become tenable. At the outset, lobotomy, the predecessor to psychosurgery, also started out as a challenging surgical venture. But it didn't take long before Dr. Freeman came along with his ice-pick-like instrument, enabling surgeons to perform dozens of lobotomies a day in their offices.

Streamlining psychosurgical techniques is now more likely because of the recommendation by the National Commission for the Protection of Human Subjects of Biomedical and Behavioral Research that the government become actively involved in encouraging such research. Whether this all-out effort will actually result in new methods to alleviate mental illness, as the commission hopes, or eventually lead to furthering brain-control technology, is a question that must remain moot. At the moment the evidence is scarcely reassuring that it may not turn out to be the latter.

Senator Sam J. Ervin, Jr., who for three years (1971–1974) headed a Senate subcommittee investigating the government's involvement in behavior-modification programs, warned that such a trend imperiled some of the basic constitutional rights of Americans. "Whenever . . . therapies are applied to alter men's minds," he declared, "extreme care must be taken to prevent the infringement of individual rights." He added that "concepts of freedom, privacy, and self-determination inherently conflict with programs designed to control not just physical freedom, but the source of free thought as well."[36]

Those committed to viewing violence and crime as basically an individual's aberrant behavior will obviously eschew Senator Ervin's caveats and applaud such expedients as psychosurgery, and other so-called deterrents to delinquency.

But tough sentencing, barbarous behavior-modification tactics, and psychosurgery are not the answers. In the words of David L. Bazelon, Chief Judge, United States Court of Appeals in Washington, D.C., "Street crime has no nostrums apart from profound social reforms, which are generally expensive, inefficient and unpopular. But that is no excuse for simplistic rhetoric. It is always easy to concede the inevitability of social injustice and find the serenity to accept it. The far harder task is to feel its intolerability and seek the strength to change it."[37]

Notes
Index

Notes

Chapter 1/Who Owns Your Personality?

1. Vernon H. Mark and Frank R. Ervin, *Violence and the Brain* (New York: Harper & Row, 1970), p. 5.
2. U.S., Congress, Senate, Subcommittee on Constitutional Rights of the Committee on the Judiciary, *Individual Rights and the Federal Role in Behavior Modification*, 93rd Cong., 2nd sess., November 1974 (Washington, D.C.: U.S. Government Printing Office, 1974), pp. 28; 40.
3. Walter Freeman, *American Handbook on Psychiatry*, Vol. 2 (New York: Basic Books, 1959), p. 1526.
4. Richard Restak, M.D., "The Promise and the Peril of Psychosurgery," *Saturday Review*, September 25, 1973; also brief of amicus curiae American Orthopsychiatric Association, State of Michigan, Circuit Court for the County of Wayne, July 1973.
5. Elliot S. Valenstein, "Brain Stimulation and the Origin of Violent Behavior," paper presented at the Fifth Annual Cerebral Function Symposium, San Diego, March 1974.
6. Edward Hitchcock, Lauri Laitinen, and Kjeld Vaernet, eds., *Psychosurgery: Proceedings of the Second International Conference on Psychosurgery* (Springfield, Illinois: Charles C Thomas, 1972).
7. Fredric Wertham, M.D., *A Sign for Cain* (New York: Warner Paperback Library, 1966), Chapter 9.
8. Ibid.
9. Leon Eisenberg, M.D., "The *Human* Nature of Human Nature," *Science* 176 (April 14, 1972).
10. R. A. McConnell, Research Professor of Biophysics, University of Pittsburgh, Special Communication to Scientists, March 17, 1976.
11. Arthur R. Jensen, "How Much Can We Boost I.Q. and Scholastic Achievement?", *Harvard Educational Review* 39 (February 1969): 1–123.

12. John Neary, "A Scientist's Variations on a Disturbing Racial Theme," *Life*, June 12, 1970.
13. Ibid.
14. Author's interview with Dr. Richard Lewontin, February 1977.
15. Alexander Thomas and Samuel Sillen, *Racism and Psychiatry* (New York: Brunner/Mazel, 1972), p. 37.
16. Herbert Spencer, *Principles of Biology* (New York: D. Appleton & Co., 1901.
17. R. Hofstadter, *Social Darwinism in American Thought* (New York: George Braziller, Inc., 1959), p. 45.
18. P. B. Medawar, "Unnatural Science," *New York Review of Books*, February 3, 1977.
19. Judge David L. Bazelon, "No, Not Tougher Sentencing," *New York Times*, February 15, 1977.
20. James V. McConnell, "Criminals Can Be Brainwashed — Now," *Psychology Today*, vol. 3, no. 11 (April 1970).
21. *Individual Rights and the Federal Role in Behavior Modification*, p. v.
22. Ibid.
23. Robert J. Grimm, "Brain Control in a Democratic Society," paper presented at Fifth Annual Cerebral Function Symposium, March 1974.
24. "Private Institutions Used in CIA Effort to Control Behavior," *New York Times*, August 2, 1977.
25. Ibid.
26. "Control CIA, Not Behavior," *New York Times*, August 5, 1977.

Chapter 2/Guilty Brain Cells

1. Vernon H. Mark and Frank R. Ervin, *Violence and the Brain* (New York: Harper & Row, 1970), Chapter 7, pp. 92–111.
2. Ibid.
3. Ibid.
4. Ibid.
5. Ibid, p. 97.
6. Peter Breggin, M.D., Professional Bulletin a complement to the FAS Public Interest Reports, published by Federation of American Scientists, vol. 2, no. 2 (February 1974).
7. Ibid.
8. Edward Hitchcock, Lauri Laitinen, Kjeld Vaernet, eds., *Psychosurgery: Proceedings of the Second International Conference on Psychosurgery* (Springfield, Illinois: Charles C Thomas, 1972), p. 369.
9. Author's telephone interview with Petter A. Lindstrom, May 1977.
10. Hitchcock, Laitinen, Vaernet, *Psychosurgery: Proceedings of the Second International Conference on Psychosurgery*, p. 371.

11. Ibid., p. 366.
12. Ibid.
13. Ibid., p. 363.
14. Ibid., p. 373 (emphasis added).
15. Ibid., p. 364.
16. U.S., Congress, Senate, Subcommittee on Health of the Committee on Labor and Public Welfare, *Quality of Health Care — Human Experimentation*, 1973, 93rd Cong., 1st sess., February 23, 1973, and March 6, 1973 (Washington, D.C.: U.S. Government Printing Office, 1973), Part II, p. 339.
17. Ibid., p. 340.
18. Elliot S. Valenstein, *Brain Control* (New York: John Wiley & Sons, 1973), p. 54.
19. Peter R. Breggin, M.D., statement in *Congressional Record*, March 30, 1972, cited in *Quality of Health Care — Human Experimentation*, Part II, p. 441.
20. Veterans' Administration Communication, August 26, 1943.
21. Author's interview with Peter R. Breggin, M.D., Spring 1975.
22. Valenstein, *Brain Control*, p. 313.
23. Walter Freeman, *American Handbook on Psychiatry*, vol. 2 (New York: Basic Books, 1959), p. 1523.
24. Ibid., Chapter 76.
25. Ibid., p. 1535.
26. Ibid., p. 1524.
27. Vernon H. Mark, Frank R. Ervin, and William H. Sweet, letter, *Journal of the American Medical Association* 201, no. 11 (September 11, 1967).

Chapter 3/Behavioral Surgery

1. E. D. Adrian and B. H. C. Matthews, "The Berger Rhythm: Potential Changes from the Occipital Lobes in Man," *Brain* 57, no. 4 (December 1934).
2. Elliot S. Valenstein, *Brain Control* (New York: John Wiley & Sons, 1973), p. 29.
3. Adrian and Matthews, "The Berger Rhythm."
4. Valenstein, *Brain Control*, pp. 28–29.
5. Ibid., pp. 28–29.
6. Ibid., p. 91.
7. Ibid., pp. 98–101.
8. Ibid., p. 100.
9. Ibid., p. 101.

10. Arthur A. Ward, Jr., M.D., "The Anterior Cingular Gyrus and Personality," special paper, *Res. Publ. Assoc. Nerv. Ment. Dis.* 27 (1948): 438–445.

11. Vernon H. Mark, and Frank R. Ervin, *Violence and the Brain* (New York: Harper & Row, 1970), p. 142.

12. Oregon State Senate, Human Resources Committee, March 20, 1973.

13. Author's interview with Dr. Seymour S. Kety, during Science Writers Seminar, A Biologic View of Mental Illness, New York, May 3, 1974.

14. Dr. Robert J. Grimm, presenting statement of ACLU of Oregon before the Oregon State Senate, Human Resources Committee, March 20, 1973.

15. Edward Hitchcock, Lauri Laitinen, Kjeld Vaernet, eds., *Psychosurgery: Proceedings of the Second International Conference on Psychosurgery* (Springfield, Illinois: Charles C Thomas, 1972), p. 209 (emphasis added).

16. Ibid., p. 204–209.

17. Author's interview with Dr. M. Hunter Brown, March 1974.

18. American Psychiatric Association Survey of Members of the Association of Neurological Surgeons, reported to the National Commission for the Protection of Human Subjects of Biomedical and Behavioral Research, June 11, 1976.

19. Mark and Ervin, *Violence and the Brain*, p. 32.

20. Ibid., p. 32.

21. Ibid., p. 7 (emphasis added).

22. Author's interview with Dr. M. Hunter Brown.

Chapter 4/Reshaping the Child

1. U.S., Congress, Senate, Subcommittee on Health of the Committee on Labor and Public Welfare, *Quality of Health Care — Human Experimentation,* 1973, 93rd Cong., 1st sess., February 23, 1973, and March 6, 1973 (Washington, D.C.: U.S. Government Printing Office, 1973), p. 350.

2. Ibid., p. 356.

3. Ibid., p. 349.

4. Ibid., p. 351.

5. Rosemary C. Sarri, ed., "Under Lock and Key," National Assessment of Juvenile Correction (Michigan: University of Michigan, December 1974).

6. Ibid.

7. Ibid.

8. Ibid.

9. Ibid.

10. Ibid., citing *Standards and Guides for the Detention of Children and Youth* (New York: National Council on Crime and Delinquency, 1961).
11. Robert C. Maynard, "Crime Tests at Age 6 Urged," *Washington Post*, April 5, 1970.
12. Dr. Arnold A. Hutschnecker, "A Plea for Experiment," *New York Times*, October 2, 1970.
13. Joseph B. Treaster, "Youthful Violence Grows and Accused Are Younger," *New York Times*, November 4, 1974.
14. Author's interview with Dr. Stephan Chorover, 1974.
15. Richard D. Lyons, "Health Institute Gives Guidelines on Behavior Modification Issue," *New York Times*, July 9, 1975.
16. Ned O'Gorman, "The Children," *New York Times Magazine*, June 1, 1975.
17. L. Straufe, M.D., and M. Stewart, M.D., "Treating Problem Children with Stimulant Drugs, *New England Journal of Medicine* 289, no. 8 (August 1973).
18. Author's interview with Judge Justine Wise Polier, September 1975.
19. Hebert E. Rie, Ph.D., Views reported in Nancy Hicks, "Drugs for Hyperactive Child Scored," *New York Times*, June 26, 1974; see also Herbert E. Rie, "Hyperactivity in Children," *Am. J. Dis. Child.* 129 (1975): 783–789.
20. Daniel Safer, M.D., and E. Barr, M.D., "Depression of Growth in Hyperactive Children on Stimulant Drugs," *New England Journal of Medicine* 287, no. 5 (August 3, 1972).
21. Ben F. Feingold, M.D., *Why Your Child Is Hyperactive* (New York: Random House, 1975).
22. Leon Eisenberg, M.D., "Symposium: Behavior Modification by Drugs: The Clinical Use of Stimulant Drugs in Children," (lecture for the American Academy of Pediatrics, Chicago, October 21, 1971) *Pediatrics* 49, no. 5 (May 1972).
23. Jack Horn, "Taking the Next Step . . . ," *Psychology Today*, August 1975.
24. Thomas Rose, ed., *Violence in America* (New York: Random House, 1969), p. 339.
25. Fredric Wertham, M.D., *A Sign for Cain* (New York: Warner Paperback Library, 1966), p. 6.
26. Ibid., p. 203.
27. Ovid Demaris, *America the Violent* (New York: Cowles Book Co., 1970), p. 360.
28. U.S., Congress, Senate, Subcommittee on Constitutional Rights of the Committee on the Judiciary, *Individual Rights and the Federal Role in Behavior Modification*, 93rd Cong., 2nd sess. November 1974 (Washington, D.C.: U.S. Government Printing Office, 1974), p. 14.
29. Ibid., pp. 28–30.

30. "Two Views of the Seed Program," *St. Petersburg Times*, September 16, 1973.
31. Ibid.
32. "The Study of the Advisability of the 'SEED' in Dade County," Comprehensive Health Planning Council of South Florida, April 20, 1973, cited in *Individual Rights and the Federal Role in Behavior Modification*, pp. 186–191.
33. Ibid.
34. Ibid.
35. Catalogue, Farrall Instrument Company, Grand Island, Nebraska.
36. Ibid.

Chapter 5/*Prisoner Guinea Pigs*

1. Leroy F. Aarons, "State Tries Brain Surgery to Control Violent Prisoners," *Sacramento Bee* (California) February 27, 1972.
2. R. K. Procunier, Department of Corrections, Sacramento, California, correspondence of September 8, 1971, to Robert L. Lawson, Executive Officer, California Council on Criminal Justice, Sacramento.
3. Stephan L. Chorover, "Big Brother and Psychotechnology," *Psychology Today*, October 1973, pp. 43–54.
4. Benjamin H. Bagdikian, *The Shame of the Prisons* (New York: Simon & Schuster, 1972), p. 10.
5. Edward Bunker, "One Can See Brutality," *The Nation*, November 29, 1975.
6. Matthew L. Myers, American Civil Liberties Union, Testimony before the National Commission for the Protection of Human Subjects of Biomedical and Behavioral Research, January 9, 1976.
7. Ibid.
8. "Judge Sets Alabama Prison Standards," *New York Times*, January 14, 1976.
9. Jessica Mitford, *Kind and Usual Punishment: The Prison Business* (New York: Alfred A. Knopf, 1973).
10. "Judge Sets Alabama Prison Standards."
11. Author's interview with Matthew L. Myers, February 1976.
12. Author's interview with Arpiar G. Saunders, Jr., ACLU, February 1976.
13. Angela Y. Davis et al., *If They Come in the Morning: Voices of Resistance* (New York: Third Press, 1971).
14. U.S., Congress, Senate, Subcommittee on Constitutional Rights of the Committee on the Judiciary, *Individual Rights and the Federal Role in Behavior Modification*, 93rd Cong., 2nd sess., November 1974

(Washington, D.C.: U.S. Government Printing Office, 1974), pp. i–ii.

15. Bertram S. Brown, "Behavior Modification: Perspective on a Current Issue," National Institute of Mental Health (Washington, D.C., 1975).
16. Edward M. Opton, Jr., Wright Institute, Berkeley.
17. *Individual Rights and the Federal Role in Behavior Modification*, p. 31.
18. Project START Operations Memorandum, October 25, 1972.
19. *Clonce* v. *Richardson*, 379 F. Supp. 338 (1974).
20. Author's interview with Arpiar G. Saunders, Jr.
21. Ibid.
22. *Sanchez* v. *Ciccone*, No. 20182-4; 3061-4 (D.C.W.D. Mo. 1973).
23. *Individual Rights and the Federal Role in Behavior Modification*, p. 264.
24. " 'Behavior Mod' Behind the Walls," *Time*, March 11, 1974.
25. Diane Bauer, "Legislators Hit Patuxent," *Washington Daily News*, May 22, 1972.
26. Author's interview with Matthew Myers.
27. Cited by Matthew Myers in interview with author.
28. Author's interview with Matthew Myers.
29. Ibid.
30. Diane Bauer, "Legislators Hit Patuxent."
31. Arthur L. Mattocks and Charles C. Jew, "Assessment of an Aversive 'Contract' Program with Extreme Acting-Out Criminal Offenders," manuscript (1971), cited by Jay Katz, *Experimentation with Human Beings* (New York: Russell Sage Foundation, 1972), p. 1016.
32. Sterling W. Morgan, Martin J. Reimringer, and Paul F. Bramwell, "Succinylcholine: As a Modifier of Acting-Out Behavior," *Clinical Medicine* 77, no. 7 (July 1970).
33. Mattocks and Jew, "Assessment of an Aversive 'Contract' Program."
34. "Scaring the Devil Out," *Medical World News*, October 9, 1970.
35. Mattocks and Jew, "Assessment of an Aversive 'Contract' Program."
36. *Knecht* v. *Gillman*, 488 F.2d 1136 (8th Cir. 1973).
37. *Individual Rights and the Federal Role in Behavior Modification*, p. 557.
38. Ibid., p. 559.
39. Lloyd H. Cotter, M.D., "Operant Conditioning in a Vietnamese Mental Hospital," *American Journal of Psychiatry* 124:1 (July 1967).
40. National Committee to Support the Marion Brothers, News Release, June 1975.
41. Ibid.
42. Ibid.
43. James Vorenberg, "Warring on Crime in the First 100 Days," *New York Times*, October 20, 1974.

44. *Individual Rights and the Federal Role in Behavior Modification*, pp. 63–64.
45. Donald E. Santarelli, Administrator, LEAA, Press Release, February 14, 1974.
46. Computer Printout Listing Behavior-Related Projects, LEAA, cited in *Individual Rights and the Federal Role in Behavior Modification*, p. 38.
47. Ibid., p. 34.
48. Ibid., p. 38.
49. Author's telephone interview with Dr. L. Alex Swan, 1976.
50. *Individual Rights and the Federal Role in Behavior Modification*, p. 40.
51. Ibid., pp. 40–41.
52. Ibid., p. 43.
53. Ibid., p. 33.
54. Ibid., p. 34.
55. Ibid., p. 33.
56. U.S., Department of Justice, "Behavior Modification Programs: The Bureau of Prisons Alternative to Long-Term Segregation" (Washington, D.C., August 5, 1975).
57. Edgar H. Schein, Professor of Organizational Psychology at M.I.T., "New Horizons for Correctional Therapy," a lecture delivered at symposium in Washington, U.S. Bureau of Prisons; printed as an article in *Corrective Psychiatry and Journal of Social Therapy* 8, no. 2 (second quarter 1962).
58. Groder's description of an Asklepieion session: "Eight of them walked into the room and sat down — and I proceeded to rip them off, one after the other. I just shit all over them about all the things that had come to my attention that were so obvious to me about the trickiness, the lies, the misrepresentations — their aimed dedication to stupidity — the whole ball of dirty wax." *Science*, August 2, 1974, p. 423.
59. Steve Gettinger, "Martin Groder: An Angry Resignation," *Corrections Magazine*, July/August 1975.
60. Rob Wilson, "U.S. Prison Population Sets Another Record," *Corrections Magazine*, March 1977.
61. James V. Bennett, *I Chose Prison* (New York: Alfred A. Knopf, 1970), p. 226.

Chapter 6/Predicting the Violent among Us

1. Author's interview with Dr. J. M. Van Buren, National Institute of Neurological and Communicative Disorders and Stroke, April 1974.
2. Vernon H. Mark, Frank R. Ervin, and William H. Sweet, letter, *Journal of the American Medical Association* 201, no. 11 (September 11, 1967).

3. *Report of the National Advisory Commission on Civil Disorders* (The Kerner Report) (New York: E. P. Dutton & Co., Inc., 1968), pp. 128–129.
4. Vernon H. Mark and Frank R. Ervin, *Violence and the Brain* (New York: Harper & Row, 1970), p. 5.
5. Ibid., p. 160.
6. Ibid., pp. 157–158.
7. Author's interview with Frank R. Ervin, March 1974.
8. Michael Crichton, *The Terminal Man* (New York: Bantam Books, 1973), p. 246.
9. Dr. William H. Sweet, testimony at Hearings on H.R. 15417 before the Senate Committee on Appropriations, 92nd Cong., 2nd sess., May 23, 1972.
10. Dr. Louis Jolyon West, Proposal for UCLA Center for the Study and Reduction of Violence, 1972.
11. Author's conversation with director of Oklahoma City Zoo, September 1977.
12. Dr. Earl Brian, Secretary of California Health and Welfare Agency, announcement, cited by Committee Opposing Psychiatric Abuse of Prisoners, April 5, 1973.
13. Dr. Louis Jolyon West's proposal.
14. Ibid.
15. Saleem A. Shah and Loren H. Roth, "Biological and Psychophysiological Factors in Criminality," *Handbook on Criminology* (New York: Rand McNally, 1974), pp. 107–108.
16. P. A. Jacobs et al., "Aggressive Behavior, Mental Subnormality and the XYY Male," *Nature* 208 (1965): 1351–1352.
17. Ernest Hook, "Behavioral Implications of the XYY Genotype," *Science*, July 1973.
18. Dr. Louis Jolyon West's proposal.
19. Ibid. (emphasis added)
20. "Opponents and Proponents of the Life-Threatening Behavior Project," *UCLA Daily Bruin*, February 26, 1974.
21. California State Legislature Hearings, May 9, 1973.
22. "Task Force on Alternatives to Violence," The Southern California Psychiatric Society (November 1973).
23. Isidore Ziferstein, M.D., statement at Hearings of the California Council on Criminal Justice, Berlingame, California, July 1973.
24. Ibid.
25. Author's interview with Dr. Isidore Ziferstein, February 1974.
26. Ernst A. Rodin, M.D., "Psychomotor Epilepsy and Aggressive Behavior," *Archives of General Psychiatry* 28 (February 1973).
27. Author's interview with Frank R. Ervin.
28. Mark and Ervin, *Violence and the Brain*, p. 87.

29. Ibid., p. 158.

30. Richard H. Wasserstrom, correspondence of August 8, 1973, to California State Senator Anthony Beilson, confirming Wasserstrom's July 23rd letter of resignation.

31. Isidore Ziferstein, M.D., "A Critique of the Project on Life-Threatening Behavior at UCLA," undated, unpublished, quoting Seeley from a KCET–TV (California) program, March 10, 1974.

32. John A. Gardiner, correspondence to California Council of Criminal Justice, June 12, 1973.

33. *San Francisco Examiner and Chronicle*, April 1, 1973.

34. Dr. Louis Jolyon West, correspondence of January 22, 1973 to J. M. Stubblebine, M.D., Director of Health, Office of Health Planning, State of California.

35. Committee Opposing Psychiatric Abuse of Prisoners, April 5, 1973, cited in U.S., Congress, Senate, Subcommittee on Constitutional Rights of the Committee on the Judiciary, *Individual Rights and the Federal Role in Behavior Modification*, 93rd Cong., 2nd sess., November 1974, p. 352.

36. Ibid., p. 38.

37. The Center for the Study of Crime and Delinquency, 5600 Fisher's Lane, Rockville, MD 20852.

38. Jane E. Brody, "Babies' Screening Is Ended in Boston," *New York Times*, June 20, 1976. See also Jon Beckwith and Jonathan King, "The XYY Syndrome: A Dangerous Myth," *I.Q., Scientific or Social Controversy? New Scientist* 64 (November 14, 1974): 474–476.

Chapter 7/Eroding the Legal Protections

1. *Kaimowitz* v. *Department of Mental Health*, Civil no. 73–19434–AW (Circuit Court, Wayne County, MI., 1973).

2. Ibid.

3. Paul Lowinger, "Psychosurgery: The Detroit Case," *The New Republic*, April 13, 1974, p. 18.

4. *Kaimowitz* v. *Department of Mental Health*.

5. Ernst A. Rodin, M.D., "Results of Discussions Held in Regard to Aggression Surgery," memorandum to Jacques S. Gottlieb, M.D., August 9, 1972.

6. *Kaimowitz* v. *Department of Mental Health*.

7. Ernst A. Rodin, M.D., "Psychomotor Epilepsy and Aggressive Behavior," *Archives of General Psychiatry* 28 (February 1973): 210–213.

8. A paper presented by Ernst Rodin, M.D., at the Winter Conference of Brain Research in Colorado, January 1971; later cited in Willard M. Gaylin et al., eds., *Operating on the Mind* (New York: Basic Books, Inc., 1975), p. 78.

9. The Medical Committee for Human Rights is a national organization composed of health workers and lawyers who are involved in activities designed to improve community health programs. The Ann Arbor chapter of the Medical Committee filed the original complaint.

10. Jo Thomas and Dolores Katz, "Surgery May Cure — or Kill — Rapist," *Detroit Free Press*, January 7, 1973.

11. *Kaimowitz* v. *Department of Mental Health*.

12. Ibid.

13. Ibid.

14. Benjamin M. Cardozo, *Selected Writings of Benjamin Nathan Cardozo* (New York: Bender, 1947), pp. 317–318.

15. *Kaimowitz* v. *Department of Mental Health*.

16. Ibid.

17. *Olmstead* v. *United States*, 277 U.S. 438 (1928), at 478, Justice Brandeis's dissent.

18. Sol Rubin, counsel for the National Council on Crime and Delinquency, has pointed out, "The Court has always neglected the law of criminal correction, and where it has ruled on the plight of prisoners, or persons being sentenced, it has generally ruled against them." So far as the Court is concerned, Rubin declares, "The Constitution has stopped at the prison gates; to a considerable extent it stopped once a man was convicted and being sentenced." See Sol Rubin, "The Burger Court and the Penal System," *Criminal Law Bulletin* 8, no. 1.

19. He cites the case of a black man who escaped from a Georgia chain gang and sought to resist extradition on the grounds that his Georgia treatment was cruel. Even though a U.S. court of appeals agreed, the Supreme Court overturned the decision and sent him back. When a similar case arose involving the return of an escapee from the Alabama prison system, Justice Douglas, in a minority opinion, declared:

> If the allegations of the petition are true, this Negro must suffer torture and mutilation, or death itself, to get relief in Alabama . . . I rebel at the thought that any human being, Negro or white, should be forced to run a gauntlet of blood and terror in order to get his constitutional rights. *Sweeney* v. *Woodall*, 344 U.S. 86 (1952).

20. When Warren Burger became chief justice, there was some hope that things would be different for the prison population. In a speech soon after his appointment the chief justice told the American Bar Association:

> We take on a burden when we put a man behind walls, and that burden is to give him a chance to change . . . If we deny him that, we deny him his status as a human being, and to deny that is to diminish our humanity and plant the seeds of future anguish for ourselves (speech to National Association of Attorneys General, February 1970).

In a later speech he urged that the states develop methods for hearing "promptly, fully and fairly" the grievances of prisoners. He urged that reform could come through rules of court, legislation, "or whatever means are available." Although the number of petitions and complaints from prisoners has increased substantially since Burger became chief justice, the Supreme Court has issued no rulings and has generally refused to review most cases involving Eighth Amendment issues except in regard to capital punishment.

21. National Commission for the Protection of Human Subjects of Biomedical and Behavioral Research, "Protection of Human Subjects. Use of Psychosurgery in Practice and Research: Report and Recommendations for Public Comment," *Federal Register* Part III, May 23, 1977.

22. Ibid.

23. U.S., Congress, Senate, Subcommittee on Constitutional Rights of the Committee on the Judiciary, *Individual Rights and the Federal Role in Behavior Modification*, 93rd Cong., 2nd sess., November 1974 (Washington. D.C.: U.S. Government Printing Office, 1974,) p. 25.

24. Peter R. Breggin, M.D., "The Return of Lobotomy and Psychosurgery," entered into *Congressional Record* 118, no. 26 (February 24, 1972).

25. Stephan L. Chorover, "Big Brother and Psychotechnology," *Psychology Today*, October 1973.

26. National Commission's Recommendations, *Federal Register*.

27. Ibid.

28. Ibid.

29. Ibid.

30. Ibid.

31. George J. Annas, "Psychosurgery: Procedural Safeguards," *Hastings Center Report*, April 1977.

32. National Commission's Recommendations, *Federal Register*.

33. Ibid.

34. Barbara J. Culliton, "Psychosurgery: National Commission Issues Surprisingly Favorable Report," *Science*, October 15, 1976.

35. Samuel Chavkin, "Therapy or Mind Control? Congress Endorses Psychosurgery," *The Nation*, October 23, 1976.

36. National Commission's Recommendations, *Federal Register*.

37. Richard F. Thompson and John P. Flynn, statements to National Commission for the Protection of Human Subjects of Biomedical and Behavioral Research, June 11, 1976.

38. Dr. Kenneth Heilman, statement to National Commission, June 11, 1976.

39. Rep. Louis Stokes (D–Ohio), statement to National Commission, June 11, 1976.

40. John Donnolly, statement to National Commission, June 11, 1976.

41. National Association for Mental Health, statement to National Commission, June 11, 1976.
42. Ernest A. Bates, M.D., position paper prepared for National Commission, June 1, 1976.
43. U.S., Congress, Senate, Subcommittee on Health of the Committee on Labor and Public Welfare, *Quality of Health Care — Human Experimentation,* 1973, 93rd Cong., 1st sess., February 23, 1973, and March 6, 1973 (Washington D.C.: U.S. Government Printing Office, 1973), Part II, p. 347.
44. National Commission's preliminary report, August 24, 1976 (emphasis added).
45. Allan F. Mirsky, M.D., and Maressa H. Orzack, M.D., "Report on Psychosurgery Pilot Study," prepared for the National Commission for the Protection of Human Subjects of Biomedical and Behavioral Research, June 11, 1976.
46. Ibid.
47. Ibid.
48. Hans-Lukas Teuber, Ph.D., Suzanne Corkin, Ph.D., and Thomas Twitchell, M.D., "A Study of Cingulotomy in Man," prepared for the National Commission for the Protection of Human Subjects of Biomedical and Behavioral Research, June 11, 1976.
49. Ibid.
50. Ibid.
51. Author's coverage of the deliberations by the National Commission for the Protection of Human Subjects of Biomedical and Behavioral Research following submission of reports by Dr. Mirsky and Professor Teuber.
52. Elliot S. Valenstein, "The Practice of Psychosurgery: A Survey of the Literature (1971–1976)," prepared for the National Commission for the Protection of Human Subjects of Biomedical and Behavioral Research, June 11, 1976.
53. Ibid.
54. The National Minority Conference on Human Experimentation (sponsored by the National Urban Coalition), Reston, VA, January 6–8, 1976.
55. L. Alex Swan, Ph.D., "Ethical Issues in Research and Experimentation in Prison," prepared for the National Minority Conference, June 6–8, 1976.
56. The National Minority Conference on Human Experimentation, "Final Summary Report and Recommendations," January 6–8, 1976.
57. Ibid.
58. Ibid.
59. Ibid.
60. The National Commission for the Protection of Human Subjects of

Biomedical and Behavioral Research, transcript of discussion on reconsideration of initial report on psychosurgery, November 13, 1976.
61. Ibid.
62. Ibid.
63. Ibid.
64. National Commission's Recommendations, *Federal Register*.
65. Ibid. (emphasis added)
66. Ibid.
67. Ibid.

Chapter 8/Surveillance Machines and Brain Control

1. John H. Fenton, "Psychologist Tests Electronic Monitoring to Control Parolees," *New York Times*, September 7, 1969.
2. Author's telephone interview with Ralph K. Schwitzgebel, Fall 1976.
3. Ralph K. Schwitzgebel, "Issues in the Use of an Electronic Rehabilitation System with Chronic Recidivists," *The Law and Society Review* 3:597–611.
4. Ibid.
5. Author's telephone interview with Schwitzgebel.
6. Ralph K. Schwitzgebel, "Development and Legal Regulation of Coercive Behavior Modification Techniques with Offenders," *Crime and Delinquency Issues* (Washington, D.C.: National Institute of Mental Health, 1971).
7. J. A. Meyer, "Crime Deterrent Transponder System," *EEE Transactions*, vol. AES–7, no. 1 (January 1971): 2–22.
8. Ibid.
9. Ibid.
10. Ibid. (emphasis added)
11. Schwitzgebel, "Development and Legal Regulation."
12. J. A. Meyer, "Crime Deterrent Transponder System."
13. Ibid.
14. U.S., Congress, Senate, Subcommittee of the House Committee on Government Operations, "Speculations on the Relation of the Computer to Individual Freedom and the Right to Privacy: The Computer and the Invasion of Privacy," prepared by D. N. Michael, 89th Cong., July 26, 27, and 28, 1966, pp. 184–193.
15. Author's interview with José M. R. Delgado, March 1974.
16. José M. R. Delgado et al., "Two-Way Transdermal Communication with the Brain," *American Psychologist*, March 1975.
17. Ibid.
18. Ibid.
19. Ibid.
20. Ibid.

21. Author's interview with Delgado.
22. *Osborn* v. *United States*, 385 U.S. 323 (1966); *Columbia Human Rights Law Review* 4, no. 1 (Winter 1972): 163–164.
23. Michael H. Shapiro, "Legislating the Control of Behavior Control: Autonomy and the Coercive Use of Organic Therapies," *Southern California Law Review* 47, no. 2 (February 1974): 239–353.
24. Alan Westin, *Privacy and Freedom* (New York: Atheneum, 1967).
25. Charles Fried, "Privacy," *Yale Law Journal* 77 (January 1968): 475–493.
26. Ibid.
27. Ibid.
28. Peter Northrop Brown, "Guilt by Physiology: The Constitutionality of Tests to Determine Predisposition to Violent Behavior," *Southern California Law Review* 48, no. 2 (November 1974): 565.
29. J. A. Meyer, "Crime Deterrent Transponder System."
30. Frank Askin, "Surveillance: The Social Science Perspective," *Columbia Human Rights Law Review* 4, no. 1 (Winter 1972): 60–88.
31. Marie Jahoda and Stewart W. Cook, "Security Measures and Freedom of Thought," *Yale Law Journal* 61 (1952): 296–333.
32. Frank Askin, "Surveillance."
33. Bernard Beck, Commentary, *Law and Society Review* 3 (1969): 611–614.

Chapter 9/It's Not Just Theory

1. *Experiments and Research with Humans: Values in Conflict*, National Academy of Sciences (Washington, D.C., 1975), pp. 44–45.
2. Author's interview with Dr. Richard Levins, February 1977.
3. *Psychosurgery: Proceedings of the Second International Conference on Psychosurgery* (Springfield, Illinois: Charles C Thomas, 1972).
4. 1976 Crime Index, New York City Police Department.
5. Selwyn Raab, "Felonies in New York City in 1976 Up 13.2%, Worst Rate on Record," *New York Times*, March 4, 1977.
6. U.S., Congress, Joint Economic Committee, "Social Stress and the National Economy: Recent Findings on Mental Disorder, Aggression, and Psychosomatic Illness," testimony of Harvey Brenner, Ph.D., Johns Hopkins University, Winter 1977 (Washington D.C.: U.S. Government Printing Office, March 1977), pp. 1–15.
7. "U.S. Report Urges Preparations for Possible Recurrence of Riots," *New York Times*, March 3, 1977.
8. Roger Simon, "The Victims' Guide," *New York Post*, March 14, 1977.
9. "A History of Eugenics in the Class Struggle," in *I.Q.: Scientific or Social Controversy?* (Boston: Science for the People, February 1976).

10. Madison Grant, *The Passing of the Great Race* (New York: Charles Scribner's & Sons, 1916).
11. C. C. Brigham, *A Study of American Intelligence* (Princeton, NJ: Princeton University Press, 1923), pp. 182–190.
12. Nathaniel Hirsch, "A Study of Natio-Racial Mental Differences," *Genetic Psychology Monographs*, January 1926.
13. "A History of Eugenics in the Class Struggle."
14. Ibid.
15. John Neary, "A Scientist's Variations on a Disturbing Racial Theme," *Life* June 12, 1970.
16. Steven S. Ross, "Scientists Honor Black I.Q. Theorist," *New York Post*, February 24, 1977.
17. Edward O. Wilson, *Sociobiology: The New Synthesis* (Cambridge, MA: Harvard University Press, 1975), p. 129.
18. *New York Times*, May 28, 1975.
19. *Science for the People* 8 no. 2 (March 1976): 9.
20. Ibid.
21. Author's interview with Dr. Richard Levins, February 1977.
22. Author's interview with Dr. Richard Lewontin, February 1977.
23. Ibid.
24. Ibid.
25. Author's interview with Professor B. F. Skinner, February 1977.
26. Ibid.
27. Ibid.
28. Ibid.
29. Ibid.
30. Alan W. Heldman, "Social Psychology Versus the First Amendment Freedoms, Due Process, Liberty and Limited Government," *Cumberland–Samford Law Review* 4, no. 1 (Spring 1973).
31. Ibid.
32. José M. R. Delgado, M.D., *Physical Control of the Mind: Toward a Psychocivilized Society* (Harper & Row, 1969), p. 254.
33. Author's interview with José M. R. Delgado, March 1974.
34. Recommendations on Uses of Psychosurgery to secretary of HEW by National Commission for the Protection of Human Subjects of Biomedical and Behavioral Research, *Federal Register* 42, no. 99 (May 23, 1977): 26319.
35. Delgado, *Physical Control of the Mind*, p. 260.
36. Ibid., p. 247.
37. Ibid., pp. 250–251.
38. José M. R. Delgado, "Evolution of Physical Control of the Brain," James Arthur Lecture, The American Museum of Natural History, New York, 1965.
39. Delgado, *Physical Control of the Mind*, p. 123.

40. Ibid.
41. Delgado, "Evolution of Physical Control of the Mind."
42. Ibid.
43. Author's interview with Delgado.

Chapter 10/Complicity

1. "The Poor," (Forum) *Individual Risks vs. Societal Benefits; Experiments and Research with Humans: Values in Conflict*, National Academy of Sciences (Washington, D.C., 1975), p. 152.
2. U.S., Congress, Senate, Subcommittee on Health of the Committee on Labor and Public Welfare, *Quality of Health Care — Human Experimentation*, 1973, 93rd Cong., 1st sess., March 7, 1973, and March 8, 1973 (Washington, D.C.: U.S. Government Printing Office, 1973), Part IV, pp. 1207–1210.
3. Ibid., pp. 1223–1232.
4. Ibid., pp. 1233–1240.
5. Ibid., Part III, p. 1035.
6. Ibid., pp. 1061–1063.
7. Ibid.
8. Ibid., p. 1064.
9. Ibid.
10. "The Poor," p. 156.
11. *Quality of Health Care — Human Experimentation,* Part III, pp. 1043–1049.
12. Ibid.
13. Jeffrey Gillenkirk, "LEAA and NIMH — Collaboration Since 1968," *Psychiatric News*, April 17, 1974.
14. Bertram S. Brown, M.D., Director, National Institute of Mental Health, memorandum to All State and Territorial Mental Health Authorities, October 15, 1970.
15. Gillenkirk, "LEAA and NIMH."
16. Ibid.
17. Ibid.
18. Jeffrey Gillenkirk, "LEAA and Mental Health — The Odd Alliance," *Psychiatric News*, April 3, 1974.
19. Ibid.
20. Jeffrey Gillenkirk, "Violence Control Project Tests LEAA's Mental Health Plans," *Psychiatric News*, April 24, 1974.
21. Boyce Rensberger, "Fraud in Research Is a Rising Problem in Science," *New York Times*, January 23, 1977.
22. Ibid.
23. Ibid.
24. Dr. Ian St. James-Roberts, "Are Researchers Trustworthy?", *New Scientist* 71, no. 1016 (September 2, 1976); and "Cheating in Science," *New Scientist* 72, no. 1028 (November 25, 1976).

25. Leon J. Kamin, *The Science and Politics of I.Q.* (Lawrence Erlbaum Associates, 1974; distributed by John Wiley & Sons, New York).
26. Boyce Rensberger, "Briton's Classic I.Q. Data Now Viewed as Fraudulent," *New York Times*, November 28, 1976.
27. Ibid.
28. Herbert Lansdell, "Psychosurgery: Some Ethical Considerations," Conference on Protection of Human Rights in the Light of Scientific and Technological Progress in Biology and Medicine, Geneva, November 14, 1973.
29. Ibid.
30. Joseph B. Treaster, "Gun Group Offers a $200 Reward to Victims Who Kill Assailants," *New York Times*, April 14, 1977.
31. James Vorenberg, "Warring on Crime in the First 100 Days," *New York Times*, October 20, 1974.
32. Rob Wilson, "U.S. Prison Population Sets Another Record," *Corrections Magazine*, March 1977.
33. Ibid.
34. Ibid.
35. Author's interview with Peter R. Breggin, M.D., Spring 1975.
36. U. S., Congress, Senate, Subcommittee on Constitutional Rights of the Committee on the Judiciary, *Individual Rights and the Federal Role in Behavior Modification*, 93rd Cong., 2nd sess., November 1974 (Washington, D.C.: U.S. Government Printing Office, 1974), p. III.
37. Judge David L. Bazelon, "No, Not Tougher Sentencing," *New York Times*, February 15, 1977.

Index